The Executioner's Bible

The Story of Every British Hangman of the Twentieth Century

Steve Fielding

JOHN BLAKE

Published by John Blake Publishing Ltd,
3 Bramber Court, 2 Bramber Road,
London W14 9PB, England

www.johnblakepublishing.co.uk

First published in paperback in 2008

ISBN: 978-1-84454-648-0

British Library Cataloguing-in-Publication Data:

A catalogue record for this book is available from the British Library.

Design by www.envydesign.co.uk

Printed and bound in Great Britain by Creative Print & Design, Blaina, Wales

1 3 5 7 9 10 8 6 4 2

Papers used by John Blake Publishing are natural, recyclable products made
from wood grown in sustainable forests. The manufacturing processes conform
to the environmental regulations of the country of origin.

Every attempt has been made to contact the relevant copyright-holders,
but some were unobtainable. We would be grateful if the appropriate
people could contact us.

Contents

Author's Note

This is my second book written for John Blake Publishing on the subject of British hangmen and follows on from *Pierrepoint: A Family of Executioners*, published in February 2006.

In writing this book I have tried where possible to avoid covering the same ground when writing about the Pierrepoint family, but, since the Pierrepoint family, and to a certain extent the people they hanged, played a large part in much of the history of execution in the last century, some repetition of facts and cases has been inevitable. Readers wishing to know the full story of the Pierrepoints would benefit from also reading that book.

Since the publication of the hardback edition of *The Executioner's Bible*, a couple of new facts have come to light. As a result, a few changes have been made to the text for the paperback.

Acknowledgements

I would like to thank the following people for their help in the research and writing of this book. First, Lisa Moore, who has helped with every stage of the book, particularly the photographs and illustrations, final proofreading and typing up the various drafts.

Thanks also to Matthew Spicer, who has been willing to share his extensive knowledge and archives, as well as to accompany me on many visits to the National Archives at Kew, where much of the research was undertaken; and to Tim Leech and Tony Homewood, who both opened their archives and shared information over the years.

This book is the result of over twenty years' research into the hangmen of England, and during that time numerous people have helped with information, a number of whom have sadly since passed away.

Former executioner Syd Dernley's contribution cannot be understated. He was pivotal in helping my original

Hangman's Record project get off the ground, and provided me with a wealth of information on modern-day executioners for this book and the previous volume, *Pierrepoint: A Family of Executioners*.

The late Frank McKue helped with information on executions in Scotland and also supplied a number of photographs.

I also thank Harry Robinson, one of the last assistant executioners, who supplied valuable information on the procedures in the last days of hanging.

I would also like to thank people who offered information and photographs relating to members of their families over the years, in particular Linda Towers, Doris Allen, Brian Allen and Sean Underhill. David Martin, David Pacey and Iain Moulds helped with information on modern-day executioners; Stewart McLaughlin helped with information on Henry Pierrepoint and Wandsworth Gaol; and Janet and Marten Buckingham helped with research and data input.

Finally, thanks to my editor, Stuart Robertson, for all his valued help on this and my previous book for John Blake.

Steve Fielding
March 2007

Introduction

It was once termed a 'Highly Skilled Mystery'; those who knew its closely guarded secrets called it the 'profession'; and during the twentieth century it was one of the hardest jobs to occupy. A competent hangman had to have nerves of steel, a strong stomach and, in later days, a good head for maths. Hanging by the neck until dead developed from a crude and brutal strangulation from a tree branch watched by hundreds, sometimes thousands, of often rowdy spectators, to a cold, clinical operation viewed by just a handful of official witnesses. Death was scientific and a prisoner was sent to his or her death with a drop worked out to the exact half-inch.

But who were these people and how did they come to take up such a role? The Executioner's Bible takes a look at how Britain recruited, trained and then disposed of its hangmen and assistants in the last century of capital punishment. It also looks at the crimes of those convicted and hanged, those often brutal killers, many of whose names have passed into the annals of criminal history. Much of the information contained in this book is being written about for the first time. Papers that were once deemed too confidential to be viewed are now easier to access, and with their opening we can begin to tell the real story of England's executioners in the twentieth century.

Chapter 1:

Execution Protocol and History

Death by hanging was the preferred form of punishment for convicted criminals in Great Britain since the dawn of Christianity. Supposedly introduced to these shores by the Anglo-Saxons, it was the usual punishment for commoners, noblemen being given a more honourable death by beheading. Over the years the practice of hanging a criminal by the neck until he or she was dead was refined to the extent that, by the turn of the twentieth century, a condemned criminal could be put to death in a quick, efficient and humane manner in times that were being measured in seconds.

During the Middle Ages there were a number of methods of execution: burning at the stake for witchcraft, beheading for treason, and most commonly hanging, often followed by the brutal drawing and quartering of the half-dead victim. In the sixteenth and seventeenth centuries there were often hundreds of executions carried out across the country each year, with the majority carried out at Tyburn.

Situated at the end of Oxford Street, adjacent to Marble Arch, where a plaque still stands to this day marking the spot, more than 2,000 people, including almost 150 women, were hanged at Tyburn in the eighteenth century, with the vast majority being men under the age of 30. The last person hanged at Tyburn was highwayman John Austin on 7 November 1783. From then on, executions in the City of London and the County of Middlesex were carried out outside Newgate Gaol.

In the nineteenth century, as the population almost tripled to more than 25 million, more than 4,000 men, women and occasionally children were hanged in Great Britain, and of these only around a third were hanged for murder. There were, at this time, more than 200 crimes that carried the death penalty. This high number was in the main due to the breakdown of crimes into more specific offences: theft from a shop, a warehouse, dwelling house and brothel, while being basically the same offence, were logged as separate offences. Similarly, with crimes of arson, burning down a house was distinguished from setting fire to a shop, or other type of building.

In reality, although the full range of offences included such obscure specific crimes as damaging London Bridge and impersonating a Chelsea Pensioner, there were fewer than 20 offences that resulted in the ultimate penalty. These were in the main murder and attempted murder; crimes of violence such as cutting and maiming (grievous bodily harm), along with arson, sex crimes, forgery, uttering (passing counterfeit monies) and coining. Likewise, a vast array of robbery offences was punishable by death, such as highway robbery (in many cases, this was street robbery), mugging, housebreaking and burglary, robbery in a dwelling house, and horse, cattle or sheep theft.

A hundred and twenty-nine people were hanged in 1800, and in the following year that number almost doubled. These figures fluctuated annually but there were still on average 80 executions a year in the years leading up to the ascension to the throne of Queen Victoria. As transportation first to America then later to Australia gradually became commonplace instead of a sentence of death, the number of executions began to decline to such an extent that in 1838 there were just six executions in the whole of England and Wales – five for murder and one for attempted murder.

After 1840, only two people were executed for attempted murder: Sarah Chesham, who made an unsuccessful attempt to poison her husband at Chelmsford in 1851, and 26-year-old Irish tramp Martin Doyle, hanged at Chester ten years later for the horrific attempted murder of a woman at Holmes Chapel, Cheshire.

Doyle was the last man to be executed in the nineteenth century for a crime other than murder, and a year later the Criminal Law Consolidation Act decreed that the number of capital crimes be reduced to just four (murder, high treason, piracy and arson in Royal Dockyards).

Hangings were carried out in public until May 1868, from when they were continued within the walls of county prisons, under the provisions of the Capital Punishment within Prisons Act of 1868. This Act received Royal Assent on 29 May 1868, three days after the execution of the Fenian terrorist Michael Barrett outside Newgate Prison. Convicted of causing an explosion at Clerkenwell in London that resulted in the deaths of seven people, Barrett became the last man to be publicly hanged in Great Britain. A crowd numbering many thousands watched as hangman William Calcraft carried out his duties in public for the last time.

Three months later, on 13 August 1868, the first private

execution in Great Britain following the Act took place at Maidstone Gaol, when 18-year-old Thomas Wells was hanged for shooting his employer, the stationmaster at Dover Priory railway station. Wells was hanged by Calcraft in the former timber yard at the gaol, out of site of the cell blocks. Press were allowed to witness the execution and recorded that Wells took a long time to die, struggling on the end of the rope for several minutes.

The new Execution Act of 1868 had come about following the efforts of reformists and humanists such as John Howard, Sir Robert Peel, Charles Dickens and several other prominent essayists, who wrote long pieces in the national press calling for an end to the grotesque spectacle of public executions, and, as public opinion grew, the Quaker movement campaigned strongly on the back of it.

Sentence of death was mandatory for anyone found guilty of murder, and remained the law up to 1957. And, between 1957 and 1964, it was the sentence passed on anyone convicted under the new Homicide Act 1957 of capital murder – that is, murder committed in the course or furtherance of theft. Before sentence was passed the prisoner would be asked if he or she had anything to say as to why sentence of death should not be pronounced. Up to 1827, men could demand 'benefit of clergy', a 'get-out clause' thought up by the church to help clerics escape execution. A woman often 'pleaded her belly', claiming to be pregnant in the hope of preventing the full sentence of the law being carried out. In 1873, Mary Cotton was heavily pregnant when she was convicted of murder, but having given birth to the child in the condemned cell she was hanged a few days later. Fifty three years later, Louise Calvert told the court she was pregnant following the passing of the death penalty on her. A medical examination found she was lying and she was hanged in due course.

When the judge was passing sentence of death, a black cap – in actuality nothing more than a small square of black silk – was placed upon his head, and he would then proceed to pronounce sentence. Prior to 1947, the sentence was,

[Prisoner's name], you are sentenced to be taken hence to the prison in which you were last confined and from there to a place of execution where you will be hanged by the neck until dead and thereafter your body buried within the precincts of the prison and may the Lord have mercy upon your soul.

In 1948, after the sitting of the Royal Commission on Capital Punishment, the sentence was modified slightly, replacing 'to be hanged by the neck until dead' with 'suffer death by hanging'. The wording of the sentence had remained similar to the ones used in the last days of public execution.

The Murder Act of 1752 ruled that the timing of the execution following conviction should take place two days after sentence, unless the third day was a Sunday, in which case it would be held over until the Monday. By 1834, the time lapse became a minimum of two Sundays between sentence and execution. Following the 1868 Act, sentence was carried into effect following three clear Sundays, with the execution usually taking place on the Monday. This meant that the executioner, who had to be in the grounds of the prison by sunset on the day prior to the hanging, would often have to arrive on the Saturday, since travelling on the Sunday was often not as easy as on other days of the week. Gradually, more and more executions were carried out on the Tuesday, and from 1902 the Home Office officially decreed Tuesday to be the first day of the working week set for execution.

Between 1900 and 1965, 1,485 death sentences were passed in England and Wales, and a few over half, 755, were carried out. Those spared were usually reprieved under the Royal Prerogative of Mercy, exercised by the Home Secretary on behalf of the Monarch. Prisoners thus saved from the gallows had their sentences commuted to life in prison, although it was very rare for someone to spend the remainder of their life in gaol, with the length of term served often barely making double figures.

Prisoners in the twentieth century often spent longer in the condemned cell than those in Victorian times. This was mainly due to the new Appeal Act of 1907, which finally allowed convicted criminals the chance to have their case reheard if they believed they had not had a fair hearing at the original trial. If a condemned man chose to appeal, the sentence was postponed pending the outcome, but once the appeal was heard, and usually dismissed – since very few appeals were successful – a new date was fixed, usually within two weeks of the appeal date. In 1941, Antonio Mancini spent almost four months in the condemned cell as his case was debated all the way to the House of Lords until all avenues had been exhausted; and in 1960 Jamaican Oswald Grey spent over six weeks in the death cell before he was hanged.

Prior to 1907 there was no chance to appeal against conviction, but the Appeal Act now gave a condemned criminal a last glimmer of hope, although most were almost a desperate last resort, often seen as such, and were duly dismissed. It was not unknown for some judges even to censure defence counsel if they felt a futile appeal had been a waste of everyone's time.

In the Middle Ages the gallows was often nothing more than a substantial tree branch to which the prisoner was tied with a rope around their neck and then 'turned off' the ladder or stool on which they had been standing. This was later refined so that a prisoner sometimes stood on the back of a horse-drawn cart while noosed and placed under a tree. The cart was then quickly removed, leaving the prisoner suspended in space.

At an execution in Oxford in April 1752, a beam was suspended between two trees for the execution of 33-year-old Mary Blandy, who found the courage to address the executioners, saying '... for the sake of decency, gentlemen, don't hang me high.' Gradually, a more conventional gallows became the norm, usually having a single upright post with a projecting beam cross-braced, the type associated with the common gibbet; or it would have two uprights and a crossbeam. The main advantage of the latter was that it was possible to carry out multiple executions at the same time. Both gallows still relied on the condemned having something pulled from beneath their feet, or being turned off a ladder. In most cases these gallows were portable structures, often erected near to the scene of the crime as a warning to the locals, and were then dismantled after the execution and stored in a local prison.

The famous 'Triple Tree' gallows was set up at Tyburn in 1571, replacing smaller and often crudely constructed gallows that sprang up in and around London. Now, with the system allowing for multiple executions, in June 1649, 23 men and one woman were hanged for a variety of burglaries and robberies. They had been conveyed to the site from Newgate Gaol in a convoy of horse-drawn carts. The Tyburn gallows consisted of three 12-foot-high pillars connected with beams forming a triangular structure. This triple gallows allowed three carts to be positioned beneath the beams at the same time.

Eventually, traffic congestion caused the gallows to be

dismantled and transferred across the city to Newgate Gaol. The triple tree structure was then replaced by a more modern portable gallows, which now had a raised platform 10 feet long by 8 feet wide beneath two parallel beams, with space for twelve criminals to be hanged simultaneously.

The condemned were placed on the trapdoors, which were opened by pushing a lever attached to a drawbar, on which rested the hinges. This new drop allowed a fall of just 18 inches and was often not long enough to allow the rope to dislocate the condemned's neck; instead they usually suffered a painful death of slow strangulation.

The first executions on the new drop outside Newgate took place on 9 December 1783, when ten convicts were hanged simultaneously. This new portable gallows was built on wheels and brought out when needed by a team of horses. By the mid-1820s, a new, more compact gallows was constructed with the double-beam gallows replaced with a single beam.

Other prisons, including York, Hertford and Maidstone, copied this new design, large enough for three prisoners to be hanged side by side. The platform stood around 6 feet high, shielded by heavy black cloth drapes to conceal from view the suspended prisoner, who would usually be struggling in the throes of a painful death.

Following the passing of the 1868 Act, providing for all executions to take place within the walls of county prisons, there was no standard design for a gallows and they varied from county to county. Some used a gallows consisting of two upright posts with a crossbeam, and a platform with either single or double trapdoors constructed over a brick-lined pit, often up to 12 feet deep. These deeper pits were needed because modern executioners were now successfully advocating drops of 9–10 feet. They were frequently erected in the prison yards and were often open-air.

In a number of big city prisons, where executions were frequently carried out, they had purpose-built execution sheds erected in the prison grounds. Again, these varied in design and resembled a modern detached garage or a Victorian seaside photographic studio. These sheds were often located a fair distance from the main prison building, which meant a long walk for the prisoner from the condemned cell to the gallows.

Several folklore tales sprang up from when prisoners had to make their last walk to the gallows in the grounds of a prison. One prisoner, faced with a long walk during a heavy rainstorm, is alleged to have told his warders that he didn't feel like going outside, because the weather was too wet.

'What are you complaining about?' the warder replied. 'I've got to walk back in it!'

In 1885, when faulty workmanship was held partly responsible for a drop that failed to fall at the Exeter execution of John Lee, the Home Office commissioned Lieutenant Colonel Alton Beamish to design a standard gallows. Consisting of two uprights and a crossbeam, the new structure was built using 8-inch-thick sections of oak. The beam ran the length of a 12-foot platform, which housed an 8-by-4-foot-wide trap containing two 3-inch-thick heavy oak trapdoors set level with the surrounding floor. A metal lever set into the floor of the execution chamber released the trapdoors when pushed.

Bad weather at Exeter was also blamed for trapdoors' failure to fall when the condemned person stood on the drop. Incessant rain made the thin wooden door swell and the extra weight meant the two doors, with a gap between them of just a few millimetres, became stuck fast and, when the trap was sprung, the doors held firm.

In 1881, a new gallows was built at Newgate, consisting of

two stout uprights supporting a crossbeam, with an iron band fixed to the centre from which a chain was suspended, and to which the rope was attached. This arrangement allowed for multiple executions, because extra chain and rope attachments could be added when required. Attached to each upright was a pulley arrangement to assist the raising of the trapdoors and for helping with the removal of the body from the noose following execution. The lever was located on the platform and the thick, heavy, wooden trapdoors would strike large bales of cotton, which helped muffle the crash when the drop fell. The trapdoors were stained a dark wood colour with the remaining woodwork painted a dull buff colour.

By the turn of the century a new scaffold designed to be constructed in the wing of a prison, directly adjacent to the condemned cell, became standard practice. This avoided the necessity of the final long walk to the scaffold, often down staircases and along several corridors, which could be a distressing sight if the condemned prisoner lost their nerve, or became overcome with fear. The sheer terror of being hanged still caused this breakdown at the last moment, but the new positioning speeded up the whole process from several minutes to a matter of seconds. The first person executed on the new one-level gallows was Matthew Chadwick in December 1890, at Kirkdale Gaol, Liverpool.

This design, with just a few alterations, remained in use until abolition, the only significant difference being the change from a single- to a twin-beam arrangement running parallel to each other about 2 inches apart. Attached to the beams were two heavy metal brackets drilled with a series of holes, through which a cotter pin was inserted, and to which a length of link chain was attached and onto which the rope was attached.

This arrangement allowed for a much more accurate

adjustment of the drop, allowing it to be calculated and rigged to within a quarter of an inch. The beams were normally 8 feet above the trapdoors and set into the wall at each end of the chamber, allowing for the dispensation of the upright beams. Trapdoors were caught by rubber-lined steel springs to stop them bouncing back and hitting the criminal. The hangman would chalk a 'T' mark on the joint across the door directly beneath the beam, to which the prisoner's toes were aligned (this is one of the origins of the phrase 'toe the line').

Britain's last working gallows, at Wandsworth Gaol, South London, was tested and serviced every six months and kept in full working order, until being dismantled in 1992. The working parts are now kept in storage at the Galleries of Justice in Nottingham.

The earliest hangmen, up to the days of William Calcraft and Bartholomew Binns, used a halter-style noose: one continuous piece of rope, usually over an inch thick, with a loop worked into one end of the rope and the other end fed through it. (The coil type of noose we have all seen in cowboy films, and used at the end of 2006 at the execution of Saddam Hussein in Iraq, was never commonplace in Great Britain.) During the reign of the chief executioner James Berry in the late 1880s, the halter-style noose was improved by feeding the rope through a brass pear-shaped eyelet woven into one end of the noose, making it more free-running.

Following a report by the Aberdare Committee in 1888, when Berry was censured for displaying ropes he had used at executions in public places, the Home Office, and not the hangman, henceforth supplied ropes. A contract was agreed with the rope maker and marquee erectors John Edgington & Co., of Old Kent Road in London, to manufacture and supply ropes.

The new execution rope consisted of a 13-foot length of Italian hemp that was five-eighths of an inch in diameter, bound with a thin layer of soft chamois leather around the neck area of the rope, which prevented rope burns on the neck following execution. Hemp was chosen because it was soft and strong with a less coarse surface than other types of rope. Early examples had no leather covering and the noose was kept in place using a stiff leather washer. Following suggestions from a number of hangmen, in particular Tom Pierrepoint, a serrated-toothed rubber washer was used to hold it in place.

The ends of the rope where they were spliced together had a natural waxy resin covering known as gutta-percha. The gutta-percha had a tendency to split and crack when cold and had to be heated with a candle to make it supple and soft to avoid sharp shreds cutting into the prisoner's neck. In the early 1950s the gutta-percha covering was phased out and replaced with vulcanised rubber.

The length of the rope was crucial. If a drop was too short, there was a risk that the condemned prisoner's neck would not break and they would suffer a painfully slow death by strangulation. And if the drop was too long, there was the risk of decapitation. The positioning of the eyelet under the angle of the jaw was very important, since it was vital that the head be thrown backwards by the rope so that the force was transmitted into the neck vertebrae rather than being thrown forward and the force taken on the throat, which tended to cause strangulation. It was also crucial that the noose be put on the right way round so that it rotated in the correct direction with the eyelet ending up under the jaw.

To help the hangmen allow an exact drop as calculated, the elasticity was removed from a new rope on the night before an execution. To do this, the noose was stretched by the use of a sandbag about the same weight as the prisoner. This was attached to the noose and dropped through the trap, and then left suspended overnight. This stretch was nearly always around a half-inch and a piece of copper wire attached to the rope, marked at the end with a chalk line, allowed the executioner to work out the amount of stretch.

It was common for the hangman, having positioned the noose on the prisoner, to leave the remaining rope to loop down behind the prisoner's back, but following an unfortunate incident at Durham Gaol in August 1883, at the execution of James Burton, a change was needed. As Burton fell through the trap, the slack rope became entangled in his arm and as a result he received a shorter drop than planned and his body swung violently in the pit. The hangman, William Marwood, and the prison warders present on the drop had to haul Burton back onto the scaffold, untangle the stray rope, and then push the unfortunate man back into the pit. Burton swung violently at the end of the rope, his neck unbroken by the fall, and was left to die by painful strangulation. It was an unsavoury end to the hangman's career. Although Marwood was not dismissed for this horrific incident, he was already ill and died just a short time later.

To prevent a repetition, new procedures were put in place. Henceforth, the rope was coiled and placed above or to the side of the prisoner and secured with twine or packthread. When the trapdoors opened the force of the drop snapped the thin cotton and allowed the rope to uncoil without fear of its fouling.

Another procedure adopted was the placing of stout boards across the trapdoor to allow the prison warders to keep upright any prisoner who may have fainted on the drop. The warders would support the prisoner by slotting their arms under their shoulders so that the falling weight pushed the hand away, described by hangman Albert Pierrepoint – nephew of Henry and Tom Pierrepoint, whom we shall meet later – as similar to the way a railway signal would fall.

It was customary to put a white cotton hood over the prisoner's head before placing the noose around their neck. In the early days of public execution it was used to spare the crowd the sight of the convict's face contorted in agony as the short drops administered meant death was often through slow strangulation. In later days it was used to prevent the prisoner seeing that the hangman was about to pull the lever and thus trying to jump at the crucial moment, or to spare a noosed prisoner the sight of another condemned person when two were hanged side by side.

The prisoner's hands were usually pinioned in front of him using a cumbersome leather bodybelt. This type of belt had been used by Calcraft and was also used by Marwood and Berry. The main drawback was that it could be difficult to secure if the prisoner put up a fight, and even if they succumbed without a struggle it still took several minutes and dragged out the painful last moments of a condemned prisoner's life for longer than was necessary.

During the sitting of the Aberdare Committee, Dr James Barr, the medical officer at Liverpool, was given the responsibility of training the first executioners, who all had to receive instruction to the Home Office standard. Among the first to receive instruction was James Billington, and his method of pinioning was to place the prisoner's hands behind their back and secure them with a thin leather strap. This speeded up proceedings and knocked several minutes off the time taken to carry out an execution. Until abolition it was adopted as the standard method. As longer drops now became the norm it became commonplace to secure the prisoner's legs and a similar leather strap, only slightly longer, was used. The main advantage of strapping the legs was to stop the condemned person from trying to jump or kick their legs when the drop opened.

William Marwood is often credited as being the pioneer of the long-drop method of execution, but the thinking behind it probably originated with doctors in Ireland. Marwood had read about their theory, understood the logic behind it and put it into practice once he was given the chance. At his first execution, when he assisted George Smith of Dudley at the hanging of Frederick Horry at Lincoln prison in 1872, Marwood's plan was to use a drop significantly longer than anything William Calcraft used, and when it was found that death had been instant, and that the prisoner had died from a broken neck and not strangulation, it was adopted at once.

Hanging now became a scientifically calculated method of administering a humane death. By allowing the prisoner to fall a predetermined distance, calculated by using factors such as age, weight, height and muscle condition, the drop was designed to dislocate the prisoner's neck by a sharp jerk when the rope became tight. The body accelerated under the force of gravity, and with the head constrained by the noose, the resulting stop at the end of the rope delivered a terrific blow to the neck, which, combined with the downward momentum of the body, fractured the vertebrae and ruptured the spinal cord, causing immediate deep unconsciousness. Instant death usually followed. Due to its position under the angle of the left jaw, the head was snapped backwards with such force that the neck was broken between the second and third, or fourth and fifth cervical vertebrae, and the use of the brass eyelet fastened into the noose allowed for a more certain break.

The accurately measured and worked-out drop removed most of the prisoner's physical suffering and made the whole process far less traumatic for the officials, who now had to witness it in the confines of the execution cell instead of in the open air.

By the late nineteenth century, there was a considerable amount of experimentation to determine the exact amount of drop, and James Berry, who became a hangman in 1884, had two unfortunate experiences in 1885. At Worcester in May, he hanged 65-year-old poacher Moses Shrimpton, who had shot a policeman, and six months later, at Norwich, he hanged Robert Goodale for the murder of his wife. In both cases, the force of the drop decapitated the condemned men, but there were extenuating circumstances. In the case of Shrimpton his age and weak muscle condition meant that the long drop of 9 feet was too far, while in Goodale's case he was a grossly overweight man. Berry sensed that the man's weight might cause problems, so he shortened the planned drop of nearly 8 feet, to 5 feet 9 inches, but even this was too long and produced a ghastly result.

In 1887, the Lord Aberdare Report was commissioned to examine execution protocol and procedure following these incidents and the unsuccessful attempt to hang John Lee at Exeter a few months before Shrimpton was beheaded on the gallows. The Aberdare Committee heard evidence from a number of medical officers who had witnessed executions and one, Dr Marshall, described a hanging in 1886 thus:

I descended immediately into the pit where I found the pulse beating at the rate of 80 to the minute, the wretched man struggling desperately to get his hands and arms free. I came to this conclusion from the intense muscular action in the arms, forearms and hands, contractions, not continuous but spasmodic, not repeated with any regularity but renewed in different directions and with desperation. From these signs I did not anticipate a placid expression on the face and I regret to say my fears were correct. On removing the white cap about 10 minutes after the fall I found the eyes starting from the sockets and the tongue protruded, the face exhibiting unmistakable evidence of intense agony.

In 1892, the Home Office issued executioners with a table of drops, which was revised in 1913. Experience showed that this table was only a rough guide and an experienced executioner would adapt this table and make his own extra calculations – usually adding around 9 inches.

Following an execution in the Victorian era, a black flag was hoisted on the flagpole above the main gate, where crowds of people often gathered. Cheers would frequently break out if the killer had been convicted of a crime that horrified the public. At the execution of Herbert Bennett, hanged at Norwich in 1901, the flagpole snapped as the flag was hoisted and many people took this as a sign that the prisoner was innocent, as he had maintained to the last.

Although the crowds that gathered would see or hear nothing of the execution, these congregations continued outside prisons until abolition. They were often made up of families of the condemned or the victim, and, as public opinion moved towards abolition, notable figures such as Mrs Violet Van der Elst, who dedicated her life to the abolition of the death penalty, would demonstrate loudly. Stunts included hiring aeroplanes to fly past streaming anti-hanging banners or dropping leaflets, and mass protests often meant the police had to put barricades around the walls of the prison to keep the crowds back.

Chapter 2:

Billington & Sons

A s the Victorian age drew to an end, the executioner charged with taking the death penalty into the twentieth century was Preston-born James Billington. Billington had had a lifelong fascination with hanging. In 1859, by the time he had reached 16, his family had relocated a dozen or so miles south to Bolton and it is probable that as a young man he witnessed public executions at nearby Salford's New Bailey Gaol or outside Liverpool's Kirkdale Prison. In his twenties he worked for a time in a cotton mill and had diverse interests such as being a club singer, wrestler and long-distance clog walker.

By the turn of the 1880s, Billington was now a Sunday school teacher and ran a barber's salon on Market Street, Farnworth. Here it seems his interest in becoming an executioner grew. He made replica model gallows in his back yard and studied the long-drop technique that William Marwood had instigated in the previous decade, using a variety of weights and dummies. Various tales sprang up from those days, one being that, besides using dummies to perfect his technique, Billington also practised on stray cats and dogs in the area.

A touring escapologist gave a newspaper interview around the turn of the century and boasted he had escaped the hangman's noose. As part of a stunt he had allowed the hangman to secure his arms as he would at an execution, and, although he was able to wriggle free, Billington informed him that, if this had been a real execution, by the time he had managed to free his arms he would have already been hanging at the end of a rope. The escapologist also claimed the hangman had told him he had hardened himself to the demands of his office by killing rats with his teeth.

In 1883 a vacancy arose following the death of Marwood, and Billington was one of over a hundred men who applied for the post. His knowledge of the methods and keen interest in the subject were enough to see him shortlisted, and he secured an interview with the panel appointing a successor. He was one of three men invited to London at his own expense to face the selection committee, but his application was overlooked in favour of that of another candidate.

Unperturbed, Billington wrote to other prison authorities offering his services, including those at Nottingham and York. The commission at Nottinghamshire rejected his first request to carry out an execution there in late 1883, mainly on account of the fact that the person Billington had offered to execute had been convicted of manslaughter and would therefore not have been sentenced to death even if found guilty.

Billington was, however, able to persuade the Yorkshire authorities to employ him on the next occasion a hangman was required and his services were engaged for an execution detailed to take place at Leeds on Tuesday, 26 August 1884.

With this date in his diary he then received another offer, this time from the governor of Tullamore Gaol in Ireland, requesting his services for an execution scheduled to take place two weeks before the Leeds engagement.

Catherine Dooley, a farmer in King's County, had been convicted of the murder of her cousin, whom she had beaten to death with an axe before hiding the body beneath a haystack. Her execution was to take place on 12 August 1884 and Billington had already reached the prison before learning that the prisoner had been reprieved. He received his fee in full, along with travelling expenses, but returned home still unproven on the scaffold.

There was to be no reprieve on his second engagement, when Joseph Laycock, a Sheffield hawker, was executed at Armley Gaol, Leeds, for the murder of his wife Maria and their four children. On the evening of 10 July, Laycock stopped a policeman in the street and complained about his wife drinking with another man. Told by the officer there was nothing he could do about it, he made his way home. At 10 p.m., with their four children asleep in bed, he sat down to supper with his wife. Laycock took out a bottle of beer and offered Maria a drink and, when she refused, he told her she might as well have a drink while she still had the chance. A short time later neighbours heard screams coming from the house and found the bodies of Mrs Laycock and the four children. They had all had their throats cut. Laycock also lay on the bed with a self-inflicted neck wound, and pleaded with neighbours to let him die, but his wounds were not life-threatening and he was placed under arrest and taken into custody.

Laycock pleaded insanity at Leeds Assizes and, although there was evidence of a history of insanity in the family, he was found guilty and sentenced to death. He was in tears when Billington entered the cell. 'You will not hurt me?' he cried, to which the hangman replied, 'No, tha'll nivver feel it, tha'll be out of existence i' two minutes.' Billington carried out the execution to everyone's satisfaction but any hopes he had of taking the mantle of chief executioner were thwarted.

Although it was less than a year since he had failed in his bid to become the new chief executioner, and the fact that the man appointed instead had already been dismissed for incompetence, Billington still found himself second fiddle to a newly appointed chief, the other unsuccessful candidate.

James Berry was a former Bradford policeman who had originally been the first choice to replace Marwood, but interference from members of his family when it was learned he was to be appointed led the committee to offer the role to a Dewsbury railway worker, Bartholomew Binns.

Forty-five-year-old Binns's short-lived reign was littered with numerous complaints of drunkenness and incompetence. At one execution, the governor noted that the executioner, who appeared drunk, placed the rope around the culprit's neck and pulled the lever, but it was more down to luck than skill whether he died by hanging or not. Between 6 November 1883 and 10 March 1884, Binns executed 8 men and 2 women, four of these at Liverpool. At his last execution, at Kirkdale Gaol, he turned up drunk and, mindful of the incompetence Binns had shown five days earlier when he hanged two women with little finesse or skill on the same scaffold, the governor sent for a local man, Samuel Heath, who had assisted Binns with that execution. Binns was adamant that Heath would not be his assistant and insisted he would carry out the work alone. When he again botched the execution, causing the prisoner to drop into the pit and painfully choke to death, Binns was dismissed.

Berry succeeded Binns and became the chief executioner of

Great Britain and Ireland, but not the exclusive one. Billington was now recognised as a competent hangman, and, although he had already had one offer to carry out an execution in Ireland, for the remainder of the decade he had to be satisfied with an annual trip to Leeds or be offered work that Berry was unable to accept.

Following the end of Berry's tenure as chief executioner after he had had several run-ins with prison officials, the Home Office took steps to avoid a repetition of selecting unsuitable candidates, making sure that any future executioners would be vetted and trained before being allowed to carry out official duties. An official list was published in late 1891 and contained the names of the three men who had been trained in the duties of executioner. Billington topped the list ahead of Francis Gardner of Berkshire and Robert Wade of Accrington. Although all three had been instructed in their duties, only Billington had actual experience of executions.

However, Billington had to wait until December 1891 to carry out an execution outside of Yorkshire, when he travelled to Shepton Mallet to hang Henry Dainton, a 34-year-old stonemason from Bath. Dainton was convicted of the murder of his wife, who was found drowned in the River Avon in the September. When the body was identified, police went to Dainton's home and found a bundle of saturated clothes and a pair of muddy boots. Placed under immediate arrest, Dainton was lucky to get to the police station alive, being almost lynched by an angry mob that had formed outside the front door. ·

It was the first of three executions in eight days for Billington, who had now taken over as chief following Berry's resignation that summer. A week later he travelled to Durham to hang a man who had shot dead the woman who rejected him, leaving the prison immediately to carry out an engagement at Hereford. Thick fog caused chaos on the railways with Billington not arriving at the gaol till nine o'clock the following morning. The authorities were notified of the delay and the execution was put back an hour. On arrival, Billington went at once to the gallows, where he rigged the drop and quickly tested the equipment. Once Billington and the officials were satisfied that all was ready, the prisoner was brought to the scaffold, where Billington in his haste made a rare mistake. As the body fell into the pit, it swung from side to side violently and there was noticeable twitching in the arms for several seconds.

This minor indiscretion did nothing to damage his reputation, and Billington began to average a score of executions a year as he became the recognised chief executioner, the most notable of his early customers being poisoner Dr Thomas Neil Cream.

In 1881, Cream, a Glasgow-born medical graduate, was sentenced to life imprisonment in Chicago for murder. He had poisoned the husband of his mistress using strychnine. Cream implicated himself when he contacted the District Attorney's office and advised them to have the body exhumed. After serving ten years, he was released and returned to England, settling in London. During the winter of 1891, four prostitutes, Ellen Donworth, Matilda Clover, Emma Shrivell and Alice Marsh, died as a result of strychnine poisoning. Cream had persuaded the women to take tonics he had prepared with promises that they would cure a variety of ailments, ranging from acne to migraine. Again, as he had done in Chicago, Cream incriminated himself by contacting the police, offering to reveal the identity of the Lambeth Poisoner in exchange for a large sum of money.

In June 1892 he was arrested after a prostitute came forward to say he had tried to get her to swallow a tablet he had prepared, but she had managed to spit it out without his noticing. Analysed, it was found to contain strychnine and a chemist testified that he had sold Cream the poison.

Hanged at Newgate on 15 November, Cream claimed on the scaffold, 'I am Jack the –' but he died before he could finish the sentence.

Although Billington was convinced he had hanged Jack the Ripper, the fact that Cream was safely locked away in Chicago's Joliet State Penitentiary while the Ripper was at large is enough to dismiss him from the list of suspects.

In August 1893, when Billington travelled to Chelmsford to carry out the execution of a 34-year-old police killer called John Davis, he had as an assistant a man whose name wasn't on the official Home Office list. Fifty-year-old William Warbrick was a lay preacher living in Bolton, who changed his name from Wilkinson when, following the death of his mother in 1896, he discovered he was born before his parents had married.

Born in Blackburn, he had witnessed several public executions at Liverpool's Kirkdale Gaol, including a double in 1862 that had drawn a crowd of almost a hundred thousand spectators. Warbrick had become close friends with Billington, and was persuaded by him to apply for the post of hangman following moves by the Home Office to ensure that assistant executioners were engaged. Billington told Warbrick he wanted a friend he could trust to be his assistant.

Warbrick wrote to the Home Office and sent proof of his preaching as testimony of his respectability. He was engaged sight unseen. This did not put him on the official list of executioners as such, but he was allowed to attend as assistant. Within days he received a letter from the governor of Newgate requesting his services at the execution of an Italian prisoner due to be hanged on 16 August. On the following day he received another letter, this time from the governor of Chelmsford, engaging him for a double execution there on 15 August. By the time Billington and Warbrick set out for Chelmsford, the Newgate prisoner had been reprieved, as had one of the Chelmsford prisoners.

Warbrick was eager to get to the prison in good time, and, although the execution wasn't scheduled to take place until 8 a.m. on the Tuesday morning, the hangmen left Bolton railway station at midnight Sunday, reaching London at 5 a.m. They spent the day sightseeing before travelling to Chelmsford in good time. When they arrived it was found that Warbrick's services were no longer needed, since there was now only one hanging scheduled, and the Essex authorities didn't want to pay for an assistant hangman if it wasn't really essential.

After supper, Billington rigged the gallows in preparation for the following morning. The condemned man, Davis, had murdered a police sergeant at Purleigh, Essex. When the officer's battered body had been found lying in a ditch, there were several sacks of corn close by. Four well-known local poachers came under investigation after some corn had been stolen from a local farm. When the men were detained, two were found to have bloodstains on their clothing, which they claimed had come from animals.

All four stood trial and the jury found two not guilty but the other two, John Davis and his younger brother Richard, guilty of murder. John Davis made a full confession, which partially exonerated his brother, who was granted a last-minute reprieve.

In April 1894 Billington carried out three executions in three days. On 2 April he executed Mrs Margaret Walber at Liverpool. Fifty-three-year-old Walber had been married for five years and ran a small shop with her second husband, but their relationship had run into trouble mainly because of his drinking and womanising. In May 1893, she discovered he had been seeing an old girlfriend and, in a rage, she locked him in their flat and threatened to poison him if he tried to escape. A few months later, following sounds of a disturbance in the flat, James Walber was found beaten to death. Margaret Walber blamed her son for the crime, claiming that he had beaten him with a chain, but evidence suggested otherwise, and she was convicted at Liverpool Assizes.

Following the execution of Walber, Billington hanged wife killer Philip Gardner at Leeds, and from there travelled down to Birmingham for the execution of Frederick Fenton, who had shot dead his fiancée after she discovered he had lied to her about his financial standing.

Billington's busy year ended with another hectic week, when he hanged four men in three days in December. On 10 December, former Royal Marine John Newell walked to the gallows for the murder of his wife. On the following day Samuel Emery was hanged at Newcastle, having been convicted of stabbing a woman to death on a road outside Tynemouth. Emery showed no fear on the morning of his execution and later Billington said he was gamest man he had ever hanged.

The hangman left the prison immediately and caught a train south, where he had his final engagements of the year. Billington was to hang two men at Winchester: Cyrus Knight, a carter who had cut the throat of his wife, before turning the razor on himself; and William Rogers, a sailor who had shot dead the woman he lived with. As they were led to the gallows, Rogers kicked off his shoes and declared that he would not be hanged in them. 'I'll not die in those. It was them that brought me here.' Knight's self-inflicted throat wound opened up when the drop fell, spraying blood onto the body of the man hanging beside him.

One of the prisons Billington frequented more than others

was London's Newgate Gaol. He hanged 27 people there during his reign as chief hangman, including three women. In 1896 alone he hanged six people there and on one occasion participated in his first experience of a triple execution.

On 14 February 1896, the body of Henry Smith, a wealthy, 79-year-old retired engineer, was found battered to death in the kitchen of his home at Muswell Hill. He had been bound and gagged, and evidence suggested he had been tortured, presumably to get him to reveal the combination of his safe, which now stood empty. Henry Fowler and Albert Milsom, two well-known thugs in their early thirties, had been seen in the area on the day before the crime, but the only clue the police had was a child's toy lantern discovered outside the house. When detectives traced the toy to Milsom, a manhunt was launched. They were traced to Bath, and although Fowler strongly denied any involvement with the crime, Milsom cracked under interrogation and made a full confession.

Convicted on overwhelming evidence at the Old Bailey, as sentence was passed Fowler made a vain attempt to strangle his former friend, whom he blamed for his predicament. They were to hang alongside another man, William Seaman, a sailor with a long criminal record, who had been convicted of a double murder in Whitechapel.

On the morning of the execution, Billington and his two assistants, William Warbrick and Robert Wade, led the condemned men onto the gallows. Wade had been on the official list now for almost five years, yet his experience to date had been limited to barely a handful of engagements, all as assistant. Fearing there may be a fight on the scaffold, prison authorities posted extra warders on condemned duty and decided to place Seaman between the two Muswell Hill murderers. Taking his position on the drop, Seaman remarked it was the first time in his life he had been a peacemaker. As

Warbrick went to strap Milsom's ankles he found he was using a new leather strap and was having difficulty getting the fastener through one of the eyelets. Unaware that his assistant was having trouble, and with his view blocked by the number of warders flanking the condemned men, Billington pulled the lever with Warbrick still kneeling on the drop. As the floor opened beneath him, Warbrick plunged headfirst into the gaping pit but had the foresight to grab onto the legs of Milsom and was able to prevent a serious accident. As one hangman later claimed, 'It's a nasty drop through the trapdoors, even without a noose around your neck!'

The three executioners remained in the prison, because they had a further engagement on the following day with the notorious Amelia Elizabeth Dyer, a 57-year-old grandmother whom the press had dubbed 'the Reading Baby Farmer'. A former member of the Salvation Army, Dyer had previous convictions for child cruelty before she moved to London in 1895. She placed advertisements offering to take children in for adoption, and on 31 March, for a fee of £10, she took charge of Doris Marmon, a four-month-old baby girl. Two days later police found the bodies of two young children floating in the River Thames; both had lace knotted around their necks, and one was identified as Doris Marmon.

Mrs Dyer was questioned, and when more bodies of young children were pulled from the river, again all with lace knotted around the neck, she was eventually charged with multiple murder and stood trial at the Old Bailey, on the same day as Milsom and Fowler. She pleaded guilty but insane, but the prosecution alleged that the motive for the killings was financial gain, and the jury took just five minutes to find her guilty of murder. Following conviction, she admitted the killings and said, 'You can tell if it's one of mine if it has a lace tied around its neck!'

James Billington was taken ill on the evening following the triple execution and for a time it looked as if responsibilities would be passed to Wade; but, despite a fitful sleep, he had recovered sufficiently in the morning. In another part of the prison the condemned woman also spent a restless night tossing and turning in her bed. She had made a number of threats following conviction that she would not walk to the drop and would cheat the gallows, and as a result extra warders were posted in her cell to see that justice was not prevented from being done.

It rained incessantly throughout the night, but despite the weather large crowds gathered outside the prison gates. On the stroke of nine the executioners escorted the woman to the gallows, where she was given a drop of just 3 feet 6 inches, sufficient for her 15-stone frame to make death instantaneous.

Billington's next engagement was at Reading a month later, where he hanged a trooper in the Royal Horse Guards. Charles Wooldridge had met his wife-to-be, Laura, while stationed at Windsor, and, when his commanding officer refused permission to marry, they wed in secret. The marriage was an unhappy one, mainly due to his drunken violent outbursts. In the early spring he was posted to London and, because the army didn't recognise his wife, she was unable to go with him.

They parted on bad terms, and, with her marriage seemingly over, Laura began a relationship with another soldier. On 29 March, she agreed to meet Wooldridge in London, but he failed to turn up. By now he had learned of her affair with the other soldier, and, after borrowing a razor, travelled to her house at Windsor. Although she was reluctant to let him in, he managed to persuade her that he needed her to sign some papers. No sooner had he entered than he pulled out the razor and slit her throat.

Wooldridge was in due course convicted at Berkshire Assizes and taken to Reading Gaol to await execution. The playwright Oscar Wilde was at the prison, serving a two-year sentence for homosexuality, and, after seeing the prisoner at exercise, was inspired to pen the classic work 'The Ballad of Reading Gaol', which he dedicated to the soldier following Wooldridge's execution on 7 July.

On 21 July Billington officiated at the last triple execution to take place in Great Britain. There was no incident of note at the Winchester execution, at which he was again assisted by Warbrick.

When Billington carried out a double execution at Leeds in August 1897, the two convicts were both named Robinson. Joseph Robinson had shot dead his wife at Barnsley in Yorkshire, while Walter Robinson had killed his cousin with a razor after she had reported him to the police following threats he had made to her. Although the two prisoners were not related, the hangmen were. Billington had with him at the execution his eldest son, Thomas, aged 24, participating at his second hanging.

Although the names of James Billington and Robert Wade appeared on the official list of hangmen and assistants – where it was noted that they had received training to be executioners – as we have seen, Warbrick was allowed to attend executions as an assistant after merely writing to the Home Office and sending in testimonials. In Thomas Billington's case it was simply the recommendation of his father that gained him this position. Thomas began to assist his father often, and, although his address was listed as Higher Market Street, Farnworth, he more often than not resided at his father's new home, the Derby Arms public house on Churchgate, Bolton, where Thomas also worked as a barman.

Of the eleven executions in which James Billington officiated in 1898, on the seven occasions where an assistant is recorded, the name of Thomas Billington is listed. Besides James Billington, there was only one other man carrying out executions as a chief as the end of the century approached, and his name also didn't appear on any official list of hangmen. Huddersfield rope maker Thomas Henry Scott had previously assisted James Berry as far back as 1889, but in recent times he carried out the majority of work as assistant to Billington or as chief executioner in Ireland, although Scott did carry out two executions in England as a number one, both at Stafford in the early 1890s. Scott was busy in Ireland in January 1899, when he carried out three executions in five days. A former hangman, the bungling Bartholomew Binns, assisted him on these jobs, one at Kilkenny, two in Armagh.

In the summer of 1899 Thomas Billington disappeared from home for a time and, on three occasions in July, James had no assistant with him. On 19 July, at St Albans, he executed a teenage girl, Mary Ansell, who was alleged to have poisoned her sister by sending her a cake laced with phosphorous poison. Caroline Ansell was an inmate at an asylum in Watford and, when she received a cake from her sister, she ate some and shared the rest with other inmates. A short time later several were taken ill, and Caroline, who had eaten the largest share, died. Mary aroused suspicions when she tried to prevent an autopsy being sanctioned, and when the results found large traces of poison she was arrested on suspicion of murder and subsequently convicted. She was hanged on a scaffold erected in the prison grounds and, although it was rumoured she had confessed on the night prior to her execution, it is believed many years later another member of the family confessed on his deathbed.

A week later Billington was engaged to carry out an execution at Lincoln, but when the day arrived he was too ill to travel and, rather than lose the engagement, and the fee, he suggested his second son William offer to go in his place. Unaware that the hangman standing before him was a complete novice, the governor of Lincoln Gaol accepted William's story that he carried out executions in the presence of his father and allowed him to continue.

The execution passed off without incident but later that morning the governor penned a note to the Home Office.

H.M. Prison Lincoln
25.7.1899
717 Edward Bell
Convicted 4.7.99 Lincoln County Assizes
Crime. Wilful Murder
Sentence. Death

Gentlemen,
    I have the honour to state that the above
execution was carried out by William Billington,
son of Billington the executioner, who was
expected. The Under Sheriff received a telegram
signed 'Billington' saying 'will arrive at 4
o'clock' whereas at 6 p.m. the son arrived saying
he had left his father too ill to come, and that
his father must have sent the telegram as he had
not done so.
    I at once saw the Under Sheriff and the son
Billington stated to him that though he had never
carried out an execution without his father being
present, yet in the presence of his father he had
done so without assistance. The Under Sheriff

considered himself satisfied that the son should
carry out the execution ...

... a warder reported to me that he did not seem
at all confident as to how he should tie the rope to
the beam, and when the assisting warder offered to
tie it for him Billington allowed him to do so ...

The Home Office treated the matter as serious and wrote
to both James and William Billington asking for their accounts
of what had happened. They in turn replied.

Lever Street
Bolton

August 4th 1899

Dear Sir

I am in receipt of your letter. I was away on
Thursday and it was 10 o'clock when I got home
last night but on Sunday night 24th July at about
11 p.m. I was taken bad with the influenza.

So I sent for my son for I could not wire or write
to you so I sent my son to Lincoln to tell you that
I was very bad in bed and that I would come on
Monday night if I was any better.

Then I told my son to tell the sheriff and
Governor that you could carry out the execution
as well as my Father.

I am sir yours obediently
James Billington
To The Governor
Lincoln Gaol

Billington & Sons

Aug 5th 1899
Bolton
Sir,

In answer to your letter on the 5th instant, I must
tell you that I have never been to an execution
before. And I am very sorry that I told you I had,
but I should not have under-took it if I had not
been confident that I could do it in a proper manner
as my father had given before. I remain

Your Obedient Servant
W Billington
87 Mill St Bolton

To the Governor of Lincoln Gaol

William's apology seems to have been accepted and, although there had been no untoward incident, the authorities were aware that a revision and overhaul of the system of recruiting executioners was needed. They did, however, manage to 'get one back' on the Billingtons for the subterfuge. The governor had told Billington junior following the execution that he was unable to pay him, since he had no authority to pay unauthorised executioners, and this was concurred by the under-sheriff.

With Thomas still indisposed, William assisted his father again two weeks later and a further four times that year, while letters passed to and fro between government and prison officials with a view to tightening up proceedings.

The first execution of the new century was at Newgate with William Warbrick assisting James Billington in the execution of Louisa Masset, convicted of the murder of her son. Warbrick's friendship with James Billington seemed to have diminished by this stage, possibly on account of the events at Newgate in June 1896, but more likely connected with the fact that his services at executions were no longer being called for. Although he had been initially reluctant to take up the role, once he found he could live with the cold-blooded killing of a fellow human being he looked forward to the exciting trips across the country, seeing new towns and cities and getting paid into the bargain. Once Billington began to tell prison officials he would prefer to use his son as assistant, a practice that was accepted without question, Warbrick found these trips few and very far between.

As a result he took to writing to the Home Office, attempting to blacken the Billington name.

29 Stone Street
Tong Moor
Bolton
Dear Sir,

  I hear that Wm. Billington has applied to be put on the list of executioners. If that is so, will you please allow me to say that I think it will be a mistake if you accept him, for some reasons:

  First he is only a boy and also he is a very forward young fellow & he is very fond of drink & I am afraid that he would be no credit to himself or to the Home Office.

  I know what I am saying because I call at the house for club money and I have done since he was a baby, so that I hope you will pause before placing him on the list. With kind regards.

  From yours truly
  (signed) W Warbrick

Unfortunately for Warbrick, the Prison Commissioners had had chance at close quarters to monitor the behaviour of all executioners and assistants over the previous few months and had come to their own conclusions. First, they noted a shortage of qualified persons on the list. They agreed that a certain amount of nepotism had taken place to the detriment of qualified persons already on the official list, but, in regard to both Wade and Warbrick, they believed that neither man was suitable to be promoted to chief executioner and was therefore of little use to the commissioners.

Replying to his letter, they told Warbrick the Prison Commissioners had no power to influence the sheriff in his discretion to select an executioner or assistant. With regard to the Billingtons, they felt that James was beginning to lose his nerve and that the once teetotal Sunday school teacher now seemed uncertain and had a fondness for drink. They found William Billington a more suitable prospect than his father and they also made recommendations that new assistants, along with the untrained members of the Billington family who wished to be placed on the official prison list of executioners, should be trained as a matter of urgency.

William Billington was the first assistant to be formally trained by staff when he turned up for a week's tuition at Newgate Gaol on Monday, 5 February 1900. One imagines it must have been an unusual set of circumstances: a warder whose only experience of executions was of observation, training a man who had already assisted on a handful of executions and on one occasion had looked a condemned man in the eye before placing the cap on his head and the noose around his neck, and then pulling the lever that sent him into oblivion.

William Billington finished his short course of training without any problems and was officially invited to assist his father on his next engagement, again at Newgate and again that of a woman convicted of the murder of a child. He assisted his father throughout the year, being the only assistant used until December, when the governor of Manchester's Strangeways Gaol engaged Warbrick for an execution there.

After an eighteen-month period away from home, Thomas Billington returned and assisted his father on an execution at Cork on 11 January 1901. It was only the second time Billington senior had crossed to Ireland, normally the domain of Thomas Henry Scott, but since two executions were scheduled that day – Scott was on duty in Belfast – Billington and his son crossed the sea to hang Timothy Cadogen, convicted at Cork Assizes in December 1900 of the murder of William Bird. Bird was a land agent and a dispute had arisen between the two men over a piece of land from which Cadogen had been evicted. In February 1900, Cadogen had walked into Bird's office and shot him dead as he was dealing with a client. In the condemned cell, Cadogen had failed in an attempt to cut his own throat using the metal tip of his boot.

On the following morning, it was recorded in the local paper that, once Cadogen was led onto the drop and Thomas had strapped his ankles, he moved to the lever while his father secured the cap and noose in place. Seeing that all was ready, Thomas pushed the lever, sending Cadogen to his death. This was contrary to standard procedure, but one wonders how many other times this had happened as Billington allowed his sons to gain more and more experience at executions.

Regardless of who actually pushed the lever, the execution passed off without a problem, and, with the prisoner removed from the noose, the Billingtons wasted no time in preparing to depart. They caused uproar when the coroner learned that the hangmen refused a request to attend the inquest, and following their departure from the gaol a summons was issued requiring their attendance. The inquest was postponed pending the return of the hangman, but James Billington notified them he did not plan to attend the inquest, something he had never attended in the past. James never returned to Ireland. The inquest was never reopened and technically Timothy Cadogen has never officially been certified dead.

Rival executioner Thomas Henry Scott, who carried out the execution at Belfast, was to officiate at just one further execution, when two months later he travelled from his home in Huddersfield to hang John Toole at Dublin. When a shortlist of those selected for training was compiled in 1900, Scott was declared to be unsuitable due to his dependency on strong drink, and, although his career in England never moved into the twentieth century, he stayed around to carry out the execution of Toole, the first to take place at Mountjoy Gaol, on 7 March 1901, before disappearing from the scene.

Reasons for Thomas Billington's disappearance in 1899 varied, but it coincided with the death of his wife, which may have had some bearing on events, but in a letter to the Home Office in the previous year James had written that his son Thomas had left home and joined the army.

Thomas Billington assisted his father again in March 1901 before receiving a letter from the Home Office notifying him that he must apply for training if he wished to continue assisting his father and be placed on the official list of executioners. He agreed and became the third new assistant to graduate from Newgate in three months.

Thomas and William shared assistant duties throughout the summer, but by November a new name appeared on the list of assistants when Manchester furniture salesman Henry Pierrepoint received his first appointments to assist James Billington. The second of Pierrepoint's engagements was to assist at an execution in Manchester.

Patrick McKenna had been sentenced to death on 13 November 1901 for the murder of his wife at Bolton after she had refused to give him a few pennies to buy more beer. McKenna was a regular customer in the Derby Arms and knew Billington and his sons well. In a strange twist, William Billington had helped in McKenna's arrest, as he had been passing the scene of the crime shortly after it had taken place. He was one of a number of men who managed to pin down the killer and bundle him into an outside toilet, where he was detained until the police arrived.

While McKenna's guilt was never in doubt, there had been much sympathy for him locally, and following his conviction, while he awaited his execution in the condemned cell at Strangeways, great effort went into securing him a reprieve.

For several days Billington, who suffered badly from bronchitis, had been confined to bed with a fever and sickness. He was barely able to rig the gallows and it was clear to his assistant that Billington was now a sick man. After completing their preparations, the hangmen returned to their quarters, where Billington collapsed crying out, 'I wish I'd never have come.' The following morning on the stroke of eight the hangmen entered the cell. McKenna sobbed loudly as he made the few short steps to the gallows, the prayers of the priest drowned out by his pitiful cries for the Lord to help him. Following the execution, they bade their farewells at Manchester's Victoria railway station, where Pierrepoint helped Billington into the carriage. On reaching home, Billington retired to his sickbed.

With a number of engagements already in James Billington's

diary, the authorities entrusted these to his second son William, the first of the new batch of assistants to pass out from Newgate, and therefore the highest in seniority, despite Thomas's longer record of service and more advanced years.

A few days after McKenna's execution, William and Thomas carried out an execution in Newcastle. On 10 December the brothers were again in action at Durham and three days later they carried out the execution at Northampton of a shoemaker who had stabbed his wife to death with a metal file.

As William and John spent the night in the prison in readiness for the execution at 8 a.m., in the early hours of 13 December 1901 their father's condition deteriorated rapidly. James Billington was given the last rites by the rector of the nearby parish church and died at 2.15 a.m. He was just 54 years old.

Newspapers quickly began linking his sudden death with his grim duties at the execution of McKenna, but, while he may have hastened his demise venturing out in the cold weather to execute his former friend, he was already a very sick man. Within a month, further tragedy struck the family, when Thomas Billington died. Already a widower himself, Thomas had been suffering acutely from colds, which later turned into a fatal case of pneumonia.

When William next officiated at an execution he had as his assistant his younger brother John, who, although aged just 21, had already applied and attended a course of instruction at Newgate in February 1902.

In May, with one John Ellis as his assistant, William hanged 21-year-old George Woolfe for the murder of a young woman on Tottenham Marshes. It was the last execution at the soon-to-be-demolished Newgate Gaol. Assisted by Henry Pierrepoint, William also carried out the first execution at

Pentonville in the September. Pentonville had now taken over from Newgate as centre of execution for persons convicted north of the river Thames, with Wandsworth serving for those whose crimes were committed south of the water.

William and John Billington began to form a regular partnership and, although Henry Pierrepoint was now undertaking executions as a 'number one', the Billington brothers carried out more than twenty executions in 1902.

William carried out two executions alone in Ireland in early 1903. It was an unusual case of two people being convicted of the same crime but being hanged in separate prisons two days apart. On 7 January, 25-year-old Joseph Taylor was hanged at Kilkenny for the murder of John Daly at Clonbrack, Queen's County, in June 1902. Taylor had become friends with the Daly family, but soon began an affair with John Daly's wife, Mary, some fifteen years older than Taylor. On the night of the murder Daly's son saw Taylor standing over his father and savagely kicking him as his mother looked on.

Two days later Mary Daly was hanged at nearby Tullamore. She had been sentenced to death, having been found guilty as an accessory after the fact, in the murder of her husband. Mary had been convicted largely on the testimony of her son, who claimed he heard his mother urge Taylor to kill her husband.

1903 was one of the busiest years on record for executions. Besides the earlier trip to Ireland, Billington, assisted by his brother and Henry Pierrepoint, carried out the first executions at Holloway Prison in north London. Amelia Sach and Annie Walters – 'the Finchley Baby Farmers' – were two nurses convicted at the Old Bailey of the murder of a young child. Sach ran a nursing home in East Finchley, London, where for hefty sums unmarried mothers would be cared for during pregnancy and then helped to find a suitable foster home for their newborn child. In reality the children were passed on to Walters, who would often administer a few drops of morphine-based drugs, or smother the child with a pillow. Sach denied passing children to Walters, but a search of her home revealed more than three hundred articles of baby clothing, and detectives believed the pair may have been responsible for around twenty deaths.

Later that month the brothers carried out the last execution at Ruthin Gaol, north Wales. Their visit caused great excitement in the region:

Great curiosity was evinced both in Denbigh and in Ruthin to see the hangman Billington ... From appearances no one would think for a moment the two quiet-looking, pale-faced persons attired in dark cloth suits, with bowler hats, were the men who would be chief actors in the launching of a human being into eternity ... They bore absolutely no luggage – that had previously been forwarded to the prison to await them ...

Upon arrival at the jail Billington had hardly put his hand to the bell when the ever-attentive warder inside opened the door and admitted them Once inside the two men remained there, attending to every detail associated with the execution of the wretched man Hughes ... Billington announced everything to be in perfect order before he retired early. Billington and his brother slept close to the condemned cell in which their prisoner was sleeping his last earthly sleep...

(Denbighshire Free Press, 21 February 1903)

William Hughes was a collier and former soldier who had shot dead his wife in revenge for her having had him imprisoned for non-payment of maintenance.

In April of that year the brothers were at Wandsworth, where they executed George Chapman, an alias of Polish immigrant Severiano Klosowski, who had poisoned a barmaid at the pub he ran in Southwark. Evidence later suggested he had murdered several other barmaids in previous public houses he had tenanted. Chapman had also worked as a butcher in Whitechapel during the terror spree of Jack the Ripper, and, like that of Dr Cream, whom their father had hanged ten years earlier, Chapman's name had been linked as one of the possible killers.

Besides officiating at five double executions that year, William also hanged Samuel Dougal at Chelmsford. Dougal was a thrice-married soldier and philanderer convicted of the murder of Camille Holland, whose body was found buried in a ditch at Moat Farm, Essex, four years after she had disappeared. In 1890 Dougal had applied to become a hangman, but was rejected due to his criminal record, and in 1896, he was cashiered from army service in Canada after being convicted of forgery. After serving a two-year sentence, he returned to England, where he met Camille Holland, a wealthy spinster. No sooner had he moved in with her than she caught him frolicking with a servant girl and told him to pack his bags. A week later, Holland disappeared and Dougal told neighbours she had gone on a yachting holiday and that he had been left in charge of the farm.

Over the next four years, a succession of women came and left the farm, and eventually neighbours alerted the police with their suspicious. Investigations into Holland's bank transactions led police to arrest Dougal on a charge of forgery; they then conducted a thorough search of Moat Farm, which revealed the bullet-riddled body of Camille Holland.

Dougal's execution caused a controversy when an overzealous chaplain badgered him into confessing his guilt on the scaffold. Three times, as Dougal stood noosed and bound on the gallows, he was asked if he was guilty. At the third request Dougal, who was now swaying and seemingly ready to collapse, confirmed he was and Billington pulled the lever. The conduct of the chaplain was later questioned in Parliament, and, although in his defence he said he felt Dougal had wanted to confess and therefore he gave him every opportunity to do so in what little time he had left, he was nevertheless censured for his behaviour.

Although he had completed his training only in February 1902, John Billington quickly rose up to become a senior executioner, and in early December 1903 he was engaged to carry out an execution at Manchester as chief executioner. A week later he was back assisting his brother and two days later an article appeared in a local newspaper.

A statement has appeared to the effect that William Billington contemplates resigning his work as hangman after having held the gruesome post for nearly two years from the time it became vacant on the death of his brother, who did not long survive the father.

Billington has informed a Press representative that his absence from business at Bolton causes a considerable loss and this is advanced as the reason for relinquishing the post. It is not expected that the present assistant hangman will seek the position his brother is about to vacate. (Bolton Evening News, 10 December 1903)

Any thoughts of retirement may have been premature, for on 29 December, for the first time, both brothers acted as chief executioner on the same day. William Billington officiated at Liverpool at the execution of Henry Starr, who had killed his wife at Blackpool, while at Leeds John executed Emily Swan and her boyfriend, John Gallagher, who had been jointly convicted of the murder of Swan's husband.

Hooded and noosed on the gallows Swan found the courage to wish her partner in crime 'good morning'. Gallagher replied, 'Good morning, love', while Swan managed the last words – 'Goodbye, God bless you' – before the trapdoors opened.

Acting as William's assistant at Liverpool was Henry Pierrepoint, who, as we have seen, had already carried out a number of executions as a chief, but for the next year or so was destined to play the role of assistant.

For William Billington the New Year of 1904 opened, as had the previous one, with a trip over to Ireland. In what turned out to be an eventful year for the chief executioner, William carried out his duties in all parts of the kingdom. Further trips to Ireland in April, when he hanged two men on consecutive days at Kilkenny, were sandwiched among journeys to Gloucester, Leeds, Birmingham, Liverpool and Glasgow.

On 16 August the Billington brothers were in action again as chief executioners. John officiated at Leeds while at the same hour William officiated at Birmingham, where Samuel Holden, a 52-year-old market porter and former soldier, was hanged for the knife murder of the woman with whom he lived. Holden had shown no fear at being hanged and walked to the scaffold smoking a cigar.

William carried out a double execution at Pentonville in December. It was his last execution in England. A week later travelled down to Cardiff to execute Eric Lange, a thirty-year-old Russian seaman convicted of the murder of John Jones, landlord of the Bridgend Tavern, at Ystrad, in the Rhondda Valley. Lange had broken into the pub, looking for items to steal. His presence disturbed the landlord's wife, whom he struck with a blunt instrument when she began screaming. When the noise woke Jones, Lange stabbed him with a knife in the ensuing struggle.

On the morning of the execution, Lange asked Billington and his assistant John Ellis, if they would pinion him with his arms in front rather than behind him. They declined his request.

It was William Billington's last execution on the mainland. With his brother now the chief executioner in Great Britain, William Billington was to officiate at just one further hanging, when he travelled to Cork to dispatch John Foster, an ex-policeman in the Royal Irish Constabulary, who had murdered William Regan, a former American soldier. The two men lodged together but in December Regan's body was found floating in the River Lee. A blood-covered iron bar discovered on the riverbank eventually led police to Foster, who was arrested after trying to pawn the dead man's gold watch and chain. Taken into custody, he was found to have bloodstains on his clothing. William Billington was assisted by John Ellis, although first-choice hangman John Billington had originally been engaged – he had had to turn down the request due to a commitment in London.

PROCEDURE

Once a prison received a prisoner under sentence of death, letters were sent out to various prisons requesting the secondment of officers to work on condemned duties. Six warders would be rostered onto condemned-cell duty and would work in pairs in the three shifts. There would be no days off once they began their duties and the shifts rotated every week, from the nightshift, afternoon shift and to the shorter day shift.

Following conviction and arrival, the prisoner would be housed in a specially constructed condemned cell. These cells varied depending on the prison, but an article in a Sunday magazine in the 1980s described the condemned cell at Bristol in 1963 as being 25 feet long and 12 feet wide. It contained a single bed, bedside cabinet and lamp at one end of the cell with a table and three reasonably comfortable chairs at the other. At one end of the cell was a door leading into the bathroom and another door to the toilet. The guards had to stay with the condemned prisoner in the bathroom and the toilet in case he tried to pre-empt the sentence.

In the middle of the room was a locked door, which led across a narrow corridor to another door – the execution chamber. There was no mention in the article as to whether the door was concealed. In some cells a single wardrobe concealed the door that led to the gallows, but in others the door was left unhidden. This second door was used by the prisoner going out to exercise and led to a narrow corridor into which the prisoner turned left or right and headed out towards the exercise yard.

What the prisoner didn't realise was that the wall

facing the door, usually containing a row of coat pegs, was a false partition that could be removed in a matter of minutes revealing a walk-on gallows floor. Thus, five or six paces would take the prisoner from the condemned cell to the trapdoors. In this arrangement the prisoner would be unaware how close he was from the gallows.

Imagining it may be minutes before he meets the end, with the door open and the scaffold clearly visible, he could see that he was now just seconds away from standing on the trapdoors. Some resisted, but, with the trapdoors being so close, warders would help drag the prisoner to the noose.

Some hangmen, John Ellis in particular, preferred to leave the prisoner in the company of their assistant, walking in front and waiting for the assistant to bring the prisoner onto the drop. Albert Pierrepoint usually walked a pace or two in front of the prisoner and on reaching the drop would stop, turn around and, with outstretched arms, position the prisoner on the chalked 'T' mark on the edges of the trapdoor.

As the assistant swooped down to secure the ankles, the hangman would withdraw a white cap, usually worn like a foppish handkerchief in his top pocket, whip it over the prisoner's head, then place the noose, pulling it tight into position under the left ear with the 'eye' facing to the front.

By this time the assistant would have stepped back. If not, a tap on the shoulder would be the signal to move. The hangman would then reach across to the lever, remove the safety pin and push it, releasing the trapdoors and allowing the prisoner to drop to his death.

With shades of what had happened to his father and older brother four years earlier at the same gaol, William Billington was issued with a summons for failing to attend the inquest after the execution. The coroner postponed it for a week, allowing the hangman time to return, but, when it was learned that Billington had left in a hurry to catch a boat back to the mainland, and had not deliberately shunned the inquest, it was allowed to proceed.

John Billington's career outlasted that of his brother by just four months. In August, as John Billington travelled to Knutsford for a rare execution in the rural Cheshire prison, William Billington was incarcerated in the newly refurbished Wakefield Gaol serving a one-month prison sentence.

On 20 July he had been charged with failing to maintain his wife and their two children, who had been admitted to the Bolton Union Workhouse a few months earlier. He had been issued with a separation order and ordered to pay the sum of 16 shillings a week. His wife reported that the hangman had failed to pay her a single penny, while Billington responded by saying that she was now living with another man. Billington told the court he had been out of work for several months but had now found a job and was able to make payment.

On 15 August while his brother counted the days to his release in a prison cell, John Billington travelled over to Leeds to carry out the execution of Thomas Tattersall. Tattersall was a plasterer from Wakefield who had killed his wife by cutting her throat. Prior to his arrest he had been working at Wakefield Gaol, where one of his last jobs had been helping to construct the new gallows there.

With John's brother now off the list and indisposed in prison, and the only other two serving executioners engaged on a job elsewhere, the prison authorities found themselves with a shortage of assistants. Of the eight names on the official list in 1901, there now remained just three. Both James and Thomas Billington had died, William was in prison, Wade hadn't assisted at an execution since the previous century and Warbrick hadn't been called upon since 1900. To date this had been enough to fulfil requirements, but now there was a problem finding an assistant to help John Billington at Leeds. The governor solved it by wiring William Warbrick, whose last appearance on the gallows had been in the days of James Billington's tenure as chief.

Surprised as he was at the sudden call, Warbrick sent his acceptance and duly turned up at Leeds. On the afternoon before the execution, a rare and terrible accident occurred. As the drop was being rigged and the scaffold prepared, John Billington stepped back and tumbled through the open trapdoor that led to the pit below. Although he got to his feet at once it was found that he had suffered cracked ribs and mild concussion in the fall. John was able to carry out his duties satisfactorily on the following morning but soon after returning home he was taken ill. Two months later he died at his home in Coppull, near Chorley. The cause of death was pleurisy, attributed, the doctors believed, to his fall. He was just 25 and left a widow and young baby.

His death brought to an end a dynasty stretching back over twenty years, during which time the Billingtons had between them hanged more than two hundred men and women. It was a legacy that would not be beaten for another fifty years.

MEMORANDUM OF INSTRUCTIONS FOR CARRYING OUT AN EXECUTION, 1891

Confidential

(By order of the Secretary of State, this document is to be treated as most strictly confidential, but the responsible Works Officer should be given the opportunity to study its contents. In any case when a copy is supplied to a Sheriff he is requested to return it to the Prison Governor from whom he received it.)

1. The trap doors shall be stained a dark colour and their outer edges shall be defined by a white line 3 inches broad painted around the edge of the pit outside the traps.

2. (a) A week before execution the apparatus for the execution shall be tested in the following manner under the supervision of the Works Officer, the Governor being present:

The working of the scaffold will first be tested without any weight. Then a bag of dry sand of the same weight as the culprit will be attached to the rope and so adjusted as to allow the bag a drop equal to, or rather more than, that which the culprit should receive, so that the rope may be stretched with a force of not more than 1,000 foot-pounds. The working of the apparatus under these conditions will then be tested. The bag must be of the approved rope and leather. Towelling will be supplied for padding the neck of the bag under the noose. As the gutta percha round the noose end of the execution ropes hardens in cold weather, care should be taken to have it warmed and manipulated immediately before the bag is tested.

(b) On the day before the execution the apparatus shall be tested again as above, the Governor, the Works Officer and the executioner present. For the purpose of this test a note of the height and weight of the culprit should be obtained from the Medical Officer and handed to the executioner.

3. After the completion of each test the scaffold and all the appliances will be locked up, and the key kept by the Governor or other responsible officer; but the bag of sand should remain suspended all the night preceding the execution so as to take the stretch out of the rope.

4. The executioner and any persons appointed to assist in the operation should make themselves thoroughly acquainted with the working of the apparatus.

5. In order to prevent accidents during the preliminary tests and procedure the lever will be fixed by a safety-pin, and the Works or other Prison Officer charged with the care of the apparatus prior to the execution will be responsible for seeing that the pin is properly in position both before and after the tests. The responsibility for withdrawing the pin at the execution will rest on the executioner.

6. Death by hanging ought to result from dislocation of the neck. The length of the drop will be determined in accordance with the attached Table of Drops.

7. The required length of drop is regulated as follows: (a) At the end of the rope which forms the noose the

executioner should see that 13 inches from the centre of the ring are marked off by twine wrapped round the covering; this is to be a fixed quantity, which, with the stretching of this portion of the rope, and the lengthening of the neck and body of the culprit, will represent the average depth of the head and circumference of the neck after constriction.

(b) While the bag of sand is still suspended, the executioner will measure off from the twine wrapped round the rope the required length of drop and will make a chalk mark on the rope at the end of this length. A piece of copper wire fastened to the chain will now be stretched down the rope till it reaches the chalk mark, and will be cut off there so that the cut end of the copper wire shall terminate at the upper end of the measured length of drop. The bag of sand will then be raised from the pit, and disconnected from the rope.

The chain will now be so adjusted at the bracket that the lower end of the copper wire shall reach to the same level from the floor of the scaffold as the height of the prisoner. The known height of the prisoner can be readily measured on the scaffold by a graduated rule of six foot six inches long. When the chain has been raised by the proper height the cotter must be securely fixed through the bracket and chain. The executioner will now make a chalk mark on the floor of the scaffold, in a plumb line with the chain, where the prisoner should stand.

(c) These details will be attended to as soon as possible after 6 a.m. on the day of the execution so as to allow the rope time to regain a portion of its elasticity before the execution, and, if possible, the gutta percha on the rope should again be warmed.

8. The copper wire will now be detached, and after allowing a sufficient amount of rope for the easy adjustment of the noose, the slack of the rope should be fastened to the chain above the level of the head of the culprit with a pack-thread. The pack-thread should just be strong enough to support the rope without breaking.

9. When all the preparations are completed the scaffold will remain in the charge of a responsible officer until the time fixed for the execution.

10. At the time fixed for the execution, the executioner will go to the pinioning room, which should be as close as practicable to the scaffold, and there apply the apparatus. When the culprit is pinioned and his neck bared he will be at once conducted to the scaffold.

11. On reaching the scaffold the procedure will be as follows.

The executioner will:
1. Place the culprit exactly under the part of the beam to which the rope is attached.

2. Put the white linen cap on the culprit.

3 (a) Put on the rope round the neck quite tightly (with the cap between the rope and the neck), the metal eye being directed forwards, and placed in front of the angle of the lower jaw so that with the constriction of the neck it may come underneath the chin. The noose should be

kept tight by means of a stiff leather washer, or an India rubber washer, or a wedge.

(b) While the executioner is carrying out the procedure in paragraph (a) the assistant executioner will:

Strap the culprit's legs tightly.

Step back beyond the white safety line so as to be well clear of the trap doors.

Give an agreed visual signal to the executioner to show that he is clear.

(c) On receipt of the signal from his assistant the executioner will:

Withdraw the safety pin.

Pull the lever which lets down the trap doors.

The body will hang for a minimum of 45 minutes and then be carefully raised from the pit provided the Medical Officer declares life to be extinct. Then the body will be detached from the rope and removed to the place set aside for the Coroner's inspection, a careful record having first been made and given to the Medical Officer of both the initial and final drops. The rope will be removed from the neck, and also the straps from the body. In laying out the body for the inquest the head will be raised three inches by placing a small piece of wood under it.

Chapter 3:

A New Century

A Home Office memo written in 1900 stated that the Prison Commissioners were looking to increase the number of assistants and letters were sent to governors of provincial prisoners asking if they had any suitable men on file. At Manchester there were two suitable applicants: Henry Pierrepoint and S E Adlam. Adlam was interviewed at the prison but rejected for further consideration when the police report came back that he was unfit for office; the report on Pierrepoint was satisfactory and he was deemed suitable for training.

Born in Nottinghamshire, Henry Pierrepoint had moved to Bradford in his childhood and was working in a mill when he read that the career of local hangman James Berry had come to an end. At thirteen years of age, Pierrepoint decided that this was the career he wanted. On reaching his eighteenth birthday he moved to Manchester, where he found work as a salesman in a furniture store managed by his sister.

Four years later he applied for the post of executioner, writing directly to the Home Secretary, who in turn passed the application to the governor of Pierrepoint's local prison. Pierrepoint was invited to Manchester's Strangeways Prison for an interview by Governor Robert Cruickshank, and following a tough interrogation he was sent to Newgate Gaol for a week's training as an executioner.

Pierrepoint carried out his first executions as assistant to James Billington in the winter of 1901, but there were no further calls until March 1902, when he was engaged at Shrewsbury Prison for the first time as chief executioner. The execution passed off without incident, although he neglected to mention the case when he serialised his memoirs in later life. In April, he assisted William Billington for the first time, and for the rest of that year and the next three he assisted both Billington brothers several times as well as carrying out executions as the chief.

On 9 August 1905, Pierrepoint worked as an assistant for the last time, assisting John Billington at an execution at Knutsford. Prisoner William Hancocks had lost an arm in an accident on the railways and, devising a strap based on the principle of the body belt his predecessors had used, Pierrepoint was able to secure the man's arm behind his back allowing for a successful execution on the following morning. He posed for a picture using the belt when he wrote his memoirs in 1916.

Pierrepoint's name was moved to the top of the list of Britain's executioners following the death of John Billington, and for the next eighteen months he officiated at every execution in the United Kingdom.

In February 1907 Pierrepoint carried out the first private execution behind prison walls in St Helier in Jersey and in the following August he hanged three people in one week, including, for the first time in his career, a woman. On a hot afternoon in August he travelled to Cardiff, where he was to execute Sunderland-born Mrs Leslie James, who preferred to use the name Rhoda Willis. She had fallen on hard times and, in an attempt to make some money, placed an advert offering her services in finding places for unwanted babies, for a fee. Asked by a woman whose unmarried sister was expecting a baby to take in the child when it was born, she had also arranged to take in another child, and, finding herself unable to cope with the babies in her care, she suffocated one of them. Her landlady made the grim discovery and the police were called.

The Pierrepoint brothers – Henry and his elder brother Tom – were to be in action on all subsequent executions that year and in 1908 Henry carried out fourteen of the fifteen executions, which included trips to Scotland, Ireland and Wales. By 1909 Pierrepoint began to notice that a number of engagements were being given to his former assistant, John Ellis. Ellis acted as his assistant five times during 1909 and tensions between the two gradually began to build.

In August 1909, Pierrepoint was engaged to execute Madar Dal Dhingra, an Indian engineering student who was studying at London University. Dhingra had attended a concert at the Imperial Institute in Kensington in July 1909 and, as the audience departed, he shot dead Sir William Curzon-Wylie, the aide-de-camp to the Secretary of State for India. He tried to shoot himself immediately after the murder, but failed and was apprehended. At his trial he refused representation and said that Sir William had been assassinated, as he was an enemy of his people. When sentenced to death, Dhingra said he was proud to lay down his life for the people of his country.

Henry Pierrepoint began the New Year of 1910 with a trip

to Dublin to hang Richard Hefferman. Hefferman had formed a friendship with Mary Walker, who had helped him find work in the post office, where she was also employed, and, when she was found on a canal bank having been stabbed to death, Hefferman was soon arrested.

Along with his brother, Pierrepoint travelled via Holyhead to Ireland, where he found that a bureaucratic error meant his name had been released to the crew as one of the passengers. This potentially dangerous situation was averted when he was ushered to a quiet part of the boat, where he could travel undisturbed.

Arriving at the prison, the hangmen were informed that the condemned man had tried to take his own life by running head first into the cell wall, resulting in a fractured skull. When this had failed Hefferman had then attempted to cheat the hangman by trying to rip out his throat with his bare hands. To prevent a further attempt, the prisoner was sent to spend the last days of his life heavily sedated in the prison hospital.

On the morning of the execution, Hefferman was crying hysterically and repeatedly kissing the large crucifix held by one of two priests there to administer the last rites and witness the execution. The execution was delayed for a time as the priests showed no inclination to allow it to proceed, and eventually the procession was made to the gallows, where Pierrepoint and his brother had to force the priests clear of the trapdoors before pushing the lever.

William Murphy, a former soldier from Leigh, near Bolton, lived with Gwen Jones and her children in Holyhead. Jones was separated from her husband but, when Murphy left his home in Holyhead to look for work in Yorkshire, she returned to him. When Murphy found out, and failed to persuade her to come back to him, he cut her throat and threw her body into a ditch. He was hanged by Pierrepoint on

15 February 1910, becoming the last man to be hanged in North Wales.

In July Pierrepoint travelled to Essex to execute Frederick Foreman at Chelmsford. Foreman had been convicted of the murder of Elizabeth Ely, with whom he lived in an old disused railway carriage. Foreman was charged with her murder following the discovery of her badly beaten body lying in a field. Death was in fact due to exposure.

When Pierrepoint turned up at the prison to carry out the execution it was clear that he had been drinking, and, as he met his assistant Ellis in the gatehouse of the prison, the old feud between them came to the boil. He called Ellis an 'Irish bastard' and punched him in the face, before a warder broke up the fight. The hangman and assistant carried out the execution on the following morning, but, on arriving home, Ellis wrote to the prison complaining of Pierrepoint's behaviour, and when it reached the ear of Home Secretary Winston Churchill he ordered the hangman's dismissal. An official memo was circulated that with immediate effect the name of Henry Albert Pierrepoint had been removed from the list of persons.

He made vain attempts to get his name reinstated in the following year but the commission refused to reconsider their decision and he later uprooted his family from Huddersfield, where he been working in the gas works, to his wife's home city of Manchester, where he died in 1922 shortly after the publication of his memoirs.

John Ellis was born in the Balderstone district of Rochdale, Lancashire, on 4 October 1874. His father Joseph ran a barbershop on Oldham Road, and after he left school it was expected that Ellis would follow into the family business, but at the age of sixteen he started work in the local Eagle spinning mill. In February 1898, following an accident at work that left him with a painful back injury, he left the mill and set up as a hairdresser, but this was a short-lived venture and he was soon working at another mill, this time at Tweedale & Smalley at Castleton, where he was employed as a labourer. He then moved to Balderstone Mill as a warehouseman between January and April 1900. On 12 April 1900 he set up business at 451 Oldham Road, Rochdale, as a barber, and it was while working there that he applied to become an executioner.

On 18 March he attended Strangeways Gaol for an interview with Governor Cruickshank. Ellis had produced references from previous employers and impressed the governor sufficiently for him to pen the short memo to the Home Office once he had left the gaol.

> ... I beg to report that I consider him well qualified for the office he seeks. From the nature of his testimonials I have deemed it unnecessary to ask the police to furnish me with a report as to his character. He can get away from his employment at any time.

The Home Office, however, wrote back that it would be prudent to have a police check on Ellis and in due course it came back as totally satisfactory. In early May he attended Newgate Gaol for a course of training and on 5 May medical officer James Scott wrote that he had seen Ellis at training and in his opinion he was 'likely to discharge his duties satisfactorily if he is called upon'.

The training went well and on 8 May 1901 Ellis was notified that his name had been added to the list of executioners and assistants, at a rate of £10 plus expenses for the executioner and £2.2.0 for the assistant.

Ellis got the first chance to earn his 2 guineas when he was invited to assist William Billington at an execution in Newcastle.

Sixty-seven-year-old John Miller had been in dispute with his stepfather Joseph Ferguson over some property owned by Mary, his mother. Siding with him in the dispute was his nephew, 37-year-old John Robert Miller. Both men believed they were being cut out of an inheritance. The whole family worked in the amusement industry, travelling from fair to fair, although they lived at Cullercoats in Northumberland.

On 20 September 1901, uncle and nephew entered a shop in North Shields and bought a long-blade knife. The younger Miller paid for it, telling the shopkeeper he needed it for his job as a ship's cook. Later that day, the two men called to see Ferguson. When the old man opened the door, the Millers, both the worse for drink, charged in. A fight broke out during which Ferguson was stabbed six times in the face and head. As Mary Ferguson came downstairs, her son stood beside the body of his stepfather, while the nephew, a knife still in his hand, boasted he had just killed her husband.

Both were arrested and, at their trial for murder, the elder Miller denied any involvement and claimed he had tried to stop the attack. They were sentenced to death and it was decided they would hang together. With their father indisposed, William and Thomas Billington were engaged to carry out the execution and it was decided that Ellis should be present as a second assistant.

Ellis wrote later that on the day before the execution he had met William Billington for the first time when the train from Bolton to Newcastle stopped at Rochdale, where Ellis was to board. Passing through the ticket barrier, he was attracted by the attention given by passengers on the platform to a portly man who was pacing up and down as the train stood waiting to depart. When he learned that the identity of the man was none other than William Billington, Ellis approached the hangman and said he would accompany him to Newcastle.

'Tha's doin' nowt o' t'sort,' Billington barked at him, until Ellis offered the official letter of engagement, after seeing which Billington invited him to join his carriage. Reaching the prison, the hangmen were given more details of the prisoners and learned that, as the date of execution approached, John Robert Miller had lost all his bravado and had become hysterical and very distressed.

It was therefore decided that the two men would be hanged separately. The younger Miller was to be hanged first at 8 a.m., the uncle an hour and a half later. Since there was enough room in the hangman's quarters for only two executioners, Ellis was given accommodation in an empty condemned cell next door to the nephew. He spent a sleepless night kept awake by both his own nerves and the fearful cries, shouts and threats from the highly distressed prisoner next door.

At a few moments to 8 a.m. on the following morning, Saturday, 7 December, having watched the Billingtons rig the gallows in readiness, Ellis stood outside a condemned cell for the first time and watched for the signal to begin. After the screaming and crying that had rung out from the cell throughout the previous night, the prisoner now seemed to have composed himself enough to face his death. He was staring vacantly into space as they entered and strapped his arms. Ellis was allowed to strap his ankles when they reached the drop, and after he had stepped back, the trapdoor opened and Miller dropped to his doom. Ninety minutes later the uncle followed him to the gallows without incident. Ellis returned home and gave an interview to a local reporter that found its way into the Daily Mail the following Saturday.

'An assistant hangman has been appointed in the person of Mr. John Ellis, a braid draper of Rochdale,' it read. 'He is proud of his appointment, he says, and was not nervous at his first "operation" this week.'

When word reached the Prison Commissioners they quickly wrote to Ellis.

Mr. John Ellis

Certain remarks in the Public Press regarding
your recent appointment as an assistant
executioner have been brought to the notice of the
Prison Commissioners. I am directed by them to
point out to you that the Memorandum of
Conditions, to which any person acting as
Executioner or Assistant at an execution is
required to conform, prohibits you from giving to
any person particulars on the subject of your
duties for publication, and to warn you that any
infringement of these conditions will be
attended by the removal of your name from
the list of persons qualified to assist or carry
out executions.

Ellis assisted Henry Pierrepoint at his first execution on 18 March 1902 and six weeks later assisted William Billington at an execution that marked the end of an era at the historic Newgate Gaol.

George Woolfe was a young soldier convicted of the murder of his former girlfriend, Charlotte Cheeseman. Woolfe had promised to marry her but had suddenly and callously broken off the romance, writing her a short note.

Miss Cheeseman,

Just a line. On Monday morning I made the
acquaintance of a young lady who I admire much
better than you; therefore you had better do the
same and think no more of me. I hope you will take
this as goodbye for good.

G Woolfe.

PS. I hope I shall never hear of you or see you
again, as I am thankful I have got rid of you so
easily. I have got the date I went to you, so if you
find yourself in trouble, or I mean in a certain
condition, it will be no good to put the blame on
me. I pity the man who ever gets tied to you, but I
am glad that I am free at last and now I have a
chance of being my old self again.

Unfortunately, Charlotte was too much in love and replied
to the note saying she would forgive him, and with Woolfe
appearing to have reconciled his differences with her they met
up on 25 January 1902 and were seen together in an East End
pub. The following morning, a young boy out playing
football discovered Cheeseman's body on Tottenham
Marshes. She had been battered to death with a chisel. Two
weeks later Woolfe was arrested after enlisting in the army
under an assumed name. Given a drop of 7 feet 8 inches, he
was the last man to be hanged at Newgate prison.

Ellis's next memorable executions both took place in 1903,
when in July he was present at two executions in a week at
Chelmsford, the second being that of philanderer Samuel
Dougal. Ellis was present at Manchester on 2 December, when
John Billington made his debut as chief executioner. He
assisted John Billington again at the end of the month at
Leeds, when he hanged Emily Swann and John Gallagher. Not

only was it Ellis's first double execution, but it was also the first time he had been present at the execution of a woman.

In 1905 Ellis was present at twelve executions, including one in Ireland (on his first trip there), when he assisted at what became William Billington's last engagement. He was present at the execution of Arthur Deveraux in August, and at the end of December he assisted Henry Pierrepoint when they hanged three men in three days.

On 17 November 1906, 53-year-old father-of-two John Davies called at the house of Jane Harrison at Aston Manor and after a row he cut her throat and fled. He was tried at Warwick Assizes on 10 December 1906, where his defence pleaded that the crime was not premeditated and should be reduced to manslaughter, but the jury returned a guilty verdict.

Ellis was contacted and was delighted to learn he had received the call to carry out the execution as number one instead of as assistant. It was the second occasion he had been offered a senior role. The first, to hang a Preston warehouseman at Manchester, had been cancelled when a reprieve was granted just a few days before he received this engagement.

Ellis arrived at Warwick Gaol on New Year's Eve to prepare for the execution due the following morning. With his calculations worked out and the drop rigged, the under-sheriff, perhaps mindful that it was Ellis's first time in charge, asked what the proposed drop would be. Told that he had decided on 7 feet 9 inches the under-sheriff told Ellis that he believed his calculation was wrong and that the drop was too long.

'I have seen more executions that you have, and I consider that a most unsuitable drop,' he told Ellis.

'Very possibly you have, but seeing an execution and performing one are two distinctly different things,' Ellis retorted.

Told that he thought a drop of 4–5 feet was more suitable,

Ellis told the under-sheriff he would take heed of his advice if he took full responsibility, at which he backed down and told Ellis to please himself.

Ellis spent the evening practising his pinioning technique and going over the arrangements with his assistant William Willis, who was participating in only his third execution. The occasion passed off without any undue incident, although the long walk from the condemned cell to the drop almost caused the prisoner to collapse.

Despite the confrontation between Ellis and the under-sheriff, he was invited back to Warwick that spring. Edwin Moore was a 33-year-old ex-private in the Royal Warwickshire Regiment, who had murdered his mother at Leamington Spa. Assisted again by Willis, as Ellis walked away a warder asked him if Moore was dead.

Told he was, the guard responded, 'Well, you've just hanged an innocent man.' Unperturbed, Ellis replied, 'Well, we can't help that. We had to carry out our orders.' The time span of the case was one of the quickest times on record: taking just 33 days from crime to execution.

Ellis carried out an execution in Scotland in the summer of 1908, but for most of the next couple of years he had to be content with the role of assistant. However, following the incident at Chelmsford in July 1910, when he was attacked and violently assaulted, he was exonerated of any blame and promoted to the undisputed chief executioner. His first execution in the post Henry Pierrepoint era was at Newcastle, where he put to death the man convicted of a brutal murder in a railway carriage.

Forty-five-year-old John Alexander Dickman had been convicted of the murder of a wages clerk, John Nisbet, who had been robbed of £400 and shot dead in the carriage of a slow train from Newcastle to Morpeth as it pulled into the station at Alnmouth. Witnesses told police they had seen Nisbet board the train in the company of a man identified as John Dickman, a professional gambler. When interviewed, Dickman admitted being on the train but denied the murder, but his seemingly ready replies to their questions drew suspicion upon himself and a search of his house unearthed a pair of bloodstained trousers and a number of gold sovereigns.

Placed on an identity parade, Dickman was picked out by several witnesses and a probe into his background found that he had been having trouble with mounting debts. Although the evidence against him was purely circumstantial, detectives believed they had a case. On 4 July he appeared before Lord Coleridge at Newcastle Assizes, and despite evidence that Nisbet had gunshot wounds from two different guns – suggesting two killers – Dickman alone was convicted. Passing sentence Coleridge said, 'In your hunger for gold you had no pity on the victim you slew.'

Dickman's conviction caused a massive public outcry, and a mass protest took place outside of the prison. He continued to protest his innocence while Ellis worked out the drop in the execution shed. On the following morning Ellis and Willis rose early and finished their preparations and, as they made their way from the execution shed across the grounds to their quarters, they spotted reporters perched on the roofs of houses that overlooked the prison. Prison officials went over to the first house and asked the journalist to come down from the roof but, when told he was within his rights to stay put, the officials were forced to erect a screen of heavy tarpaulin to block the view of the prisoner on his last walk to the drop.

Oblivious of events taking place outside, Dickman was asked by the chaplain if he wished to make a confession before he was hanged.

'No! I will admit to nothing. I am innocent,' he maintained.

Despite the warm weather outside, Dickman was wearing a topcoat and, as the executioners entered, he began to button it up. Ellis pinioned his arms and, as they formed a procession to the scaffold, Dickman began to resist.

'I'm not going to die with my coat on!' he shouted, 'I want it off!'

This left Ellis with a dilemma. One of the most crucial parts of the execution protocol on the morning was to get the prisoner's arms secured. Once the condemned man was pinioned, the chances of any untoward incident on the drop were drastically reduced. But Dickman seemed adamant he didn't want to move as long as he was wearing his coat. If the gallows had been in the adjacent cell he might well have had Dickman manhandled onto the drop, but, with the execution shed a walk across the grounds, Ellis decided to agree to the request. He loosened the strap and helped the prisoner out of his coat. As it was thrown onto his bunk, Ellis quickly fastened the straps and led the procession to the gallows. Dickman never spoke another word and died without making any confession.

Although many believed Dickman went to the gallows an innocent man, police investigating the case had on file another murder proven against Dickman, which they would have proceeded with had he been acquitted.

There were no further executions in Great Britain until November of that year, when Ellis was involved with four in nine days. The first took place at Lancaster, when Thomas Rawcliffe was hanged for strangling his wife. It was the last execution to take place at the historic castle prison. A week later, Ellis hanged another strangler at Liverpool before travelling down to London to play a part, on 23 November 1910, in one of the most notorious murder cases of the twentieth century: that of the infamous Dr Crippen.

A New Century

Hawley Harvey Crippen was a 48-year-old American-born 'doctor', who made history as the first murderer captured with the assistance of wireless. He came to England at the turn of the century, and although he had medical qualifications gained in America, he was unable to practise in England as a doctor. He set himself up as a seller of patent medicines, while his wife turned their spacious home at Hilldrop Crescent into a guesthouse. Mrs Crippen worked as a music-hall singer under the name of Belle Elmore and dominated the mild-mannered Crippen, who would meekly obey her commands to clean the house, do the chores, and even to polish their guests' shoes.

Early in 1910, Belle Elmore vanished. Crippen told friends she had returned to America to care for a sick relative and wasted no time in inviting his secretary and clandestine lover, Ethel Le Neve, back to the house, where she was soon seen wearing Belle's furs and jewellery. Belle had failed to notify anyone of her visit to America, and, when her theatrical friends grew suspicious, one of them contacted the police.

Scotland Yard's Chief Inspector Walter Dew called at the north London house and questioned Crippen about his wife's disappearance. He confessed that the story about her visiting a sick relation was false, and the truth was simply that she had been having an affair, and had left the country with her new lover.

But the police visit had shaken Crippen's nerve and he decided to flee the country. With Ethel disguised as a boy, they booked passage to Canada as Mr and Master Robinson, and headed for Antwerp, where they caught a transatlantic steamer. Unfortunately for Crippen, detectives returned to his house to check on a couple of points in the statement and finding the house deserted, Dew ordered a thorough search. Belle's body was unearthed in the cellar.

The renowned pathologist Bernard Spilsbury, on his first major criminal case, was able to confirm that the remains belonged to the missing woman, and that the cause of death was hyoscine poisoning.

The case now made headlines in all the world's press. For days the papers carried the story of the search for the missing couple, several mentioning that police believed Crippen might attempt to leave the country. On board in the Atlantic, the captain of the SS Montrose read the press reports and became suspicious of two of his passengers. Suspecting they might be the fugitives Crippen and Le Neve, he dispatched a wireless message to Scotland Yard. Dew caught a faster ship and was able to meet the Montrose as it docked in Canada.

Crippen was brought back to London to stand trial for the murder of his wife. Ethel Le Neve was charged with being an accessory. Tried before Lord Alverstone at the Old Bailey in October, Crippen pleaded not guilty and claimed that the body in the cellar could have been there before he moved in. He admitted that he had purchased a pair of pyjamas similar to those in which the body had been wrapped. The label on the jacket bore the manufacturer's new name, a name they had adopted in 1909 after becoming a limited company, by which time the Crippens were occupying the house at Hilldrop Crescent. This proved beyond doubt that the body in the cellar could have been buried there only while Crippen occupied the house. On 18 October he was found guilty and sentenced to death. Ethel Le Neve was acquitted and emigrated to America on the morning of her lover's execution. Crippen tried to cheat the hangman by attempting to cut his own throat with a part of his spectacles as he lay in bed on the night prior to his execution. On 23 November he was hanged at Pentonville.

In 1911 Ellis hanged William Palmer, a Manchester-born

painter who went to the gallows protesting loudly against the injustice of the sentence. A few months later Ellis officiated at his first double execution as chief executioner. On 17 October he hanged two men at Pentonville. One was Edward Hill, a fireman convicted of the murder of his wife at King's Cross. Hanged alongside Hill was Francisco Godhino, a native of Goa who had battered to death a stewardess, Alice Brewster, aboard a transatlantic liner en route from Sydney to London.

Ellis carried out the execution assisted by two new assistants, William Conduit of Manchester, who had assisted him earlier in the year at Chelmsford, and Albert Lumb of Bradford, present at his first execution. Hill collapsed in a faint while waiting for the noose to be placed around his neck and the scene was probably too much for Conduit, who never officiated at another execution.

Early in 1913 Ellis executed John Williams, known in the press as George Mackay – 'the Hooded Man', who had been convicted of the murder of Inspector Arthur Walls, shot dead at a mansion in Eastbourne after he had been sent to investigate a burglary. Williams was arrested in London after a tip-off and returned to Sussex to stand trial. Following conviction, he was visited in the death cell by his girlfriend, who had given birth to his child as he awaited execution. Refused permission to marry, she was however granted permission to visit on the day before his execution, and, holding his newborn son in his arms, Williams pressed a small piece of prison bread into his tiny hand. 'Now nobody can say your father never gave you anything,' he said.

Ellis officiated at almost all of the capital cases that resulted in execution as the country moved towards World War One, the most notable being that of George Ball, hanged at Liverpool for the horrific murder of his employer. Miss Christina Bradfield was the manageress of the family business where Ball worked. On 10 December, Ball and a fellow employee, Samuel Elltoft, were seen leaving their workplace, wheeling a cart. When Christina Bradfield's body was found in the canal the next morning, Elltoft and Ball were soon arrested. Ball was found to be in possession of the victim's watch. At their trial, he was found guilty of murder and sentenced to death, while Elltoft received four years after pleading guilty to being an accessory.

In the November Ellis hanged the oldest man convicted in Britain of murder in the twentieth century. Charles Frembd was a 71-year-old German grocer convicted of the murder of his wife at Leytonstone in the September. Louisa Frembd was found dead in bed, her nightdress covered in blood, with her husband lying next to her. Both had cut throats, although his wound was a minor, self-inflicted one. Beside the bed Frembd had left a simple note: 'Her first husband made off with himself. I cannot stand it any longer. God forgive me. Her temper done it.' Normally, a defendant of this age would have been spared the gallows, but Frembd went to his death a victim of the strong anti-German feeling at the time.

Although born in Germany, Frembd had lived in Britain for 54 years and, after the execution, the inquest recorded that the punishment had been satisfactorily carried out but that the deceased had a bruised eye caused by the trapdoor catching his head as he fell.

In 1915 Ellis executed another notorious killer whose name passed into the annals of criminal history. George Joseph Smith, the infamous 'Brides in the Bath' murderer, had graduated from petty crime to swindling and bigamy, then finally to multiple killings in order to satisfy his greed. His *fortunate* 'wives' lost only their possessions, while the unlucky ones, Beatrice Mundy, Alice Burnham and Margaret Lofty, were drowned in their baths.

Smith might have evaded arrest if detectives had not been alerted by the relatives of two of his victims who had noticed a newspaper account headlined A bride's tragic fate, which recalled the tale of a newlywed bride who drowned on her honeymoon. The similarities between this and their own tragedies aroused suspicion, and, when both separately reported it to the police, discreet enquiries led to Smith's being detained and later charged with the murder of three women.

Convicted at the Old Bailey on 22 June, he was hanged on Friday, 13 August, by Ellis and his new assistant Edward Taylor. Smith spent his final days on Earth in sheer terror at the thought of his fate and it was claimed he was dragged screaming to the gallows.

Later that year Ellis officiated at an execution at Bedford and, arriving at the prison, he found that in a cost-cutting measure no assistant had been engaged. He discovered this move only when he arrived at the gaol and immediately voiced his concerns, adding that without an assistant he would not be strapping the prisoner's legs on the drop the following morning. 'Place your feet together as soon as we get there,' Ellis told the prisoner, William Reeve, when they met in the condemned cell on the morning of the execution.

Ellis was not happy at the lack of assistant and wrote at once to the Prison Commissioners outlining his fears. Taking heed from their chief executioner, who had thus far caused them no problems, they duly reinstated assistant executioners and, when Ellis was next called upon to carry out his duties, it was at a double execution at Liverpool.

It was the first time he had carried out a double execution since 1911 and by a strange quirk of fate the two cases bore several similarities. In both cases one of the crimes had been committed on the high seas and one of the condemned men bore the name of Hill (see the case of Edward Hill and

Francisco Godhino above). Even more bizarrely, when Ellis got both men onto the gallows, prisoner Young Hill lost control of his senses and let out a fearful scream before he was silenced for ever.

Although he had shunned any form of publicity after the run-in with the authorities following his graduation to the official list in 1901, when he spoke to the press, Ellis found himself in the public gaze when, in the summer of 1916, he was engaged to carry out the execution of Sir Roger Casement, found guilty of treason after a highly public trial.

On 29 March 1917, Leo George O'Donnell, a sergeant in the Royal Army Medical Corps, was hanged at Winchester for the murder of Lieutenant William Watterton, a quartermaster officer at a hospital in Aldershot. On New Year's Day 1917, O'Donnell had announced his engagement to the lieutenant's daughter, and later that day Miss Watterton, who served in the Women's Auxiliary Service, obtained a night pass so that she and a friend could celebrate her engagement. After spending the night drinking, they returned to her father's bungalow, expecting to find him there.

When they found no one at home they waited for him to return, when, at 11.30 p.m., O'Donnell called round, telling them that the lieutenant had left earlier that night for an urgent appointment. This seemed to imply that O'Donnell had been at the bungalow earlier; and his sudden return so late in the evening made the two women suspicious.

Shortly before midnight, O'Donnell left and headed for the hospital, where he asked to be shown into the quartermaster's office – where patients' valuables were kept – claiming to have been sent by Lieutenant Watterton. Unable to produce the passkey, he was refused entry and returned to his billet.

On the following afternoon, William Watterton's body was found in a trench on a nearby training ground. He had been battered to death – there were more than 24 cuts to his head – and his pockets had been rifled. O'Donnell was arrested once it was learned that he had tried to gain entry to the offices. Held on remand, he offered a friend £250 if he would provide him with an alibi and, when tried before Mr Justice Darling, O'Donnell denied any charge of murder, with the prosecution stating that he had committed the crime in order to obtain the key to the quartermaster's office and thereby steal the valuables within. O'Donnell claimed that the real killer was a man blackmailing Watterton over an alleged affair with a young Spanish girl.

Ellis badly bungled the execution and, although O'Donnell was given a drop of 6 feet 9 inches, it was not enough to cause instant death. Filling in the official forms following the execution, the governor and chief medical officer of Winchester recorded that death had been due to asphyxiation, although they found no fault in the behaviour of the hangmen.

In November 1919 Ellis returned to Newcastle for a double execution, but, just as had happened eighteen years before, it was decided that the men should be hanged in two separate executions.

Ernest Bernard Scott was a 28-year-old colliery fireman convicted of the murder of his sweetheart, Rebecca Quinn, after she had ended their relationship. He was hanged at 8 a.m. Seventy-five minutes later Ambrose Quinn, a 28-year-old former soldier with the Flying Corps, was hanged for the cutthroat murder of his wife at Newcastle. Scott was hanged by Ellis with Taylor assisting, and at the execution of Quinn he had Robert Baxter as his assistant. They were the last executions to take place at Newcastle.

In 1920 Ellis officiated at several high-profile cases, including that of Eric Holt, who had shot dead his fiancée on sand hills close to Blackpool. A month later, on 26 May, he officiated at a rare double in Glasgow, when two men were hanged side by side for a murder in Queen's Park.

Albert James Fraser and James Rollins were army deserters convicted of the murder of Henry Senior, who had been robbed and beaten to death on 3 February in Queen's Park, Glasgow. Senior had met a girl that evening, and when she suggested they go for a walk in the park he readily agreed. Lying in wait, Irishman Rollins had grabbed and held down Senior while Australian-born Fraser had beaten him unconscious before stealing money and items of clothing. They were arrested in Belfast the following week and stood trial at Glasgow High Court on 4 May, the main evidence coming from the girl who had lured Senior to his death.

Eighteen-year-old Kevin Barry was a medical student at the University College, Dublin, and a member of the IRA. On 20 September, there was an ambush in King Street, Dublin, in which three young British soldiers were killed. Seventeen-year-old private Matthew Whitehead was killed at the scene; Henry Washington and Thomas Humphries later died from their wounds.

Barry was arrested after he was found hiding beneath a lorry after the ambush, with a German Mauser pistol in his possession. A bullet recovered from the body of Private Whitehead was identified as having been fired from the Mauser, and as a result Barry was convicted.

He was tried by a British court martial and sentenced to death, allegedly having been tortured first. The IRA claimed that Barry should be reprieved since he was a serving soldier and as such should be treated as a prisoner of war. But the British authorities disagreed and confirmed that the execution was to go ahead despite widespread protests. Due to the sensitivity of the case, and fearful of repercussions in later life, neither Ellis nor his assistant Willis made mention of this or other subsequent Irish executions when their memoirs were later published.

At the end of the year Ellis again carried out two executions in two days. On 30 December Ellis carried out an execution without an assistant. There were 3 executions across the country and a shortage of assistants. It was the last time there would be no assistant at an execution in Great Britain. On 30 December he performed a hanging at Birmingham before travelling to Manchester to carry out an execution at Strangeways.

Charles Colclough, a fish salesman from Hanley, had been convicted of the cutthroat murder of a love rival. Following his conviction at Stafford Assizes, his appeal failed, as did a petition to the Home Secretary. At 8 a.m. on New Year's Eve, as Colclough walked to the scaffold inside Strangeways Gaol, a postman walked up the street leading to the prison gates.

'Who are they tolling the bell for?' he asked one of the crowd standing in the rain. When told it was a man named Colclough, the postman looked down at the telegram in his hand. 'Hard lines, Colclough, I've got an express letter here for him.' It was a reprieve that had arrived moments too late.

Most of Ellis's work in 1921 was at Mountjoy Prison, as the troubles in Ireland led to ten executions that year. Ellis carried out the executions of seven of these men. On 14 March, along with assistants Willis and Baxter, he hanged six men in three double executions. Thomas Whelan and Patrick Moran had been convicted of the murder of two British Intelligence officers, who had been shot dead in Dublin on 21 November 1920, in what became known as Bloody Sunday, when the Irish Republican Army killed thirteen people.

Patrick Doyle, Bernard Ryan, Thomas Bryan and Frank Flood were charged with high treason after being charged with taking part in an attempted ambush at Drumcondra on

21 January 1921. Nineteen-year-old Flood was the youngest of the prisoners, and had been a close friend of Kevin Barry.

The six were all convicted by court martial and hanged in pairs at Mountjoy by Ellis, while a crowd of more than twenty thousand people protested outside. Whelan and Moran were hanged at 6 a.m., Doyle and Ryan at 7 a.m., Flood and Bryan at 8 a.m.

On 25 April, Thomas Traynor, a father of ten, was hanged at Mountjoy for the murder of a soldier shot dead in a Dublin ambush on 10 January. On returning home, Ellis penned a letter to the Irish authorities questioning the fee he had received.

3 Kitchen Lane,
Balderstone Fold,
ROCHDALE
27th April 1921

Dear Sirs,
I hope you will forgive me taking up your valuable time. I shall be pleased if you would kindly reconsider the fee of £10 which you have decided I must have for carrying out the execution of Thomas Trayner [sic] at Mountjoy Prison on April 25th, as you are aware you have allowed me £15 for single executions of Sinn Feiners. I am sure you will agree it is little enough. The risk I have, the inconvenience I am put to, also the jeers and insulting remarks I have to put up with. So long ago as 1911 I received £11.11.0 for carrying out an execution in Ireland, namely Cork, also the usual travelling expenses, at that time it was far more pleasant than it is to-day. I am always away 15

hours longer than any execution in England, if
it takes place when fixed.

I left Rochdale on Thursday night at 8.33 p.m.,
arrived back 5.10 p.m., Tuesday, so I missed four
days work, my wages are over five pounds per week.
I have been on the Home Office list as executioner
for 20 years and as far as I know there has been
no complaint about my efficiency at my work or my
conduct. Thank you very much for your letter No.
17486/48BL. I shall at all times be willing to go
to Ireland if at liberty. Hoping you will consider
this matter again. I have put £2 for loss of wages
which is rather less than what I make.

I am,
dear Sirs,
Your Humble Servant
John Ellis

Whether this matter was resolved is unclear, although it is
noticeable that Ellis never officiated in Ireland again. At the
next executions at Mountjoy a few weeks later, it was Tom
Pierrepoint and not Ellis who pushed the lever.

Ellis was also involved in several high-profile cases in 1922,
none more so than that of solicitor Herbert Rowse
Armstrong, hanged on 31 May at Gloucester for the murder,
by arsenic poisoning, of his wife. Katie Armstrong had died
in 1920, and in the summer of 1921 Armstrong was involved
in a professional disagreement with Oswald Martin and,
following a visit to Armstrong's home, Martin became
seriously ill. A relative suggested an analysis of Martin's
urine, and, when the specimen was found to contain arsenic,
Scotland Yard were informed. As they began to investigate
they decided to exhume the body of Armstrong's wife and a

postmortem revealed the presence of arsenic. Armstrong was arrested on New Year's Eve 1921.

Ellis travelled to Gloucester from Manchester, where earlier that day he had executed Preston wife murderer Hiram Thompson, whom he later described as the most callous man he had hanged. Thompson was so oblivious of his fate that he had to be shaken awake on the morning of his execution, and he told guards that he had slept far better in the condemned cell that he did at home.

After arriving at Gloucester and spying Armstrong at exercise, Ellis asked the warder for the prisoner's details and was shocked to learn he hadn't been weighed since being admitted to the gaol. Ellis demanded Armstrong be weighed at once and, when he had the information he needed, he rigged the gallows and prepared a drop of 8 feet 8 inches, one of the longest on record. At 8 a.m. the following day, Ellis entered the cell and, as he approached the prisoner, Armstrong bade the hangman goodbye.

'When we get there, look straight at me and it will be all over very quickly,' Ellis said before walking ahead and leaving his assistant Edward Taylor to escort the prisoner to the drop.

'I'm coming, Katie,' Armstrong called out as Ellis reached for the lever.

On leaving the prison, Ellis bumped into a Rochdale Hornets rugby player whom he knew well and they shared a drink in a pub near the railway station until it was time for Ellis to catch his train home.

A week later he travelled to Pentonville to hang Henry Jacoby, an 18-year-old pantry boy who had been convicted of the murder of a wealthy guest. At 8 a.m. on 14 March, a maid at a London hotel entered the room of Lady Alice White and found her severely injured and close to death. She had been attacked with a hammer, and died on the following day.

As there appeared to be no sign of a break-in, nor had anything been stolen from the room, detectives thought it was more likely to be an inside job.

Jacoby became under suspicion when he started suggesting various theories about the crime. A search of his room revealed two bloodstained handkerchiefs, and he was arrested. At his Old Bailey trial the defence claimed Jacoby had entered the room after hearing what he believed was an intruder, and in the darkness he had lashed out with the hammer. It was only when he realised what he had done that he concocted a number of false statements.

Jacoby's subsequent execution caused a great deal of controversy when a reprieve was granted for the well-to-do Ronald True, who had been convicted of murder at the same Assizes. It was felt that a number of True's upper-class friends had used their influences to secure a reprieve, while Jacoby, from much humbler origins and with no influential friends to fight his cause, had gone to the scaffold.

Assisted by newly appointed assistant Tom Phillips, Ellis wrote later that he had seen Jacoby playing cricket with warders on the afternoon before his execution. As they waited outside the condemned cell on the following morning Governor Blake looked at the large clock on the wall and then at his pocket watch.

'All right, Ellis, let's get this over with,' he said as the warder opened the cell door.

'I want to thank you, sir, and all the officers for the kindness you have shown me,' Jacoby said as he walked bravely to his death. Ellis wrote later that when he went to see the governor before leaving the prison Blake's eyes were red as if he had been crying.

On 10 August at Wandsworth, Ellis carried out the double hanging of Reginald Dunn and Joseph O'Sullivan, two members of the IRA convicted of the murder of Field Marshall Sir Henry Wilson, the retired chief of the Imperial General Staff, who had been shot dead on his doorstep on 22 June 1922, shortly after announcing that he was to stand for election in Ulster. Dunn and O'Sullivan were ex-patriots living in London, who considered themselves dedicated to the Irish cause, and had fled the scene pursued on foot by two police officers and several members of the public. They were eventually cornered after seriously wounding the policemen and one of the other pursuers, and were lucky to escape with their lives as the crowd attempted to lynch them. They were both convicted of the murder at the Old Bailey and sentenced to death by Mr Justice Shearman. As the judge concluded the passing of the death sentence – '... and may the Lord have mercy on your soul' – Dunn remarked loudly, 'He will, my Lord!'

Intelligence reports suggested that the IRA were planning to spring the prisoner before execution and, as a result, the place of execution was kept secret and armed police guarded the entrance to both Pentonville and Wandsworth prisons. Although no attempt was made to free the prisoners, large demonstrations took place outside both prisons.

In December 1921, Londoner Irene Wilkins placed an advertisement in the capital's Morning Post under the situations-wanted column: 'Lady cook, 31, requires post in a school. Experienced in school with forty boarders. Disengaged. Salary £65'.

On the day it appeared, she received a telegram telling her there was a position available at a Beech House and that she should catch the 4.30 train from Waterloo to Bournemouth Central. 'Car will meet.'

She telegraphed her acceptance and boarded the train before she learned that Beech House did not exist. The following morning her body was discovered on a piece of waste-ground on the outskirts of Bournemouth. She had been battered to death, and evidence suggested that she had resisted a sexual assault, although she had not been raped.

Copies of telegrams sent from the Bournemouth area were examined and, although evidence had been made to disguise the writing, they had all been written by the same hand and all contained the same spelling mistakes. A tyre mark close to where the body was found was identified as having been caused by a Dunlop Magnum. Owners of cars fitted with these tyres were questioned, including chauffeur Thomas Henry Allaway, who aroused suspicion by fleeing the area almost at once.

After he had been arrested at Reading, a specimen of his handwriting carried the telltale spelling mistakes. Witnesses identified Allaway as the driver of a car seen meeting the Waterloo train on 22 December, and the post office clerk who took the telegrams recognised him by the sound of his voice.

Assisted at the Winchester execution by Edward Taylor, Ellis was alleged to have made another blunder. He failed to get Allaway's feet in line over the drop and placed the knot in the wrong position, so that when the trapdoor opened and the prisoner plunged down, the rope swung violently from side to side instead of hanging still.

Allaway died slowly from strangulation and, when asked by the governor, 'Was death instantaneous?' Ellis replied, 'Well, almost!'

Later that day the governor commented on the execution in the LPC4 book.

```
Although the trial drops with the dummy were
satisfactory the execution itself was not
satisfactory for the following reasons:
    The prisoner when dropping hit first the edge of
```

the pit behind him and then rebounding hit his
forehead on the opposite edge causing a broken
bruise (there was blood on the cap). Thus his fall
was broken twice and he did not therefore receive
the full drop.

This undoubtedly accounted for death being due
to asphyxia. I am told now that the same thing
happened at his last execution 29.3.17 but it was not
reported. Death then was also due to asphyxia and
it was also done by Ellis. On all previous occasions
death has been due to dislocated vertebrae.

An inquiry was set up and Ellis was asked to give evidence.
He told the panel that he was concerned that the trapdoors of
the gallows at Winchester Prison were too narrow and that the
walk from the cell to the gallows was too long. The pit was 1
foot 10 inches narrower than the standard gallows of 10 feet
8 inches, such as the one at Pentonville. The chairman found
that Ellis was free from blame: 'I submit that the accidents in
the two cases at Winchester were due to the opening being too
narrow and I consider that a wider opening should be
provided before another prisoner is hanged there.'

On the night of 3 October 1922, Percy Thompson and his
wife Edith were returning from a visit to the theatre in Ilford
when a man surprised them and stabbed Percy several times
in the chest, fatally wounding him. Police were immediately
suspicious of 28-year-old Edith Thompson's version of events
and under questioning she revealed that she was having an
affair with 20-year-old Frederick Bywaters, a steward on a
P&O liner. He was later found to have been the attacker.
Investigations soon produced letters written by Edith to her
boyfriend, in which she described how she had tried to poison
Percy's food and attempted other ways of killing him.

When they stood trial together at the Old Bailey in December 1922, it was clear from the outset that the prosecution deemed Edith to be equally responsible for her husband's death, despite the confession from Bywaters that he alone carried out the killing and that his lover was unaware of his intentions. In the end it was the letters Edith had sent Bywaters that told against her, and they were jointly convicted of the murder. Their appeals failed and the executions went ahead as scheduled. Ellis was engaged to hang Mrs Thompson, with Willis given the task of hanging her partner in crime at Pentonville.

On 9 January 1923 at Holloway, Ellis, assisted by Baxter and Phillips, carried out the most unpleasant execution of his career. Mrs Thompson had been in a distressed state since word had got back to her that there would be no reprieve. Ellis advised warders that she should be given a glass of brandy prior to his entering the cell at 9 a.m. After resetting the trapdoors, the hangmen spied into the cell before returning to their quarters.

Ellis was relieved to see that the prisoner seemed to have calmed down but, as they approached the condemned cell a few minutes before the appointed hour, they were horrified to hear the prisoner's distressed cries and moans. After entering the cell, they had to pick up the prisoner, who had collapsed on the floor, and, once Ellis had strapped her wrists, she sank back into a chair in sheer terror.

Knowing that it was highly unlikely she would be able to walk to the drop unaided, he decided to strap her ankles in the cell and ordered Baxter and Phillips to carry the stricken and barely conscious woman to the gallows. As she was placed on the drop and supported by four warders, Ellis could see that she was unconscious and he quickly placed the cap over her head, adjusted the noose and pulled the lever.

The execution of Edith Thompson undoubtedly had a profound effect on Ellis. In the following months he took to drinking heavily and would often sit at home staring into space. Nevertheless, he didn't let the execution cause him to tender his resignation, but it was not far from coming. Ellis made three trips to Scotland that year, the second of which was to hang Susan Newell at Glasgow's Duke Street prison.

Thirty-year-old Newell had strangled a newspaper boy who would not give her an evening paper without the money. She was the first woman to hang in Scotland for over fifty years and, unlike Edith Thompson, the prisoner did not go to pieces and seemed to have accepted the situation better than the hangman. Ellis made just a token gesture to secure her wrists with the leather strap and, on reaching the gallows, she objected to his placing the hood over her head. Thrown into confusion, he paused for a moment. As the hangmen held the white cap while he remained unsure what to do, Newell managed to free her arms from the strap. Willis noticed what had happened and quickly adjusted the strap while Ellis decided to grant her request, placed the noose over her head and pulled the lever.

In the following month Ellis made his last visit to Scotland and a few days after Christmas he travelled to Leeds to officiate at his first execution in Yorkshire as chief executioner. Perhaps unbeknownst to him, it was also to be his last. On 28 December John Eastwood was hanged for the murder of his wife. There are no reports of any undue incident at Leeds, although, interestingly, neither Ellis nor his assistant Seth Mills officiated at an execution again.

It is possible that Ellis decided to offer his resignation when he was engaged to carry out another execution at Holloway at the end of February. Dora Sadler was a 37-year-old nurse who had murdered the two young children of her employer at

Kensington. She had become so attached to the children that she became jealous of the mother and, following a series of quarrels, she was given notice to leave her job. That evening, 11 November 1923, as she and the children slept in the nursery, she switched on the gas and on the following morning the children were found dead from gas poisoning. Sadler was discovered unconscious and later charged with murder.

She was sentenced to death in January 1924, and Ellis would have received a letter inviting him to carry out the execution at Holloway. Although probably reluctant to revisit the site of his most upsetting execution, he still felt he had responsibilities to the state. Sadler's appeal was rejected on 4 February, and a further letter confirming that the execution was to go ahead would have been sent. Four days later a reprieve was granted and Ellis probably breathed a heavy sigh of relief. Maybe the realisation that he now no longer wanted to put to death a fellow human being persuaded him to pen his resignation letter, which was announced in the press in March 1924.

Looking back over the 23 years on the scaffold, Ellis later wrote that he found it hard to believe that he had survived it. He said that he was glad he no longer had to travel the length of the country to and from early-morning hangings, while trying to run his hairdressing business.

Fellow hangmen and others who saw him in action, particularly in the early days, stated that he had nerves of steel, but behind the front of ice-cold determination he was constantly afraid of making errors, more so as he took to drinking heavily.

In retirement his health soon deteriorated as he continued to drink heavily, and after a drinking bout in 1924 he attempted to commit suicide, shooting himself in the jaw. At Rochdale Magistrates' Court he was charged with attempted suicide (suicide was a criminal offence in England and Wales until 1961), and sitting in the dock with his face heavily swathed in bandages he made commitments to curb his drinking and assured the magistrate that he would not make another suicide attempt. In return for this promise he was bound over for twelve months and discharged.

Shortly after his bungled suicide attempt, he entered into an agreement with Thompson newspapers in Dundee for a series entitled 'Revelations of My Life'. It ran for over six months, and in it he gave candid and frank accounts of many of his notable cases; but, perhaps fearing reprisals from the IRA, he neglected to make any mention of his trips to Mountjoy, or the execution of Sir Roger Casement.

In 1927 Ellis was persuaded to take part in a drama production, *The Life and Adventures of Charles Peace*. Peace had been executed at Leeds in 1879 for the murder of a Manchester policeman during the commission of a burglary. Playing the role of Marwood, the executioner who had officiated at Peace's hanging, Ellis added much to the appeal of the play, but it also attracted a great deal of controversy with many people considering his involvement inappropriate. The play opened in December at Gravesend, but audiences quickly dwindled and it closed after just a few weeks.

Ellis apparently had some financial involvement in the production of the play, for when it closed he kept the scaffold and took it home to Rochdale. Ever enterprising, he then used the scaffold as part of a sideshow in which he demonstrated the execution craft for a few pennies, pinioning members of the public and demonstrating how an execution took part by hanging his assistant Leo Scott. It was a popular attraction at fairgrounds and seaside resorts in the following year.

By the early 1930s the economic climate was poor and, with times being hard in Rochdale as elsewhere, there was often little enough money for food, let alone haircuts, so with his hairdressing business floundering Ellis found himself attempting to supplement his income by selling towels in local pubs. With his health failing and his drinking heavy, the end finally came for him on 20 September 1932. After drinking heavily, he became violent and threatened his wife and daughter with a razor. As his family fled the house in terror, he turned the razor on himself.

John Ellis had been a mild-mannered man whose suicide was attributed to the stresses of his role as hangman, and the nightmares he began to suffer after the executions of Mrs Thompson and young Jacoby. It was also attributed to the slump in his business as a hairdresser and the failure of his other ventures.

Ellis had served for 23 years as a public executioner, carrying out more than two hundred hangings in all parts of the country. It was a total that was to remain unbeaten for over twenty years.

Chapter 4:
The Road to The Gallows

It had been a shortage of assistant executioners that prompted Henry Pierrepoint to suggest that his elder brother apply for the post. Seven years his senior, Thomas William Pierrepoint was working as a quarryman and helping out with the family carrier business when the idea was first put to him.

Tom Pierrepoint was taught all he would need to know about the profession in the barn at the back of the shop Tom's wife ran at Town End, Clayton, a village on the outskirts of Bradford. Shown everything his brother had learned, not only on the training course at Newgate Gaol but from the wealth of practical experience he had gained working with James Billington and his sons over the previous four years, Tom Pierrepoint wrote out his letter of application and was subsequently invited to Pentonville for a one-week training course. The staff at Pentonville quickly realised that the elder Pierrepoint had received expert training and he breezed through the course and practical test.

He became a regular assistant to his brother in the spring of 1906 and was present at many executions, including that of baby farmer Rhoda Willis. On 5 November the brothers were on duty at Reading, where William Austin was hanged for the murder of the daughter of the family he lodged with at Windsor. At Lincoln Gaol they hanged farm worker William Duddles for the murder of his wife with a hammer, and at Cardiff George Stills, a Glamorgan colliery worker who had battered his aged mother to death while drunk.

In November 1908, following the conviction of Bradford murderer John Ellwood – who had killed a cashier at a local office – local interest had been immense. Henry Pierrepoint was constantly bombarded by questions from locals asking if he was going to 'top' Ellwood. With his name not yet bandied about in the press, brother Tom had often shared in conversation about the fate of Ellwood with his customers, unaware that he would be later assisting at the Leeds execution.

Rumours had spread that Henry Pierrepoint had refused the Ellwood engagement because it meant hanging someone from his hometown, and when he arrived at the gaol the large crowds milling around the prison gates were the same people both Pierrepoints had recognised as their inquisitors in the previous weeks.

Ellwood had boasted to his guards that he knew Pierrepoint well, and that he was going to cause the hangman plenty of trouble, but, spying the prisoner at exercise, neither of the brothers recalled having seen the condemned man before.

Leeds now had a new permanent scaffold constructed in the garage where the prison van was stored, and, after working out the drop and rigging the gallows, the hangmen made their way back to their quarters in the prison hospital, passing two prison officers busy digging a grave in the small plot of land used to bury hanged murderers.

Although many condemned men had bragged they would make trouble on the morning of their executions, it was usually an idle boast. Few fought for their lives; few were dragged kicking and screaming to the gallows. The vast majority, when the time came, were more often than not too overcome with fear to do more than meekly submit to pinioning. But, despite the rarity of trouble on the drop, it was always planned for. On the night before the execution, Pierrepoint drilled into the warders their duties on the following morning: they would stand on wooden planks laid across the trapdoors, at either side of the prisoner, ready to hold onto the prisoner's arms should he struggle or faint.

When Tom Pierrepoint followed his brother along the corridor to the condemned cell he found that the usual official witnesses had been supplemented with several extra uniformed guards, and, as they waited for the under-sheriff to arrive outside the cell, Henry Pierrepoint took a last opportunity to size up the prisoner. Gazing secretly through the spyhole, he found Ellwood dressed in his own clothes but, rather than sitting at the table, he was standing talking to the warders close to the cell door.

On the stroke of nine, a warder opened the door and the hangmen briskly strapped the prisoner's wrists before he realised what was happening and had a chance to resist. The threats to cause trouble were now worthless. When Pierrepoint bared his neck before leading him to the drop, Ellwood snarled viciously at him, 'Harry, you're hanging an innocent man!' The walk to the scaffold was only 20 yards but Ellwood walked slowly, turning his head, glaring at warders and maintaining his innocence.

Reaching the drop, Tom Pierrepoint hastily secured his ankles, as his brother adjusted the rope.

'You are killing an innocent man,' Ellwood barked, and, as the hangman reached to place the white cap over his head, the prisoner spoke one more time.

'It's too tight,' he complained, before he was silenced for ever.

Tom Pierrepoint assisted his brother several times in 1909, including trips to Pentonville – where they executed the Reubens brothers and Indian assassin Madar Dal Dhingra – as well as Bodmin, Wakefield and Stafford. He also travelled to Ireland for the first time, when he assisted his brother at Mountjoy at an execution they were later not paid for, mainly due to an administrative mix-up.

When the brothers travelled together to Cambridge on 13 June, neither knew it was to be the last time they would work together. James Hancock was a 54-year-old Yorkshire-born labourer who had moved to Cambridge a decade or so earlier, to run a coal-hawking business. Hancock had been having a relationship with Eliza Marshall, the sister of Alfred Doggett, Hancock's rival coal dealer at Chesterton. When Hancock's love life began to sour, he turned violent towards her and she went to her brother for sanctuary. On 4 March 1910, the two men quarrelled in a stable where Hancock kept his horses, which ended with Doggett being stabbed to death with a carving knife. Hancock was hanged on 14 June, one month before Henry Pierrepoint carried out the execution at Chelmsford that was to lead to his dismissal.

When Henry Pierrepoint was dismissed, there was the need to promote an assistant when two executioners were needed on the same day in August. John Ellis was already engaged at Newcastle when the governor at Leeds received two men under sentence of death, and, with Pierrepoint off the list, the most experienced assistant, by just a matter of months, was his brother Tom. He wrote to confirm his availability and, with echoes of what happened five years before, Harry Le Mesurier, the governor at Leeds Gaol, was left with the problem of finding an assistant executioner.

Since the end of the Billington's tenure in 1905, the only men engaged at executions had been Henry Pierrepoint and John Ellis as chief executioners with Tom Pierrepoint and William Willis acting as assistants. As before, the problem was solved by contacting William Warbrick, five years since he had last been engaged, asking if he was free to 'carry out duties at Leeds on August 9th'. Warbrick confirmed his availability for the double execution but by the time he travelled to Leeds one of the men had been reprieved.

Tom Pierrepoint's first job was to hang a fellow Bradfordian, John Coulson, who had murdered his wife and young son by cutting their throats with a carving knife. Calculating a drop of 6 feet 1 inch, Pierrepoint carried out the execution without a problem, death was instant, and the family name was restored to the top of the list of qualified executioners.

Large crowds waited around outside the gates at Armley following Coulson's execution, including a number of photographers who hoped to photograph the hangmen. Pierrepoint and Warbrick avoided being recognised by equipping themselves with small reporters' notebooks, and left the gaol by the front gate holding the books in their hands as if they were members of the press group that had witnessed the execution.

There were no further executions that summer, but the next hanging took place at Lancaster Castle, where Pierrepoint assisted Ellis for the first time. With Tom aware that Ellis was responsible for his brother's sacking, it was the start of a frosty relationship between the two men that was to last throughout the whole time they worked together. Pierrepoint assisted Ellis again at Pentonville at the end of December, and a week later he returned to Leeds to carry out his second senior engagement when he hanged Henry Ison, who following a drunken quarrel had beaten his common-law wife to death with a heavy poker.

Tom Pierrepoint now found, as Ellis had a few years earlier and as Stephen Wade would many years later, that, although an assistant had received promotion to number one, most under-sheriffs still chose to rely on the most experienced man on the list, and so offers to him to officiate as a chief executioner were limited. Not only that, chief executioners were seldom offered the role of assistant, so they could go many months, sometimes years, without being called into action. However, several officials bucked this trend. Those in Yorkshire and Durham in particular always seemed to go against the majority, and preferred to appoint the local man regardless of whether he was top of the list or not.

As the country approached World War One, Pierrepoint found engagements quite erratic. In some months his diary was bustling; other times he went several months without work. In 1911 he assisted Ellis a number of times, at Liverpool, Pentonville and Wandsworth, none of which produced any untoward incident, and at the end of the year Pierrepoint was again engaged as a number one when he officiated at Stafford, where George Loake, a retired engine driver, paid the ultimate penalty for the brutal murder of his estranged wife, whom he stabbed to death at Walsall. In the following year he assisted again at Pentonville, where Frederick Seddon was hanged, and carried out three executions as number one.

When he travelled to Norwich in November to hang Robert Galloway, a sailor who had strangled a woman in

Norfolk, he had as his assistant George Brown. Brown had been one of three new assistants appointed in the autumn of 1910, making up the shortfall following Henry Pierrepoint's sacking, and to prevent the necessity of having to rely on old assistants such as Warbrick, who had failed to convince the authorities of his worth a decade before.

Three weeks after the Norwich execution, Pierrepoint hanged Gilbert Smith at Gloucester for the murder of his wife. Another new assistant was engaged, Albert Lumb of Bradford, and the two men travelled down from Yorkshire to carry out the job, which passed off without incident.

1913 was a lucrative year for Tom Pierrepoint, when all the engagements he was offered were as number one. On 29 January he officiated at Pentonville and six weeks later he hanged boxer Edward Palmer, who had cut his wife's throat at Bristol. His income was further supplemented with fees from senior executions carried out at Wakefield, Dorchester, Birmingham, Newcastle and Cambridge, and he rounded off the year with another trip to Wakefield on New Year's Eve, when he hanged George Law, a Sheffield engineer who had strangled his landlady.

Pierrepoint assisted at the last two executions to take place at Lewes Gaol in Sussex, both in the summer of 1914. In July, Herbert Booker was hanged for the cutthroat murder of Ada Stone in a train carriage at Three Bridges, Crawley. Both were returning from Crystal Palace and sporting Liverpool Football Club rosettes, having just watched their team lose to Burnley in the FA Cup final. A month later he assisted Ellis at the last execution at Lewes when Percy Clifford, a soldier, was hanged for the murder of his wife.

Tom Pierrepoint carried out his first Shepton Mallet execution later that year, when Henry Quartley was hanged for the murder of a neighbour whom he blasted to death with a shotgun following some long grievance. He was assisted by George Brown, and had another new assistant when he travelled to Wandsworth in 1915 to hang Robert Rosenthal, convicted of treason at Middlesex.

1915 was to be a barren year for Pierrepoint: apart from the trip to London, the only other executions were at Wakefield, where he hanged two men, a week apart, in December. They were the last men hanged at Wakefield, which, despite having a purpose-built gallows, had ceased as a place of execution when its prison status was reclassified.

Pierrepoint's diary was quiet during the rest of the war: there were no engagements in 1916 and just two in 1917. In March he hanged John Thompson at Armley Gaol in Leeds, a shepherd who cut the throat of a teenage girl at Beverley, and a month later he was back at Armley to dispatch cutthroat murderer Robert Gadsby. On 18 December he travelled to Newcastle for the execution of William Cavanagh, who had stabbed a sailor during a brawl.

By the time Pierrepoint returned to Leeds in the winter of 1918, the war in Europe had ended. John Walsh, a Wakefield collier, had strangled his sweetheart, and was one of four men to die on the gallows at Armley within a month. In January, three men were hanged in two days, beginning on 7 January with Benjamin Hindle Benson, who had cut the throat of his girlfriend when he caught her in bed with a lover after arriving home from the war unannounced. The following day, assisted again by Robert Baxter, he hanged two soldiers who had committed a brutal murder during the course of a robbery at a Pontefract jeweller's shop.

In the summer of 1918, two young deserters, Lance Corporal George Cardwell and Private Percy Barrett, were on the run and staying in lodgings near Pontefract. Yorkshireman Caldwell and Londoner Barrett had been away from their unit since the spring and, to make ends meet, had found work labouring at a colliery while lodging with Cardwell's sister.

On the afternoon of 16 August, the deserters committed the robbery at the jeweller's shop, which was run by an elderly widow, Mrs Rhoda Walker. Later that evening, she was found slumped behind the counter, battered about the head and suffering from horrific wounds. She died in hospital the following day.

Witnesses reported seeing two soldiers near the shop, one of whom sported a wound stripe (awarded to Allied soldiers who were wounded in combat) on his Army Service Corps uniform. Four days later police in London arrested two soldiers selling rings in a London pub. One of the men sported wound stripes on his uniform and both were arrested on suspicion of the Pontefract murder.

Both protested their innocence but were hanged side by side. Cardwell, despite being a deserter, had fought with extreme courage and bravery during the war and had been recommended for both the Distinguished Service Medal and the Military Medal. The six wound stripes he wore on his arm, which helped lead to his arrest, were the result of his having been wounded in action in France in 1915.

Pierrepoint wasn't recalled into service until early January 1920, when he was back at Leeds to deal with Lewis Massey, who had been convicted at Leeds of the murder of his wife. Willis assisted, as he did on Pierrepoint's next execution, at Lincoln. Pierrepoint carried out two executions at Leeds in the spring and on 30 December he was in action again at Leeds when three hangings were carried out on the same day. He was assisted by Edward Taylor, who had assisted him a month earlier at Durham.

At the end of May 1921, Pierrepoint was contacted by

officials in Ireland and asked if he was willing to carry out executions scheduled there on 7 June. Accepting the invitation, and assisted by Baxter, he hanged three men: at 7 a.m. Patrick Maher and Edmund Foley, who had been convicted of the murder of a police sergeant during an attempted rescue of prisoners in 1919, were hanged side by side; an hour later, William Mitchell, who had shot dead a justice of the peace during a robbery, walked to the gallows.

Anxious to keep the hangman's identity secret, as Ireland was going through a volatile period, the newspaper announced his name as Mr Harte. The expense sheet makes interesting reading:

EXECUTIONER	£. s. d.
Balance of Fee	20. 0. 0.
Rail Fare Clayton–Bradford	0. 11. 0.
Manchester–Bradford (return)	0. 11.8.
Fare Manchester–Holyhead	0. 16. 7½.
Board Holyhead (Saturday & Sunday)	0. 15. 0.
Fare Holyhead–Dublin	1. 0. 0.
Loss of Time	3. 0. 0.
Fare Dublin–Belfast	0. 18. 10.
Food Belfast	0. 5. 6.
Fare Belfast–Manchester	1. 10. 7½.
Board Liverpool (Sunday)	0. 15. 0.

ASSISTANT	£. s. d.
Balance of Fee	8. 0. 0.
Cab Home–Station	0. 1. 6.
Rail Fare Hertford–King's Cross	0. 3. 6.
Tube King's Cross–Euston	0. 0. 1½.
Fare Euston–Holyhead	1. 18. 6.
Board Holyhead (Sunday)	0. 10. 0.

Fare Holyhead–Kingstown	1. 0. 0.
Fare Dublin–Belfast	0. 18. 10.
Food Belfast	0. 5.6.
Fare Belfast–Euston	2. 17. 7½.
Breakfast (Liverpool)	0. 2. 6.
Tube & Rail Fare Euston–Hertford	0. 3. 7½.
Cab Station–Home	0. 1. 6.
Loss of Time	2. 10. 0.
Total	**£ 48. 7. 5.**

It seems clear that it was far too dangerous for the hangmen to return home by boat from Dublin, since those looking for reprisals would probably have staked out the port on the lookout for the English executioners. Travelling to Belfast and sailing to Liverpool was probably the safest option at a time when the troubles in Ireland were at their height.

Pierrepoint was next called into action in the spring of 1922, when he travelled to Durham to hang James Williamson, who had killed his wife with a cutthroat razor. His only other execution that year was a double at Lincoln Gaol, where George Robinson and Frank Fowler, two farm labourers, both convicted of separate murders at Lincolnshire Assizes, were hanged together. Spurned lover Robinson had killed his girlfriend, while Fowler shot dead a bride of three days.

In January 1923 the executions of Edith Thompson and Frederick Bywaters took place in London. Both were to hang in separate executions – she at Holloway, he at Pentonville – and the original dates had clashed with a prior engagement Pierrepoint had at Armley Gaol, Leeds. On being invited to execute Bywaters at Pentonville, Pierrepoint reluctantly had to turn down the request, so it was then offered to Willis, but following the appeals of both the Leeds murderer and Thompson and Bywaters, the revised execution dates would have left Pierrepoint free to execute Bywaters. Instead, aided by new assistant Tom Phillips, Pierrepoint carried out the execution of Chinese laundryman Lee Doon at Leeds four days before the Ilford killers went to the gallows, with Pierrepoint doubtlessly rueing the lost fee.

In April Pierrepoint carried out the execution of Daniel Cassidy at Durham. After gatecrashing a New Year's Eve party, Cassidy had shot dead his son-in-law. In August, Pierrepoint returned to the northeast, when Hassan Muhamed, an Arabian sailor, went to the gallows for the murder by shooting of his bride-to-be at South Shields. On both occasions he was assisted by recent recruit Robert Wilson, who, despite having been on the list for three years, had carried out fewer than half a dozen executions.

Pierrepoint's last executions of the year were all at Mountjoy Gaol, Dublin. William Downes, a 25-year-old former soldier, was one of a gang of thieves who raided a factory at Ashdown in October, stealing a large sum of money and a number of bicycles, which they used to make their escape. Pursued by Irish Free State CID officers, the men were cornered at Castle Knock, and in the ensuing fight Downes was placed under arrest and held in a police car guarded by Captain Thomas Fitzgerald, while the other officers rounded up the rest of the gang. Having waited for the captain's attention to be distracted, Downes whipped out a revolver and shot him dead before fleeing the scene, only to be quickly rearrested.

He was sentenced to death by hanging on 30 October, less than two weeks after committing the murder. A newspaper article claimed that the new Irish Free State authorities had to advertise for an executioner for the job, which was carried out by Pierrepoint on 29 November 1923. The hangman's identity was specifically not disclosed to the press.

It's unlikely that Baxter assisted this time, since, following the formation of the Irish Free State, Pierrepoint was free to choose his own assistant. His nephew claimed in his book many years later that Pierrepoint would take friends from Bradford to act as his assistants. If he believed they had the correct nerve and discretion he would instruct them in their duties in the same barn behind the shop where his younger brother Henry had trained him almost two decades before. These men were often recorded in the press as Joseph Robinson, and their identities remain one of the unsolved mysteries of Pierrepoint story.

On 12 December Pierrepoint and his assistant returned to Dublin to carry out a double execution, and three days later they carried out a single execution. Unlike that of the previous visit to Mountjoy, none of the three executions was politically motivated.

Pierrepoint carried out the execution of Matthew Nunn at Durham in January 1924, when his conduct was questioned by the prison chaplain, who claimed that the hangmen barged into the cell and manhandled the prisoner into the corridor before the priest had time to put on his surplice and lead the procession. On 13 March he returned to Dublin to hang Jeremiah Gaffney, who had shot dead a man in Kerry.

By the time Pierrepoint travelled to Leeds in June, John Ellis had tendered his resignation and Pierrepoint's name was now at the top of the list, but any thoughts he had of having the monopoly on all executions were soon dashed when both Willis and Baxter began to receive offers to officiate as a number one.

One afternoon in late August, while having tea with his nephew Albert, Tom Pierrepoint read in the paper that Ellis had tried to commit suicide. Throwing down the paper, he turned to his nephew and said he should have done it years ago.

A few days after Ellis's failed suicide attempt, Pierrepoint travelled to Wandsworth to hang Patrick Mahon, who had murdered Emily Beilby Kaye at Eastbourne. Mahon's wife had started the murder investigation when she found in his pocket a ticket for a left-luggage locker at Waterloo Station. Believing her husband may have been cheating on her, she asked a former policeman to check it out and, presenting the ticket, he found it related to a Gladstone bag that contained bloodstained clothing, a kitchen knife and a tennis-racket case with the initials EBK.

Scotland Yard posted a detective to question Mahon when he collected the case. He was detained and asked to account for the bag's contents. Mahon finally confessed that the bloodstained clothing belonged to 38-year-old Emily Kaye, with whom he had been having an affair. He claimed she had fallen and banged her head, receiving fatal injuries, and, fearful of the consequences, he had dismembered the body and disposed of the dissected body parts. Police went to a cottage Mahon had rented and discovered the remains of the corpse in a trunk with saucepans on the stove filled with boiled body parts.

Mahon was composed as the date of his execution approached. This was in contrast to when he had first been brought into the cell, when he had to be dragged half-conscious along the corridor in sheer terror. It appeared he had knowledge of the hanging procedure. On the morning of his execution, once assistant William Willis had strapped his ankles and stepped back, with the cap and noose in place Pierrepoint reached for the lever and, sensing the hangman was ready to spring the trap, Mahon jumped with bound feet as the floor beneath him collapsed. Instead of falling plumb through the drop, the noosed prisoner fell back, crashing into the edge of the platform before dropping into the pit and swinging violently on the end of the rope.

In August 1925, Pierrepoint travelled to Dublin to carry out two executions on the same morning. At 8 a.m., 24-year-old Michael Talbot was hanged in the men's prison for the murder of his uncle, Edward Walsh. Talbot had been having an affair with Annie Walsh, his aunt, who blamed her nephew for the killing. Talbot confessed he had been in league with Walsh, who was hoping to claim insurance money following her husband's death. Ninety minutes after Talbot walked to the gallows, Walsh was hanged in the women's prison, spending her last hour crying and praying.

It was the first time Tom Pierrepoint had officiated at the execution of a woman, but less than a year later he hanged another woman, this time at Manchester's Strangeways Prison, one of eleven executions he carried out in 1926.

Louie Calvert was a 33-year-old prostitute and thief, who had married during the previous year with her husband unaware of her past. Arthur Calvert had proposed marriage when she falsely told him she was pregnant, and when she could not conceal her deceit any further she told him she was staying with her sister in Dewsbury until the child was born. Leaving her home in Leeds, she crossed the county but on arriving in Dewsbury she returned to prostitution, taking lodgings with Mrs Lily Waterhouse, an old woman she had known previously. Calvert placed an advertisement offering to take in a child for adoption, which she planned to pass as her own newborn baby, and soon took possession of a baby girl.

Calvert might have got away with her deception, but, as she made plans to return to her husband, her landlady noticed items had gone missing and reported the theft to the police. The older woman was advised to take out a summons and, when she failed to turn up in court, officers called at her house, where she was found battered and strangled in a bedroom. Police traced Calvert to Leeds. She opened the door to them wearing the dead woman's clothes and boots.

In 1928 Pierrepoint carried out five executions in four days, travelling to Manchester, Lincoln, Durham and Leeds. The Manchester and Durham engagements had originally been planned as double executions. At the end of the month he hanged a former policeman at Birmingham, but the most notorious entry in his diary came that spring, when he dispatched Patrick Kennedy, convicted along with his accomplice Frederick Browne of the murder of PC George Gutteridge in Essex.

Pierrepoint hanged Kennedy at Wandsworth at the same moment Baxter hanged Browne at Pentonville. Although each now received a fair share of executions, both were warned that 'touting for business' – writing to the under-sheriffs offering to carry out an execution rather than waiting to be asked – was contrary to their terms of engagement and could lead to dismissal.

In 1930 Parliament had its first major review of capital punishment since the Aberdare Report fifty years before. As the debate raged, newspapers were split between those wanting to keep it as a deterrent and not for retribution, and those supporting a total abolition. While the issue was under review Labour Home Secretary J R Clynes granted a large number of reprieves, with just four executions taking place that year. Clynes was the first home secretary of the twentieth century to support the abolition of capital punishment, and was pleased to find the committee recommending that the death penalty be suspended for a trial period of five years. The decision did not meet with the approval of the Shadow

Cabinet and, with Conservative Members refusing to sign the report, the government's failure to bring in any new legislation saw the proposal defeated.

In the February, Pierrepoint was interviewed in a local newspaper. Describing him as a youthful-looking sixty years of age, the reporter interviewed him at the local foundry where he had recently found work, having finished his carrier business. Asked for his thoughts on the death penalty, Pierrepoint said, 'Why should a murderer be nursed for the rest of his life? I think it would be encouraging people to murder if the death penalty were abolished, but it would make no difference to me either way.'

In March 1931 Pierrepoint hanged Alfred Rouse at Bedford. In what became known as the Blazing Car Murder, Rouse, a bigamist and travelling salesman, had murdered an unknown man whose body had been found inside a burned-out car in Northamptonshire.

The first execution of 1932 took place in Belfast, where fairground entrepreneur Edward Cullens was hanged for shooting dead a business rival. A month later, Pierrepoint was assisted by Robert Wilson, who was also his assistant when they travelled to Manchester to hang 32-year-old George Alfred Rice, convicted of the rape and murder of a nine-year-old girl. Despite the horrific crime, Rice was still visited regularly by friends and family, telling them at the last visit that he was prepared to meet his end bravely.

Rice had been listening to the words of the priest, but, when the door opened and the hangmen entered, he began begging for mercy, and, as Wilson helped Pierrepoint strap his wrists, the condemned man slumped to the floor in a heap and had to be carried, terror-stricken and shrieking, across the corridor onto the gallows.

Pierrepoint had just one further engagement in his diary

during the summer of 1932: to go to Winchester prison to hang a sailor who had murdered his girlfriend. However, a week before the scheduled execution a reprieve was granted. In the weeks following the appointment of his nephew Albert as a new assistant, all those on the official list were sent an official agreement and bond, which they had to sign in the presence of a witness. Tom Pierrepoint had already signed a similar bond many years before and it appears that, unknown to the aged hangman, his failure to return the signed bond saw his name temporarily removed from the list. Subsequently when the under-sheriff of Oxford received a man under sentence of death, he was unable to appoint Pierrepoint and chose to select an untried executioner.

The matter was resolved when Pierrepoint signed the bond, and in the following year he was restored to the list, officiating at every execution except for three that Robert Baxter carried out at Pentonville. Assisting on several of Pierrepoint's engagements was his nephew, who had now been officially placed on the list.

On 3 January 1934, Tom Pierrepoint was at Hull, where he hanged Roy Gregory, a Scarborough boot-maker who had murdered a young child. Leaving the gaol, he travelled straight to Ireland, where he carried out an execution at Dublin without the aid of an assistant.

At the end of the year Pierrepoint and his nephew carried out the execution of Ethel Lillie Major, the daughter of a Lincolnshire gamekeeper who had poisoned her husband with strychnine. The hangmen reached Hull on the afternoon of 18 December, where, after receiving the condemned woman's details, they worked out a drop of 8 feet 6 inches. 'I shall be very surprised if Mrs Major isn't calmer than any man you've seen so far,' Pierrepoint reassured his nephew, who had shown concern at the hanging of a woman. Ethel

Major walked bravely to the gallows. She was the last person hanged at Hull, where her ghost is reported to haunt the gaol to this day.

In 1936 Tom Pierrepoint hanged two women. Dorothea Waddingham had poisoned two women in her care home in Nottingham after wills had been made out in her favour. She was hanged at Birmingham. Three months later he hanged Charlotte Bryant at Exeter. Between these trips he also hanged Parsee doctor Buck Ruxton at Manchester.

Ruxton had been convicted of the murder of his wife Isabella and their twenty-year-old maid, Mary Rogerson, at Lancaster. The women had disappeared in September 1935, with Ruxton telling relatives his wife had taken Mary away to have a pregnancy terminated. Meanwhile, two dismembered bodies were discovered in a ravine in Dumfriesshire. The body parts were wrapped in a copy of a Sunday paper available only in Lancaster and Morecambe, and this led police to Buxton. Ruxton had strangled both women before dismembering them in a bathtub.

Pierrepoint carried out every execution in 1938, the first time since the days of Ellis during World War One that one hangman had officiated at all executions in one calendar year. In February 1940, he hanged Peter Barnes and James Richards, IRA men convicted of a bomb outrage in Coventry, and in the summer he carried out another double execution at Durham, of two men convicted of the murder of a policeman.

1941 was to be the last year that Tom Pierrepoint could claim to be the undisputed chief executioner. He carried out two executions at Dublin, as well as trips to Liverpool, Durham and Manchester, and in July he travelled to Wandsworth to hang George Armstrong, a Newcastle-born spy who was the first Englishman to be executed for treachery during the war.

A month later he returned to Wandsworth to execute two spies and the year ended with a trip to Leicester, where 61-year-old Thomas Thorpe was hanged for the murder of his wife. On 1 May 1942 Harold Hill was hanged for the horrific murder of two young schoolgirls, Doreen Hearne and Kathleen Trendle, who had vanished while walking home from school at Penn, Buckinghamshire. It was the first execution at Oxford for a decade and Pierrepoint was assisted by his nephew.

On Easter Sunday 1942, a Royal Ulster Constabulary patrol had been ambushed by members of an IRA gang. They gave chase and later stormed a house where PC Patrick Murphy was shot dead. Six men, aged between eighteen and twenty-one, were arrested, including nineteen-year-old Thomas Joseph Williams, who had received three gunshot wounds during the incident. The six men were all convicted at Antrim Assizes and sentenced to death. Pierrepoint and his nephew Albert were engaged and discussions took place as to the best way to carry out the executions. But just four days before the executions were scheduled the six were taken out of their cells for an interview with their solicitor.

'I have good news for you all, with one exception,' they were told. Five were to be reprieved and, presumably because he had fired the shot that killed Murphy, Williams wasn't spared. After a tearful goodbye, the others were transferred to another part of the gaol, and Williams was hanged on 2 September, walking bravely to his death, given the extremely long drop of 8 feet 9 inches.

On more than one occasion Tom Pierrepoint's temperament and conduct was being questioned and, following an execution at Wandsworth, Governor Ben Grew outlined his concerns as to the aged hangman's conduct.

I was not favourably impressed by the attitude of
T. W. Pierrepoint the executioner ... I formed the
opinion that Mr Pierrepoint at his advanced age –
I believe his age is 72 years – has passed his
peak of efficiency and is becoming less tactful
and more abrupt in his methods ...

It wasn't to be the last time that official correspondence on
Pierrepoint passed among official channels. In the following
year all governors were asked to make a report on his
behaviour at executions. The following report is typical.

H.M. Prison
Liverpool,
10th February 1943
Execution of Ronald Roberts

In accordance with instructions I beg to submit
the following report. Mr. T.W. Pierrepoint carried
out the execution in an expeditious manner and
his behaviour throughout was quiet and decorous.
He obviously regards speed as the hallmark of
efficiency and there hardly seems sufficient time
for him to ensure that the assistant is clear of
the trap. This zeal for speed may be related to a
desire to show that his ability is unimpaired by
advancing years. Perhaps I may also comment on
the fact that it is his practice to make an
addition of several inches to the authorised scale
of drops. He says he does so to reduce the extent
of the reflex convulsions which may follow. In the
case today I understand there was an addition of
ten inches and there were no convulsions. There
was a complete fracture – dislocation of the upper

```
cervical vertebrae but the skin was not broken or
marked except for a trivial and unavoidable graze
and the soft tissue appeared to be intact.
   H.K. Snell
   Medical Officer
```

Roberts had killed a woman who collected coupon money at Barrows-in-Furness.

On 12 March Pierrepoint carried out the first execution of an American soldier. David Cobb was a 21-year-old black soldier from Alabama, serving in the 827th Engineer Battalion (Aviation), at Desborough, Northamptonshire, convicted of the murder by shooting of Lieutenant Robert Cobner.

Cobb was sentenced to death by hanging, to be carried out at Shepton Mallet. The American military were allowed to retain most of the traditional formalities of an American execution, apart from the actual method, which had to conform to British practice using a British noose.

There hadn't been an execution at Shepton Mallet Gaol since 1926, and Tom Pierrepoint, who had officiated then, was contacted by the American authorities, with his nephew Albert engaged to act as assistant. In line with American custom, the execution was to take place on the first hour on the scheduled date. In the days of rationings and shortages, an American execution was one occasion when food and canned beer were served in abundance.

In a typical British execution the condemned prisoner was usually hanging dead on the end of the rope between ten and sixty seconds. For the wartime executions carried out at Shepton Mallet, the prisoner was escorted to the drop, and, once noosed and pinioned on the trap, had to wait for several minutes while the charges were read out and the prisoner was asked if he had any last statement.

Cobb, the first of three men hanged at Shepton Mallet that year, marched bravely from the death cell to the execution chamber and calmly listened to the words of the chaplain, spoken alongside those read out stating the sentence of the court martial.

When Pierrepoint carried out the execution of Charles Arthur Raymond at Wandsworth later that year, his conduct was again questioned. This time his lack of dexterity and speed were questioned and the commissioners penned a reply to Governor Grew's report:

20.7.43
Re: Thomas William Pierrepoint
    The commissioners thank you for your report
on the above named who acted as executioner in
the case of Charles Arthur Raymond on 10.7.43.
Owing to wartime difficulties of replacements and
favourable reports from other prisons, the
Commissioners are inclined to allow Mr Pierrepoint
to act. Particular attention should be paid to
his technique.

1944 was to be the last year Tom Pierrepoint carried seniority over his nephew, performing all executions carried out in Great Britain and Ireland, with the exception of five in London at which his nephew officiated. On 11 August Pierrepoint carried out a double execution at Shepton Mallet, when two Americans became the first men to be executed for rape for almost a hundred years, and on 1 December he and his nephew carried out the execution of Charles Kerins at Dublin. In September 1942, Detective Sergeant Denis O'Brien was ambushed and shot dead by a gang of men as he left home to go on duty at Dublin Castle. IRA member Kerins refused to recognise the court and neither put forward a defence nor made any statements. Albert Pierrepoint later claimed that, as they returned to the mainland, both he and his uncle were issued with death threats by the IRA.

The year 1946 marked the fortieth anniversary of Tom Pierrepoint's appointment as a hangman. On 8 February he carried out the first execution to take place in Glasgow for almost twenty years and a month later his last execution at Durham, when former soldier Charles Prescott was hanged for shooting dead his girlfriend's sister. She was not the intended victim but had been struck by a bullet fired through a window from outside the house. A month later, when he executed Glasgow hard man Paddy Carraher, the prisoner broke free as Pierrepoint went to pinion him in the cell, and turning on his guards he managed to punch a warder, breaking his nose.

In what was his busiest period for many years Pierrepoint was in action four times as summer approached, including two visits to Manchester. He was now walking with a stick and stricken with arthritis. The end of his career came without warning when he carried out the execution of John Caldwell at Glasgow.

That summer Pierrepoint was officially notified that his name had been removed from the list and on 9 November he wrote to the Prison Commissioners.

19 Northside Terrace
Lidget Green
Bradford
Yorks
7th November 1946
Dear Sirs,

   Having received official notification a few months ago that owing to my advanced age my name had been removed from the list of public executioners I wish to bring it to your notice that I held the post of

Above left: James Billington – the country's chief executioner at the turn of the 20th Century.

Above right: John Billington – the last member of the Billington family to hold the office of chief executioner. In 1905 he was involved in a nasty accident on the gallows at Leeds Prison that was to cost him his life.

Below: William and Thomas Billington – the brothers carried out just four executions together following the death of their father in December 1901. Within weeks of this photograph Thomas had passed away.

How the Illustrated Police News depicted the last moments in the life of
Louisa Masset. Factually incorrect, the white cap seen in the hangman's
pocket would have been placed over the culprit's head before placing
the noose. Her execution at Newgate on 9 January, 1900, the first of the
twentieth century, was carried out by James Billington and assistant
William Warbrick.

The gallows at Newgate Gaol during the nineteenth century *(above)* and at the turn of the twentieth century *(below)*. It was here that the first of the twentieth century executioners learned their trade.

Henry Pierrepoint and John Ellis leave Swansea Gaol in May 1909. A year later Pierrepoint would be sacked for the violent assault on his assistant while both were on duty at Chelmsford Gaol.

Above: Samuel Herbert Dougal – hanged at Chelmsford in 1903.
In 1890 he had failed in his application to become a hangman due to
his criminal record.

Above right: 'Brides in the Bath' killer George Joseph Smith.

Below: Doctor Hawley Harvey Crippen and Ethel le Neve in the dock
at Bow Street following their arrest after a transatlantic chase.

Thomas Allaway – hanged at Winchester in August 1922. His execution was badly botched and he died, in terrible agony, of strangulation.

Inset: Mr Justice Avory, with black cap draped on his wig, sentences Thomas Allaway to death at Winchester Assizes on 7 July 1922.

Records of an Execution carried out in *Winchester* Prison on the 29 March 1917.

Particulars of the condemned Prisoner	Particulars of the Execution	—	Name and Address, in full, of the Executioner	Name and Address, in full, of the 1st Assistant to the Executioner (if any)	Name and Address, in full, of the 2nd Assistant to the Executioner (if any)
Name *Leo George O'Donnell*	The length of the drop, as determined before the execution. 6 feet 9 inches.		John Ellis The Fells Butcher Bowlee Middleton Manchester	Robert Baxter 49 Fort Vale Milford	
Register Number *1956*	The length of the drop, as measured after the execution, from the level of the floor of the scaffold to the heels of the suspended culprit. 6 feet 9 inches.				
Sex *male*	Cause of death {(a) Dislocation of vertebræ, (b) Asphyxia.] *Asphyxia*	Opinion of the Governor and Medical Officer as to the manner in which each of the above-named persons has performed his duty.			
Age *25*		1. Has he performed his duty satisfactorily?	1. *Yes.*	1. *Yes.*	1.
Height *5ft 7 ins*	Approximate statement of the character and amount of destruction to the soft and bony structures of the neck. *mark of rope on neck.*	2. Was his general demeanour satisfactory during the period that he was in the prison, and does he appear to be a responsible person?	2. *Yes.*	2. *Yes.*	2.
Build *Thick set and muscular*		3. Has he shown capacity, both physical and mental, for the duty, and general suitability for the post?	3. *Yes.*	3. *Yes.*	3.
Weight in clothing (to be taken on the day preceding the execution.) *161lbs*	If there were any peculiarities in the build or condition of the prisoner, or in the structure of his neck, which necessitated a departure from the scale of drops, particulars should be stated. *no*	4. Is there any ground for supposing that he will bring discredit upon his office by giving or by granting interviews to persons who may seek to elicit information from him in regard to the execution or by any other act?	4. *No*	4. *No*	4.
Character of the prisoner's neck *Thick and muscular*		5. Are you aware of any circumstances occurring before, at, or after the execution which tend to show that he is not a suitable person to employ on future occasions either as manner of hangman, or assistant in performing the duty, or the likelihood of his creating public scandal before or after an execution?	5. *No.*	5. *No*	5.

Above: LPC4 sheet recording the details of the execution of Leo O'Donnell at Winchester in 1917. In the first of two botched executions by Ellis at Winchester, the cause of death is recorded as asphyxia.

Below left: Edith Thompson – hanged at Holloway in 1923. The distressing scenes, as she was dragged terror-stricken and semi-conscious to the gallows, were to lead to hangman John Ellis tendering his resignation.

Below right: John Ellis and Leo Scott posing for a photograph in the years following Ellis's retirement, when he took his gallows to fairgrounds.

Thomas William Pierrepoint – the longest serving executioner of the twentieth century.

public executioner for almost 40 years during which time I carried out approximately 300 executions without a complaint of any kind.

After having carried out my duties conscientiously and satisfactorily for so long a period I thought at least I should have received some small renumeration [sic] in the way of a pension or gratuity and I ask you if you could consider this matter.

I should also like to point out that the fee for executions has not risen at any time during my term of office and I think you will agree that, that is about the only trade or profession that has not had an increase of salary during the past six years. I am now 76 years of age and I trust you will raise this matter with the appropriate authorities and they will see their way clear to grant me some renumeration [sic] for my long services.

I am Sir

Yours obediently

Thomas William Pierrepoint

The commissioners gave the letter scant consideration before penning a short reply.

Sir,

With reference to your letter of the 7th instant concerning the question of your gratuity. I am desired by the Prison Commissioners to inform you that they regret that there is no fund from which a grant could be made for you.

I am Sir,

Your obedient Servant

Establishment Officer

Pierrepoint settled into his old age and, following the death of his wife, he was cared for by his daughter. He died on 11 February 1954 at the age of 84.

Like Tom Pierrepoint, Accrington-born William Willis had become a hangman in 1906. He was thirty years of age and working as an engraver in a printing works at Miles Platting, Manchester, when he decided to apply. It was a casual remark from a friend that set him on his way. Willis was having tea with a friend one evening in 1905 when he learned that William Billington would be drinking in a local pub. Willis said he had no inclination to meet the recently retired hangman, to which his friend asked, 'Dost think thou could do that job of his?'

Willis replied, 'Of course I could. Billington's nobbut a man the same as me. If he can do it, I'm sure I can.'

That night Willis penned his application and in due course was invited to Preston gaol for an interview with the governor, designed to vet any potential recruits and to weed out the cranks and ghouls. Having sailed through the initial interview he received a letter inviting him to attend a training course at Pentonville. His wife was aghast when she learned Willis was planning to go ahead with the training.

'I'm not going to make a fool of the Home Secretary after him sending a letter,' he told her.

Willis, a former military policeman described as having a fine muscular physique, graduated from the executioner's training school in the spring of 1906, and attended at his first execution on 7 August, when he assisted Henry Pierrepoint at the execution of a sailor at Nottingham. Three months later he assisted Pierrepoint again in the execution of Edward Hartigan, who had battered his wife to death with a hammer on the day Willis had carried out his first job.

On 1 January 1907, Willis assisted John Ellis at Warwick. It was Ellis's first as chief executioner and he was to assist Ellis frequently over the next decade and a half. Willis also assisted Ellis on the latter's second execution as chief three months later, again at Warwick, but then it was to be over a year before he was next back in action.

In July 1909, he travelled up to Perth with Ellis for the execution of Alexander Edmundstone, who had killed a young wages clerk at East Wemyss, Fife. It seems that Willis became stricken with a sickness during the night and was unable to carry out his duties on the following morning, leaving Ellis no choice but to carry out the execution alone.

1910 was to be a busy year for Willis. He started by assisting Henry Pierrepoint on several executions, including that of William Murphy, the last to be hanged in north Wales. Murphy had shown a rare courage on the morning of his execution, climbing onto a chair as the hangmen entered the cell, and then jumping down saying, 'I guess it will be just like that.'

'Yes, as easy as that,' Willis reassured him before escorting the former soldier onto the drop.

He also assisted at two notable hangings that year, both which have passed into the annals of crime. On 9 August, he assisted Ellis at Newcastle, where John Dickman went to the gallows for the murder of a wages clerk, shot dead in a lonely railway carriage near Newcastle. Large crowds protested outside the gaol as Dickman walked defiantly to the drop.

In November 1910 there were four executions. On the fifteenth Willis assisted Ellis at Lancaster, where Thomas Rawcliffe was hanged for murder, by strangling, of his wife. A week later he assisted Ellis in three executions in three days, the second of which was probably the most infamous execution in prewar Great Britain, that of Hawley Harvey Crippen.

On 29 December, he assisted Tom Pierrepoint, who was

acting as 'number one' for only the second time since the dismissal of his brother in the summer. A week later Willis was at his first execution in the south of Ireland, when he worked with Ellis at the hanging of William Scanlan, who had shot dead his sister-in-law, with whom he had been having an affair, at Cork.

Willis assisted both Ellis and Pierrepoint frequently over the next few years. Notable names in his diary were police killer John Williams, a.k.a. 'the Hooded Man', who had shot dead Inspector Arthur Walls at Eastbourne; Liverpool killer George Ball, who had killed his employer and dumped her body in the River Mersey; and Eric (Frederick) Holt, a former soldier who had shot dead his sweetheart on the sand hills at Lytham St Anne's in Lancashire on Christmas Eve 1919. Holt was hanged on 13 April by Ellis and Willis, and on the following morning both were in action again at Cardiff, when Thomas Caler was hanged for the rape and cutthroat murder of a café owner.

1920 was to be a pivotal year for Willis. He assisted Tom Pierrepoint at Leeds and Lincoln, and worked with Ellis at executions in Manchester and Exeter and a double execution at Glasgow. Recently discovered letters have confirmed that Willis assisted Ellis at the execution of Kevin Barry in November in Dublin, although neither man made mention of it in their memoirs. Although there are no official records available naming the executioner and assistants, Willis was the usual assistant to Ellis on all trips to Dublin's Mountjoy Prison to execute convicted IRA men.

Willis assisted Ellis again, at Exeter at the end of November, but the next engagement was when he carried out his first as chief on 30 December, when three executions were scheduled to take place at the same time. As the most senior assistant, Willis was offered the engagement at Pentonville when both Ellis and Tom Pierrepoint were engaged elsewhere.

Marks Goodmarcher was a 58-year-old Jewish tailor's presser of Whitechapel, convicted of the murder of his married daughter, Fanny Zetoun. Goodmarcher had quarrelled with his daughter and son-in-law, and cut her throat on 23 September during the Jewish Black Fast. He committed the crime after they failed to visit him on the 'Day of Atonement' when, according to custom, Orthodox Jews who have quarrelled seek reconciliation.

Goodmarcher attempted to cut his own throat after the murder and was sentenced to death by Mr Justice Darling when his plea of insanity was ignored. Willis was assisted by Robert Baxter and although it was Willis's first time in charge he neglected to mention it when he serialised his memoirs in the late 1930s.

On the following day, New Year's Eve, he assisted Ellis at Strangeways Prison, Manchester, when Charles Colclough, a fish salesman of Hanley, was hanged for the murder of a collier George Shenton.

1921 was an unusual year for Willis: he was involved in ten executions as assistant to both Pierrepoint and Ellis, but apart from his assisting at the double execution at Wandsworth in February, and another trip to Manchester assisting Ellis, the rest of the work was at Mountjoy, including the execution of six men before breakfast on 14 March.

In the following year all Willis's work was again as assistant and included trips to Glasgow and Belfast, assisting Ellis, and a trip to Durham to assist Pierrepoint in the execution of a miner who had murdered his wife. He also acted as the second chief executioner at the double hanging of Edith Thompson and Frederick Bywaters.

John Ellis, assisted by Robert Baxter and Thomas Phillips, hanged Thompson – who, as we have seen, had to be carried to the drop unconscious – while William Willis and new assistant Seth Mills hanged Bywaters, who met his end bravely. It has often been incorrectly reported that Thomas Pierrepoint carried out the execution of Bywaters. Indeed, even his nephew Albert claims in his autobiography that this is the case.

In February 1923 Willis travelled to Londonderry to carry out the execution of William Rooney, who had murdered a mill worker at Cookstown, County Tyrone. It was the last execution at the gaol and, as with other Irish executions, he makes no mention of it in his memoirs.

The remaining executions Willis attended in 1923 were all as assistant to Ellis and, with the exception of a trip to Nottingham, they took place in Scotland: two at Edinburgh and one at Glasgow, where he was the assistant at the execution of Susan Newell.

Now an established chief executioner, he was ready to step into the role vacated by Ellis as the first-choice hangman at the majority of Northern prisons. He officiated as chief executioner at two jobs in Manchester and one in Belfast, along with acting as assistant to Pierrepoint on three executions in 1924, including those of Patrick Mahon and Abraham Goldenburg, but he was perturbed to find that he was engaged as assistant to Robert Baxter when a Frenchman, Jean-Pierre Vaquier, was hanged at Wandsworth on 12 August.

When Willis carried out the execution of Wigan coalminer James Winstanley at Liverpool on 5 August he was participating in his 106th execution. His ratio of executions was now more as chief than assistant but he must have been frustrated to find that after nearly twenty years' service he was still often engaged as assistant. Although Tom Pierrepoint claimed seniority over Willis by just a few months, he had accepted his rapid rise to chief seemingly without making a fuss; but finding Robert Baxter, with less than half the length of service of Willis, starting to get more and more work as a chief made him unhappy.

Willis's conduct now began to be questioned. On 5 January 1926 he executed John Fisher at Birmingham. Fisher, a 58-year-old machinist, shared an immaculately kept terrace house in Birmingham, with his partner of the previous fourteen years, Ida Taylor, and Jessie Dutton, Ida's daughter, who lodged with them. On Sunday afternoon, 25 October 1925, Jessie Dutton was sitting in the lounge opposite Fisher, while her mother busied herself with housework. Some sixth sense told Jessie that something was amiss and she got up, put her coat on and left the house. It saved her life.

Minutes later, Fisher rose from his chair and without warning attacked Ida with a carving knife, cutting her throat, before washing the knife, tidying up the house, leaving and closing the door behind him. Having spent the rest of the day wandering the streets, he boarded a tram, during which time Ida's body lay in the house undiscovered. The only seat was next to a policeman, and when the officer rose to alight, Fisher followed him off the tram and confessed that he had committed a murder.

Willis recalled later that he very nearly caused the most remarkable accident in the history of British execution. As Fisher was led to the scaffold in a daze, in order to prevent him from collapsing, two warders stood very close to him. Such was his haste to carry out the execution that Willis attempted to place the white cap and noose around the neck of the nearest guard. He realised his mistake at the last moment and within seconds the drop fell. If he had succeeded in noosing the guard, the speed at which executions were carried out would have ensured that, in all probability, the guard would have hanged. The story later became prison folklore and it was often quoted that Willis had been too drunk to distinguish the condemned man from the guard; but, unless he had secreted drink into his quarters from outside, it's unlikely that drink was the cause of the near-mishap.

Willis was chief executioner at Manchester and Liverpool during a week in March. At Liverpool he executed Lock Ah Tam, a seaman born in Canton in 1872. Tam had come to Britain in 1895 and had met and married his wife Catherine in South Wales before they moved to Birkenhead and raised a family. He became a well-paid and highly respected member of the Liverpool Chinese community in charge of the welfare of his fellow sailors, and it was part of his duties to mediate in quarrels and arguments between Chinese sailors.

In 1918, during a disturbance at a dockside club, he was beaten on the head with a billiard cue and from then on his personality underwent a marked change. He became a heavy drinker and gambled heavily, to the extent that he was declared bankrupt in 1924. Tam also began to quarrel with his family, but his wife remained loyal and arranged counselling for him.

On 30 November 1925, he organised a family party for the twentieth birthday of his son, Lock Ling, who had returned home after seven months in China. As the party drew to a close Tam got into a fierce quarrel with his wife. His son and two of their daughters, Doris and Cecilia, already in bed, came downstairs to see what the disturbance was. As Lock Ling hurried to fetch a neighbour his father pulled out a gun and shot his wife and two daughters. Mrs Tam and Cecilia died instantly; Doris died in hospital several days later. At his trial Lock Tam was defended by Sir Edward Marshall Hall, who failed in persuading the court that Tam was undoubtedly insane.

On 13 April, Willis carried out his last execution as chief

when he hanged ex-borstal boy George Sharpes at Birmingham. Hanged fourteen days after his twentieth birthday, Sharpes had been working on a farm on his release from reformatory and when the wife of his employer told other workers of his police record he battered her to death with a hammer.

When Willis received a letter offering an appointment at Manchester on 24 June he must have been disappointed to find that, instead of the usual role as chief executioner, he was engaged as assistant to Tom Pierrepoint. It was the seventh execution to take place at Strangeways since Ellis had retired, and Willis had officiated at the previous six without any incident of note. Although he may have taken this demotion personally, the probable reason behind it is that the person to be hanged, 34-year-old Louie Calvert, had been sentenced to death at Leeds and if the Yorkshire authorities had engaged the executioner it was logical they would employ their usual man.

Three days later he was at Pentonville for the execution of Johannes Mommers, who had been convicted of the murder of Augusta Pionbini, an Italian woman in Essex. Mommers had been lodging with the Pionbini family, and one evening took Augusta out. Later, she staggered home with a gaping wound to her throat and died. Sentenced to death at the Old Bailey, he was hanged on 27 June at Pentonville by Robert Baxter, assisted by Willis.

Willis's conduct at the execution was severely criticised and it was noted on the official execution form that he had failed to strap the legs of the condemned man sufficiently. The Prison Commissioners seemed aware that Willis may have had an issue with having to assist a man he claimed seniority to, although it was clear from reviewing the list of executions that the three men acting as executioners all had their own 'patch'.

With just the one exception, for the past three years Willis had been the chief hangman at executions carried out at Liverpool, Manchester and Birmingham; Baxter's domain was predominantly London, East Anglia and south Wales, with Pierrepoint officiating elsewhere. So in some ways Willis and Baxter were more fortunate than Pierrepoint, inasmuch as each was acting as both assistant and chief executioner while Pierrepoint's work was all as chief. Although the number one earned far more money than an assistant, his engagements were more limited. In 1926, for example, Baxter officiated at four executions as number one, in London and in Cardiff, along with jobs assisting Pierrepoint at Gloucester and Winchester, and assisting Willis at Birmingham.

At Pentonville, Willis's behaviour was such that it was made official and, after a request for more information on the matter, on 2 August the governor penned a letter to the Home Office.

... as to the personality of Willis I am not impressed, even an executioner can remain humane and decorous. Willis appears to be the reverse: he is offensive, over-bearing, ostentatious and generally objectionable in his manner. The Foreman of Works also reports that he was most aggressive on arrival when he found his tea was not prepared.

One considers cold calculated callousness as part of an executioner's make up, but brutal callousness bordering on blood lust is not desirable, and this is the impression Willis gave to me when the man was secretly paraded the previous day for the benefit of the executioner.

As to his private life I cannot say, but his

appearance, which is bloated and heavy, gives the
idea that he drinks, although during his stay
here there was nothing to indicate the slightest
sign of drunkenness.

    Maj. Benke

    Governor

Willis's name was removed from the official list of executioners on 5 August 1926. Unbeknown to him, he was now an ex-hangman and the issue came to light only after he accepted an engagement at Liverpool in the November. Having written offering his acceptance of the engagement, he then received a second letter from the under-sheriff who had engaged his services, notifying him that he had been informed by the Prison Commission that his name had been removed from the official list and he therefore had to withdraw the offer of the work.

Willis was distraught at the news and at once penned a letter to the Prison Commission asking for an explanation.

22 Bunyan Street
Hyde Rd
Ardwick
Manchester

The Prison Commissioners
Dear Sirs,

    On the 4th inst. I received a letter from the
Under Sheriff of Cheshire as follows. 'In
consequence of reports from the Prison
Commissioners I find I am unable to engage you as
executioner in accordance with my letter of the
28th inst., which letter is therefore hereby

cancelled.' and would esteem it a favour if you
accede to my request for particulars of such
report, which necessitate your instruction for
cancelling same, because to my knowledge I am not
aware of anything justifying this course. I have
been at your service for the last 20 years and nine
months and on no single occasion have my duties
been questioned through inefficiency, during the
116 executions I have been present at. Therefore
I think it is only justice to request the favour.

However should it be more convenient to
interview you personally, I await your esteemed
instructions.

I am
Yours obediently
W. Willis

The reply was short and to the point.

I am desired by the Prison Commissioners to
acknowledge receipt of your letter of the 7th
inst., and, in reply regret to inform you that they
are no longer able to recommend you as a person
suitable to assist at executions and your name
has according been struck off the list.

Willis responded by asking them to reconsider and
pointing out that he had recently assisted at Pentonville,
after which he had received the second instalment of his pay
– the 'good-conduct money', he called it – and ended by
asking them to take into consideration his long service and
to reconsider their decision, which he believed was based on
a misunderstanding.

When he received no reply to this letter he travelled down to London and called at the Home Office, but finding the person he needed to speak to was otherwise engaged he was unable to get an interview face to face. He wrote two further letters begging them to reconsider before at last receiving a curt reply: 'I am desired by the Prison Commissioners to acknowledge receipt of your letter of the 3rd inst., and, in reply to inform you that they have nothing to add to their letter of the 17th ...'

With Willis still none the wiser as to why his name had been removed, his persistence led to a tightening up of the way in which matters were dealt with. The commissioners reflected that Willis might have benefited from being told outright why his name had been removed, and letters were sent to all under-sheriffs advising them to make sure they appointed executioners from the current list of appointed hangmen and to be aware they would be notified of any changes to the names on the list, as and when they happened.

Proof that this was not taken on board was clear when Willis was engaged twelve months later for another execution at Liverpool. Thinking he may have served some form of suspension, he replied, accepting the position, only to be informed that the Prison Commissioners could not sanction the under sheriff's choice of executioner and the offer had to be withdrawn.

Willis reluctantly settled into retirement, serialising his memoirs in the *Sunday Despatch* in the late 1930s shortly before he died.

Chapter 5:

Rivalry

Robert Baxter of Hertfordshire is one of the more mysterious of twentieth-century executioners. Little seems to be known of his private life away from the gallows and there is hardly anything to shed extra light on him in any of the files held at the National Archives. This is despite his being one of the most highly regarded of executioners, who for over a decade was responsible for almost every execution carried out in the city of London.

Robert Orridge Baxter became an assistant hangman in early 1915. Although records of his training are thus far unavailable, it's not unreasonable to assume he attended the short course of instruction at Pentonville along with Edward Taylor, as both appeared on the list within a few weeks of each other. Baxter was 37 years old, and living at 49 Port Vale, Hertford, when he witnessed his first execution, at Wandsworth, as assistant to Tom Pierrepoint, on 15 July 1915.

The man executed was Robert Rosenthal, a German

convicted of treason at Middlesex Guildhall. In April 1915, a letter sent to a man named Kulbe in Holland was intercepted by the British Secret Service. Franz Kulbe was an alias of Captain Von Prieger of the German Admiralty, who was known to be active in the recruitment and control of spies. Traced to a hotel in Copenhagen, the writer of the letter was discovered to be 23-year-old Robert Rosenthal. Rosenthal was known to have spent time in England between November 1914 and April 1915, and to have sent telegrams to a number of addresses in Holland. Several of these had been intercepted and monitored and, when examined again in greater detail, were found to contain coded messages detailing the movements of the British naval fleet at Edinburgh, Portsmouth and Hull.

Rosenthal was kept under surveillance and a few days later he travelled back to England. In due course he made his way back to Copenhagen, where he was arrested on board a ship as it sailed out of Newcastle and passed into international waters. After he had initially denied any involvement with espionage, Rosenthal's demeanour changed when he was confronted with the evidence of telegrams and the letter from the Copenhagen Hotel, and, leaping to his feet, he clicked his heels and confessed that he was indeed a spy.

His trial was held in camera (in secret), and following conviction Rosenthal wrote to Lord Kitchener, apologising for his actions and offering to divulge information on an American in Berlin working for the American Relief Commission, who was spying for the enemy. Rosenthal was the only spy convicted during world War One to be hanged, while eleven other spies tried and convicted by the court martial were shot at the Tower of London. The reason he went to the gallows and was not shot was simply due to a lack of space at the Tower in the summer of 1915, as several other spies were already waiting on death row and a number of others were on remand pending trial.

Baxter was called into action to assist Tom Pierrepoint at Wakefield in December, but his next execution, assisting John Ellis for the first time, was one of the most controversial of the twentieth century. Prior to the outbreak of the war in 1914, Irish-born Sir Roger David Casement had become a hero to the British people as a result of his work in Africa. As a member of the British Consulate, Casement had been awarded a knighthood for exposing scandals and outrages in Africa and South America. In 1911 he had retired from consular service and took up the cause of Irish nationalism and independence, while retaining his British citizenship.

Following the outbreak of the war in August 1914, Casement left Ireland and went to Germany, and for the next eighteen months he lived in Berlin. He attempted to persuade the German government to support an Irish rebellion and uprising. Not only this but he also visited a number of POW camps, trying to enlist Irish prisoners in a brigade being formed to fight the British. Those who refused to join Casement were subjected to brutal treatment from the German guards.

In 1916, Casement's request for assistance was granted and the German authorities sent over a shipment of arms to be used in the planned Easter Sunday uprising. When he discovered that the majority of these guns were little more than useless – outdated and unreliable, mostly liberated from Russians on the Eastern Front – Casement sent a warning to his comrades in Ireland not to use the weapons. This message was intercepted and the shipment seized. A few days later, on Good Friday, 20 April 1916, Casement was arrested within hours of his landing by German submarine in Tralee Bay.

Taken to the Tower of London pending trial at the Old

Bailey, he was charged 'that as a British subject he had conspired with the enemy during a time of war, and had thus committed treason'. Found guilty and sentenced to death, Casement was stripped of his knighthood, and, in an effort to discredit the man whom the public had treated as a hero just a few years before, they allowed the press to publish extracts from his diaries that showed he was a homosexual. A large crowd that had been gathering since daybreak cheered when notice of execution was posted on the gates of Pentonville prison. Casement stood well over six feet tall, and, settling on 6 feet 3 inches, Ellis showed Baxter how to make a slight adjustment to the drop, to compensate for his unusually tall frame.

As Baxter escorted Casement to the drop the prisoner showed little sign of fear, declaring, 'What a beautiful morning. I die for my country,' before striding bravely onto the drop.

Baxter soon impressed the authorities with his efficiency and professionalism, and began to frequently assist both Ellis and Pierrepoint. In 1917 he assisted Ellis at the execution of Leo O'Donnell at Winchester, when it was noted that the condemned man died of painful strangulation rather than a dislocated neck.

Baxter's engagements fluctuated greatly during the latter years of the war. In 1917 he was present at more than 50 per cent of executions, and in the following year, when just seven men were hanged, he wasn't present at all. In 1919 he again had the lion's share of the assists, including two in two days at Leeds in early January, one a double, and trips to Liverpool, Glasgow and Newcastle. Baxter assisted both Ellis and Pierrepoint in 1920, and was the assistant when William Willis made his debut as a senior executioner at the end of that year.

His notable executions in 1921 include a double at Wandsworth, when Field and Gray were hanged for the murder of seventeen-year-old Irene Munro, in what became known as 'the Crumbles Murder'. Munro was a typist from London, who was holidaying alone in Eastbourne, when she met a pair of unemployed and unsavoury characters, Field and Gray, local men who spent the summer months cruising the promenade, paying attention to female holidaymakers.

On 19 August 1920, two men and a girl were seen heading in the direction of the Crumbles, a stretch of beach between Eastbourne and Pevensey Bay and on the following day a boy discovered a battered body partially buried in the shingle. It was identified as that of Irene Munro, who had been reported missing. A tip-off led police to Field and Gray, who were picked up four days later.

Baxter escorted Grey to the drop as Pierrepoint prepared his partner in crime on the drop. It was the first time he had seen Field since they had been led out of the dock cursing and each blaming the other for their predicament.

Between March and June 1921 Baxter made two visits to Dublin, where he assisted at the execution of nine men. On 14 March he assisted Ellis and Willis in the execution of six men hanged in pairs on the hour between 6 a.m. and 8 a.m. Three months later he assisted Tom Pierrepoint when three men were hanged on the same gallows for a variety of crimes, both political and nonpolitical.

There were no engagements of note in Baxter's diary for 1922, but 1923 was just a few days old when he assisted at another infamous execution, that of Edith Thompson, who was hanged at Holloway. The rest of the year was quiet, with just one assist, and, after one further assist in April 1924, his next engagement was to mark his debut as chief.

In the autumn of 1923 following the collapse of a business

venture that had almost bankrupted them and broke up their marriage, Mabel and Alfred Jones took over the running of the Blue Anchor Hotel in Byfleet. But while her husband Alfred settled in to his new role as licensee, Mabel took a holiday in Biarritz, France, where she met 44-year-old Jean-Pierre Vaquier. Despite the fact that neither spoke the other's language, they became friends, even purchasing an English–French dictionary to help them communicate, and in due course they became lovers.

She returned home to her husband, but within weeks Vaquier turned up as a guest. Jones was unaware of the Frenchman's encounter with his wife, and Vaquier informed him, with the aid of the English–French dictionary, that he was in the country on business, hoping to sell the patents on a machine he had invented. In total, Vaquier stayed at the Blue Anchor for six weeks without paying his bill, telling Jones that he was expecting a cheque, when he would settle his account.

On 29 March, Jones rose early and drank his usual glass of health salts. He complained to his wife and a barmaid about the bitter taste and died in agony a few hours later. The police had his body analysed and it was found to contain strychnine. Vaquier and Mrs Jones were both questioned and a photograph of the Frenchman appeared in the evening newspaper. On the following day a chemist from a nearby town contacted the police and told them he recognised the man in the photograph as someone to whom he had sold poison. Vaquier protested his innocence throughout the trial but was convicted on overwhelming evidence.

Baxter carried out the execution, assisted for some unknown reason by both William Willis and Thomas Phillips. Willis was unhappy at playing a subordinate role to a man over whom he had almost a decade of seniority, and it was the start of a frosty relationship between them that was to have serious repercussions for him in the coming months.

Baxter officiated at his second senior execution at Ipswich in November, and ended the year assisting Tom Pierrepoint at executions in Hull and Nottingham. By 1925 Baxter was a recognised number-one executioner, carrying out his first senior execution at Pentonville in April. He was to be the sole chief executioner at the gaol for the next decade, hanging more than a score of criminals on the gallows on which he and his fellow executioners had learned their trade.

In August 1926 Baxter assisted Tom Pierrepoint at the execution of 22-year-old Charles Finden at Winchester. Finden was a labourer from Alton, convicted of the murder of a fifteen-year-old John Thompson on 5 June. The boy worked on a farm and disappeared shortly after collecting his 15 shillings weekly wage. His body was discovered on a piece of wasteland beside the Alton-to-Basingstoke railway line; he had been strangled with a necktie and robbed of his money.

Finden was arrested on suspicion of murder on 24 June but claimed he was asleep in a field at the time of the crime. His wife told detectives he had given her a 10-shilling note and two half-crowns (each 2s 6d), which he claimed he had earned working at a local tennis court. There was no one to support his story of earning the money and he was duly convicted.

Finden was hanged on 12 August and given a drop of 7 feet 1 inch. Governor Harding at Winchester noted that, unlike in the last two executions at the gaol, death appeared to be instantaneous and that the execution had been carried out very efficiently, but added a note on the official LPC4 record of execution: 'Robert Baxter is a very quiet and efficient man and goes about his work quickly and silently and has not the overbearing way of many executioners'.

As word of Baxter's character and efficiency spread his services became more sought after. In August 1927 he carried out his first execution at Wandsworth: the execution of two labourers who had murdered the nightwatchman at the site where they were employed in Surrey. The execution passed off without incident, although it was noted that one of them received a laceration on his chin following execution, caused by a sharp edge of the metal eyelet or thimble sewn into the noose.

Nine days later Baxter was back in London for the execution of John Robinson. On 11 May 1927, staff in the left-luggage office on Charing Cross station became aware of an awful smell coming from a large trunk that had been deposited five days earlier. They reported their suspicions to the police, who, forcing entry, discovered the dismembered body of a middle-aged woman identified as 36-year-old Mrs Minnie Bonati. The pathologist, Sir Bernard Spilsbury, was able to confirm that death was due to strangulation.

The seller of the trunk and several clues, including a bloodstained matchstick and the laundry mark on some clothing left in the trunk, led police to Robinson, a Lancashire born ex-soldier. After initially denying the crime, he confessed he had killed her following a row over money and had dismembered the body with a knife purchased from the very hardware shop next to Victoria railway station at which Patrick Mahon, hanged at Wandsworth three years earlier for murder and dismembering his victim, had purchased his knife.

Baxter had to refuse the offer to assist at an execution on 6 January 1928, writing that he was unable to accept because he was already engaged to carry out an execution as number one at Wandsworth on that day. Sydney Goulter was the first of four men Baxter hanged at Wandsworth that year. January

1928 was a busy month for executions with both Baxter and Pierrepoint executing five men each. Following the execution of Goulter there were no calls until Baxter was invited to Glasgow to hang a man convicted of the murder of his mother. Pierrepoint had originally been invited to carry out the execution in the first week of January, but had to refuse because his diary already had a double execution booked for that day and also engagements pencilled in on either side of the projected date. Baxter was then offered the job and accepted, with Pierrepoint left rueing his decision when an appeal shifted the date to the end of the month, which would have allowed Pierrepoint to carry out his duties.

Three days after the trip to Scotland, Baxter travelled down to Cardiff to hang two men convicted of a vicious gangland killing following a feud on a racetrack. Thirty-one-year-old David 'Dai' Lewis was a former Welsh professional welterweight boxer, who earned a living running a one-man protection racket on the racecourses of south Wales. His simple scheme was to charge bookmakers extortionately large sums of money for basic items such as chalk and dusters for their blackboards, in return for guaranteeing the safety of their pitches.

On 28 September 1927, Lewis made the mistake of trying out his scheme at Monmouth racecourse. Monmouth was the territory of the Rowland brothers, well known to Lewis as a gang of hard men, but foolishly the ex-boxer failed to heed the warning to go home. Instead he returned to Monmouth on the following day and again plied his trade. He returned to Cardiff later that afternoon and that night, as he left a public house, he was attacked and received a fatal knife wound.

The police were tipped off that the Rowland brothers had carried out the attack, but, from his deathbed, Lewis claimed that he did not know who had stabbed him, only that he was certain that it was neither Edward 'Ted' Rowland nor Danny Driscoll, two names at the top of the police's list of four suspects. Another of the gang, John Rowland, later confessed that he had stabbed Lewis in self-defence but the police ignored the confession and charged four suspects with the murder.

Tried at Glamorgan Assizes, one was found not guilty and released; three others were convicted on the testimony of bystanders who had watched the fight from the distance. The three-day trial ended with Ted and John Rowland, along with Driscoll, being sentenced to death.

As they waited for the result of their appeal, John Driscoll went berserk, was certified insane and removed to Broadmoor. Tom Phillips, Lionel Mann and Robert Wilson assisted Baxter at the double execution. Driscoll maintained his courage to the last, laughing and joking as he was led to the drop, asking which noose was his. In contrast gang leader Rowland collapsed in terror when Baxter entered his cell and was carried semiconscious to the drop.

Four days later, Baxter was back at Wandsworth for the execution of a man who had cut the throat of his sister after she had refused to cook him supper.

Baxter and Tom Pierrepoint were now the only recognised chief executioners on the list and both were getting a fair share of work predominantly on a regional basis. Pierrepoint's domain was mainly the northern gaols and Ireland, with Baxter the main executioner for London, along with prisons in South Wales and East Anglia. It appears, though, that the long-serving Pierrepoint was not happy that Baxter, with ten years' less experience, was now seen as an equal in the eyes of the Home Office.

Pierrepoint had doubtlessly expected that, with Ellis now

retired, he would become the undisputed number-one executioner, as his brother and bitter rival Ellis had both been previously. Noting that Baxter was getting more and more engagements than Pierrepoint believed was fair, he took it upon himself to write to a number of under-sheriffs when he read in the newspapers that sentence of death had been passed in their jurisdiction. This was contrary to the terms and conditions of the hangman's agreement, but was something that had been in place since the days of James Berry, forty years before. Now frowned upon and seen as touting, this, it seemed, was something that Baxter had also taken to doing, for both he and Pierrepoint were contacted and warned that such behaviour was against the regulations and conditions they adhered to each time they agreed to carry out an execution.

There is no record of Baxter's replying to the Home Office but Pierrepoint responded, seemingly blaming Baxter for causing Pierrepoint to go to these measures.

'I never used to write but I found it out that someone else was and I was not getting my fair turn. The Junior man was getting the work and the Senior man was waiting idle.'

A total of twenty-six men were hanged that year, an almost equal split between the two, with Pierrepoint carrying out fourteen as chief, and Baxter carrying out twelve as chief and also as assistant to Pierrepoint.

On 31 May both were in action, bringing to a conclusion the horrific murder of a policeman in Essex. Early on the morning of 27 September 1927, Police Constable George Gutteridge was shot dead on a lonely country lane between Ongar and Romford. He had been shot twice in the neck and, as he lay dead in the road, a bullet had also been fired into each eye. Police suspected Gutteridge had been killed as he challenged the motorist who had stolen a car from a doctor's house a few hours earlier, which was later found abandoned in Brixton.

In January 1928 Frederick Browne was arrested for stealing a car. Browne ran a garage close to where the doctor's car had been found, and when police searched his premises they found a gun that was identified as the one that had killed the policeman. Browne was an ex-con, a petty thief and a known associate of Patrick William Kennedy, a soldier and former member of the IRA. Known as 'Two-Gun Pat', Kennedy was arrested in Liverpool and admitted being with Browne in the stolen car when challenged by PC Gutteridge. He claimed that they had been stopped and, when Browne was unable to prove he was the owner of the car, the policeman took out his notebook, and, as he did so, Browne shot him.

With fears of a disturbance if the two met on the scaffold, it was decided that they should be hanged at different prisons. Kennedy was executed at Wandsworth by Pierrepoint and assistant Robert Wilson; at the same moment over at Pentonville, Baxter and assistant Henry Pollard hanged Browne.

Baxter made two further trips to Scotland that summer, and travelled to Belfast to help Pierrepoint hang William Smiley, a farm labourer who had robbed and murdered two sisters. It was the last time Baxter worked as an assistant.

Baxter's last execution of the year was almost to cost him his career and resulted in his being summoned to take a medical examination at Pentonville to prove his fitness for the post. Twenty-year-old Trevor Edwards and his sweetheart Elsie Cook came from the same Welsh mining village near Bridgend. On the morning of 17 June 1928, he was found bleeding heavily from the neck and told a policeman summoned to the scene that he had killed his sweetheart by cutting her throat with a razor and that her body was on a nearby hillside.

Newly appointed assistant Alfred Allen, present at his first execution, assisted Baxter at Swansea on 11 December, and was involved in an almost fatal accident. Like his contemporaries, Baxter prided himself on his speed on the gallows, and as he went to work that morning it was noted by those present that he was very quick in placing the cap and noosing the prisoner. Seeing Allen strap the condemned man's legs and step back, Baxter pushed the lever and witnesses were horrified to watch as the assistant followed the prisoner into the pit. Fortunately, Allen wasn't injured. Only his pride was hurt, and, although the incident was recorded in the papers that day, no blame was attached, with the governor claiming the accident was a mixture of the hangman's alacrity and Allen's slightly defective vision.

The last part of the claim was inaccurate. It was Baxter, not Allen, who suffered from defective vision and he was indeed blind in one eye. Baxter made a statement to the governor that morning and claimed that Allen had not stepped back far enough.

'I think this is because the trapdoors are much wider than those at Pentonville ... and therefore he fell down into the pit!'

When word reached London of the incident it was decided to hold an internal inquiry into the incident and Baxter was summoned to Pentonville on 18 January 1929 for a medical examination, and to make a more detailed statement of events.

Three prison doctors found that Baxter was free from organic disease and both physically and mentally fit to act as executioner. They also noted that he had no vision whatsoever in his left eye but his right eye had normal vision for his age (now fifty). They concluded that,

We find no reason to find that Baxter is less
capable of seeing all that goes on during the
immediate preparation for the execution and
seeing that all is in order before he pulls the
lever than he was before he became blind in his
left eye. In fact we are of the opinion that Baxter
has sufficient acuity of vision to perform the
duties of an executioner efficiently.

Allan C Pearson

F J Wilfred Sass

E W A Cormack

A memo was issued outlining the actual method of
execution as carried out at Pentonville in 1928.

Executioner walks to the scaffold in front of
the condemned man. As the prisoner stands on the
chalk mark on the drop, the executioner places
the cap over the head, then places noose around
the neck, adjusts and then tightens it. Steps back
towards the lever and pulls when the engineer
draws out the safety pin.

Assistant Executioner walks immediately
behind the condemned man to the scaffold with the
leg strap in his hand. As soon as the prisoner is
on the chalk mark fastens the leg strap from
behind and steps back

Foreman of Works observes movements of both
and when all clear signals to the Engineer who
withdraws safety pin. From experience this is
perfect timing and usually the assistant
executioner has finished the job and steadied the
prisoner from behind. There is no signal between

executioner and assistant but I have never seen
Baxter fail to look down quickly and see the leg
strap is on and the assistant is standing clear.

The incident was concluded with the findings that Allen
had taken fractionally longer than normal, possibly due to
nerves, and that he had got the leg strap tangled when he first
put it around the culprit's legs. Also, the floor of the Swansea
gallows was new, the trapdoors were wider than those on the
old-style gallows, such as the one at Pentonville, and there
was no discernible mark to show where the trapdoor ended
and the floor began. There had been discussions about
outlining the edges of the trap and in this instance it had been
decided not to whiten the edges because it may cause distress
to the prisoner walking onto what was clearly the trapdoor.
It was noted that an outline should be made on the scaffold
if it would avoid a repeat of the Swansea incident.

In conclusion, the governor, Major Benke, recorded, 'I have
every faith in Baxter's efficiency and was quite impressed
with Allen during the trials.'

Baxter had made the recommendation that all future
assistants should witness an execution without taking any
part in proceedings and this was agreed and put into practice
for future graduates.

Baxter carried out just two executions in 1929, both at
Pentonville and a week apart in February, and it was to be
over a year before his services were next called upon. At a
time when Parliament was discussing the abolition of capital
punishment, the first execution in the 1930s was one of the
most notorious.

Sidney Harry Fox was the fourth and favourite son of
Rosaline Fox. Both mother and son were not averse to
breaking the law, and would often holiday in expensive hotels

across the country, leaving a trail of unpaid bills behind them. In 1927, Mrs Fox became friendly with a Mrs Morse and they took a flat together at Southsea, Hampshire. Sidney Fox soon joined them and persuaded Mrs Morse to take out a life-insurance policy in his favour. Soon afterwards she realised that Fox had made at least one attempt to gas her while she slept and ejected Fox and his mother from the flat, but not before Fox stole items of her jewellery that led to his serving fifteen months in gaol.

He was released in March 1929, and mother and son soon teamed up again. On 21 April 1929 Rosaline Fox took out a will and an insurance policy on her life. They continued to roam the southeast, leaving a trail of unpaid hotel bills until, on 16 October, they booked into the Metropole Hotel at Margate in Kent.

Two days later Fox took out a policy entitling him to the sum of £1,000, should his mother meet her death accidentally. Both that and a previous insurance policy were due to expire on 22 October. On that day Fox travelled into London, calling at the offices of the insurance companies holding the policies, and made arrangements for them to be extended by 24 hours.

On the evening of 23 October, just hours before the policies were due to elapse, Fox took his mother to dinner before escorting her to her room. With less than half an hour until the policies expired, he was seen running down the corridor, shouting that there had been a fire and calling for help. Staff found the room thick with smoke and Rosaline Fox dead. A doctor gave cause of death as accidental suffocation and on the following morning Fox collected a death certificate and set out to claim his insurance payout.

Fox was arrested in Norwich in November. His haste to collect the money and the timing of the death aroused the suspicions of the insurance companies, leading to a police inquiry that involved the exhumation of Mrs Fox. This time death was found to be due to strangulation.

Sidney Fox was hanged at Maidstone on 8 April, the last man to die on the gallows in Kent. He collapsed when Baxter entered the cell and was carried kicking and screaming onto the drop.

Again, it was to be Baxter's last execution for over a year, and, when he was next called into action it was to carry out an execution in Gibraltar on 3 July 1931, when 31-year-old Ernesto O'Pisso was hanged for the murder of an elderly woman. There was rioting in the streets and it was reported that troops patrolled with hockey sticks as Baxter went to work alone on the gallows in the prison in the Moorish Castle.

Baxter carried out two executions in Pentonville and one in Cardiff but the bulk of the work now seemed to be going to Pierrepoint, as it would continue to do for the remainder of Baxter's career as hangman. Between August 1931 and April 1935, the last year he officiated as executioner, Baxter carried out just eight engagements, all at Pentonville, and had even begun to see jobs at Wandsworth now go to Pierrepoint. It was no coincidence that his eyesight was beginning to fail him and his reactions had become slower. On 29 October he officiated at Wandsworth for the last time and both the governor and medical officer noted that his eyesight had obviously deteriorated recently. He was in action the following day at Pentonville, executing Alan Grierson, and his name was deleted from the official list a few days later.

Baxter settled into retirement and eventually died in Hertford in the late spring of 1961, aged 83.

Robert Baxter's appointment in 1915 had been to fill one of the vacancies left by the removal of Albert Lumb from the list. Living in Bradford, Lumb had joined the list at the same time as William Conduit of Manchester, and the two men appeared at executions in the months following the dismissal of Henry Pierrepoint. With Pierrepoint dismissed and the Prison Commissioners unhappy at having to call William Warbrick out of retirement, they compiled another list of applicants and narrowed it down to three, the third being George Brown of Ashton-under-Lyne, near Manchester.

Conduit's career was the briefest. He assisted Ellis at an execution at Chelmsford, in which the convict had attempted suicide before arrest. When the man fell to his death the fall opened the neck wound and sprayed blood everywhere. It was a gruesome sight for a new recruit, and, when on his second execution the prisoner was overcome with terror on the drop and screamed for mercy, it seemed that was more than enough and he tendered his resignation.

Albert Lumb's short career ended with the outbreak of World War One. He had assisted both Ellis and Tom Pierrepoint before his name disappeared from the list. There is nothing on record to show that Lumb was a friend of Pierrepoint's prior to becoming an assistant, but it is probable that he was.

George Brown remained as an assistant for almost a decade and at various times he lived in Manchester, Cardiff and Bolton. His first execution could also have been enough to upset any assistant suffering from nerves. Fifty-year-old William Palmer had been convicted of the murder of an aged widow in a lonely cottage in Leicestershire. Palmer protested his innocence from the moment of his arrest right through his stay in the condemned cell.

Brown met Ellis at Leicester Gaol on the afternoon of 18 July 1911 and viewed the prisoner in the condemned cell. He tipped the scales at 206 pounds (just over 14½ stone) and Ellis pointed out that the unusually short and thick, flabby neck would cause problems in working out a drop.

At eight o'clock on the following morning the hangmen waited outside the condemned cell for the signal to enter. Palmer hadn't slept a wink on the previous night and had frequently shouted out, 'I'm going to be murdered in the morning!'

As Ellis and Brown entered, he stood facing the door with an evil glare on his face, and, instead of the more common sight of a prisoner sitting placidly waiting to be led to the drop, they found a man ready to fight for his final moments on Earth.

'You're not going to let these fellows murder me?' he barked at the warders, and when the governor stepped forward to try to calm him down he brushed him aside. 'I'm innocent! I'm not going to allow myself to be murdered without putting up a fight!' Brown stepped into position to strap Palmer's arms as he had been instructed, but his inexperience and the confusion caused by the shouting and struggling meant that he found himself face to face with the prisoner as he struggled to avoid pinioning.

'I'll get you!' Palmer shouted at Brown, swinging his heavy hobnailed boots at Brown towards his groin. Brown stepped back quickly and, as the warders closed on him, he got into position behind Palmer and attempted to get the wrist strap in place.

In what Ellis later dubbed 'pandemonium', four warders rushed to secure the prisoner, who was fighting for his life to avoid the straps. It took the four warders and two executioners to get the straps on, but not before both Ellis and Brown received punches and kicks. Palmer was pushed face down onto the cell floor and his arms forced behind his back and the straps tightened.

The execution shed at Leicester was 40 yards from the

condemned cell and as the procession made for the door the governor addressed the condemned man one last time.

'You are only making it all the harder for yourself, Palmer,' he said. 'Pull yourself together and act like a man, not like a coward!'

'I am innocent, I'm not going to let you murder me,' he maintained, twisting and struggling to be free of his straps.

Palmer was marched to the scaffold and as they approached the threshold Ellis whispered to Brown not to strap his legs. Before the noose came into sight, Ellis whipped the hood from his pocket and placed it over the prisoner's head. Moments later he was in position on the chalk mark. Brown held him still for a moment as Ellis adjusted the noose, then leaped back and the floor opened and Palmer ceased to resist. It had been a terrifying baptism of fire for the new assistant, and, writing his memoirs many years later, Ellis, a veteran of more than two hundred executions, claimed it was the most exciting of his career.

Five months later Brown assisted Ellis in a double execution at Manchester, and three days later at Liverpool, and assisted at Manchester in December 1913, when Ernest Kelly was hanged for a murder at Oldham as thousand rioted outside the gaol at the injustice of the sentence. There was no doubt that twenty-year-old Kelly was guilty of the murder of shopkeeper Daniel Bardsley at Oldham, but the crowds were unhappy at a reprieve granted to his eighteen-year-old accomplice, who many believed was equally as guilty as, or even more guilty than Kelly.

Brown assisted both Ellis and Tom Pierrepoint over the coming years but as the war ended it was noticeable that his appearances at executions became few and far between. He last assisted in October 1919 and then disappeared from the list.

Edward Taylor passed out of Pentonville in 1915 and, like

that of George Brown, his debut execution was to be a very trying affair, when he assisted Ellis when the infamous 'Brides in the Bath' murderer George Joseph Smith paid for his crimes. It was later recorded that Smith collapsed as he was led onto the scaffold and it was believed he had died of heart failure before the rope added to the certainty of his death.

When Taylor travelled from his home in Brighton to assist Ellis at Pentonville in March 1918, he was advised before he travelled to bring his own food, for which he would be reimbursed, since there were food shortages in London at the time. Taylor was present at several executions a year, including the botched hanging of Thomas Allaway at Winchester in 1922.

It's possible that the unnerving sight of Allaway being 'hanged like a dog', as one reported later noted, caused Taylor to have doubts as to his willingness to assist, or it may have been the news in the papers that Ellis, recently resigned as the chief executioner, had attempted to commit suicide. Whatever the reasons, he assisted at just one execution in the following year, none in 1924 and finally two in 1925. He assisted Baxter at Norwich in November that year and then refused any subsequent offers of engagement. It apparently took the Prison Commissioners until May 1928 before Taylor was notified that his name had been removed from the list following his refusal to act as assistant at the last eleven executions for which he had been invited to officiate.

The first postwar assistant to join the list were Thomas Mather Phillips, who was living in Farnworth, Bolton, when he applied to become a hangman in 1918. Born in 1889 and raised in nearby Clifton, Manchester, he was working as a collier in Little Lever when he was accepted for training. Although his record is unavailable, a knowledge of the workings of the Prison

Commissioners indicates that it is likely he trained in the summer of 1921 alongside Robert Wilson of Manchester and Seth Mills of Hengoed in south Wales. Philip was invited to assist an execution at Cardiff but had to turn it down and it was then offered to local man Mills.

Phillips carried out his first execution in the spring of 1922, when he assisted Ellis at the last execution at Usk. William Sullivan was a 41-year-old foundry puddler hanged for the murder of Margaret Thomas, who had been found battered to death in her isolated cottage at Coytre, near Newport.

Phillips's second engagement was to help hang teenager Henry Jacoby and the experience of an execution that was to cause upset and sympathy from the prison staff would stand him in good stead for a job that came his way early in the following year, when he was engaged at Holloway to assist in the execution of Edith Thompson.

In April 1923 he again assisted Ellis at an execution at Liverpool, which had involved a dramatic manhunt across three counties. Fred Wood was a travelling upholsterer sentenced to death at Chester for the murder of spinster Margaret Gilchrist White, who lived with her brother in a villa at Bramhall, Cheshire.

John White had returned home after a visit to Manchester and discovered his sister's body. She had been strangled. Detectives reasoned that she had invited the killer into the house and in one room they found several half-upholstered chairs, as if someone had been repairing them. On the mantelpiece they discovered Wood's business card.

Wood was pursued across the country and finally gave himself up when he saw his poster outside a police station in Lincoln. His defence at his trial was that the woman had been taken ill while he was repairing a chair at the house and had strangled herself during a fit. Wood failed in an attempt to prise her hand away from her throat and she fell to the ground dead. Feeling certain no one would believe his story, he took a small amount of money he was owed for the work already done and fled. The jury were unconvinced and found him guilty of murder.

On 2 January 1924 Phillips assisted Tom Pierrepoint for the first time when they hanged cutthroat killer Matthew Nunn at Durham. Pierrepoint was censured for the brutal treatment of the prisoner. The priest who was sitting with Nunn as the fateful hour approached, said that the hangmen had burst into the cell and after they had pinioned Nunn's arms, Pierrepoint pushed him out of the room into the corridor.

'I have been present at a number of executions and never have I witnessed such callous haste,' he later complained to the governor.

Phillips assisted Baxter for the first time in August that year, when poisoner Jean-Pierre Vaquier was hanged, and in the following summer he assisted Willis at an execution at Manchester. Phillips also returned to Durham that year, this time for a double execution, where one of the prisoners went to the gallows chanting hymns.

In January 1928 Phillips was present at four executions. On 3 January he assisted Tom Pierrepoint at Manchester, when Fred Fielding was hanged for the murder of his sweetheart on the previous Bonfire Night, and two days later he travelled back to Durham to hang a man who had killed his wife and tried to make it look as if she had hanged herself. At the end of the month he assisted Baxter at a double execution at Cardiff and a single execution at Wandsworth.

In August 1931 he assisted Baxter at the double execution of two men convicted of the murder of Herbert Ayres. Ayres lived in an area close to railway sidings at Scratchwood, near Elstree. Resembling a shantytown, it was a community of huts, converted railway carriages and crudely hand-built shacks, populated by a transient group of casual workers, homeless people and the unemployed.

On 1 June 1931, the body of Ayres was discovered beneath a smouldering pile of rubbish. The renowned pathologist Sir Bernard Spilsbury was able to help police identify the victim and confirm he had been dead for approximately three days and had died as a result of repeated blows to the head.

A witness was traced who had been living at the camp at the time of the murder and claimed the killers were two tramps, 61-year-old Oliver Newman and 56-year-old William Shelley, known as 'Tiggy' and 'Moosh'. He told police that, while sleeping on the floor of the men's hut, he had heard a quarrel. Then he saw them attacking Ayres, whom he knew as 'Pigsticker'. He later saw the body of Pigsticker being carried towards the dump, where it was later discovered. Fearful for his own safety, he left the camp the following day.

Newman and Shelley did not deny killing Ayres, and claimed they were justified in what they had done because the victim had repeatedly stolen food from their hut. The first time, they give him a warning and a beating; when it happened again, they killed him. Showing no remorse, the callous killers walked defiantly to the gallows on 5 August 1931.

Phillips was present at a number of infamous executions throughout the 1930s and in 1936 he assisted for the first time at the execution of a woman. Charlotte Bryant was an Irishwoman who had met her husband Fred when he was serving in Londonderry in the Black and Tans. After she had followed him back to England in 1922, they settled in Coombe, Dorset, where she quickly became disillusioned with life as a farmer's wife and mother of his five children, and began a steady stream of affairs, which, it seemed, her husband chose to ignore.

In 1933, she met Leonard Parsons, who soon moved in as a lodger, and, despite his carrying on a relationship with Bryant's wife, the two men became good friends. By the summer of 1935, Bryant grew tired of the local gossip about his wife and the lodger, and, following a series of quarrels, Parsons moved out.

Around this time, Fred Bryant began to complain of stomach pains, and, although in otherwise good health, he died on 22 December. Earlier that year he had been seen by a doctor suffering from similar symptoms, and, as a result of his sudden death, an inquest was ordered. Cause of death was found to be arsenic poison and a charred tin that had contained arsenic was discovered in the garden. A chemist was found who had sold the tin to Mrs Bryant, and her daughter later testified in court that she had seen her mother trying to burn the tin following the death of her father.

Charlotte Bryant was sentenced to death at Dorchester Assizes and it was alleged that her striking black hair had turned white as she awaited execution. A few days before she was hanged she dictated to a warder a letter to the King: 'Mighty King. Have pity on your afflicted subject. Don't let them kill me on Wednesday.'

Thomas Phillips assisted Tom Pierrepoint as a large crowd gathered outside the prison gates. Fearing that the demonstrations would get out of hand, the authorities decided to bring the execution forward an hour to 8 a.m.

In 1937 Phillips assisted Alfred Allen at Pentonville in what turned out to be Allen's last execution, and during the following year he assisted Tom Pierrepoint three times. He was now noted as living at Park Parade Harlesden, having found work as a bin man for the local corporation.

Phillips finally graduated to chief executioner in March 1939. It had taken over twenty years from his original application to his finally pushing the lever, during which time he had assisted at more than forty executions. He had also had the chance to assist more executioners than any other assistant, having been present when Ellis, Tom Pierrepoint, Willis, Baxter and Alfred Allen had officiated.

On 2 January 1939, the body of seventeen-year-old Peggy Pentecost was found in a Lambeth hotel room. She had been strangled and a handkerchief forced into her mouth. Peggy had checked into the hotel on New Year's Eve in the company of a man, who had signed the register as Mr and Mrs Armstrong of Seaford. The man was soon found to be Harry Armstrong, a 38-year-old parlourman, with a number of previous convictions, including attempted murder. He told police he had an alibi for the time it was believed she was murdered. Armstrong said that he had become engaged to Peggy at Christmas and they had travelled to London, booking into a hotel, and while still booked in they had a quarrel when he learned she was also seeing another man. As a result he had left and spent that night with a woman he met in a café at Paddington Station.

He claimed her other lover must have carried out the crime, and following conviction he said he did not wish to appeal but asked for a reprieve on medical grounds. Phillips carried out his debut execution at Wandsworth, assisted by Albert Pierrepoint. Armstrong was given a drop of 7 feet 6 inches and death was instant.

In the following week Phillips was back at Wandsworth, this time as assistant to Tom Pierrepoint, and he assisted him again at the end of the year at Wandsworth when two soldiers were hanged on separate days for the rape and murder of Mabel Bundy, whose battered and bruised body had been found close to the hotel where she worked at Hindhead. Witnesses had seen her drinking with a number of soldiers from a nearby army camp that housed the 2nd Battalion of the North Staffordshire Regiment. Privates Stanley Boon and Arthur Smith were picked out at an identity parade. Along with another soldier, Boon had left a bar at closing time, shortly after Smith and Mabel Bundy. Smith said that he and the woman had sex – to which she had consented – when Boon and the other man approached. Boon in particular seemed drunk and aggressive.

It was alleged that Boon and the other man had spied on Smith as he had sex, but when the woman realised she was being watched she tried to stop. During a struggle it was said that both Boon and Smith raped her and then beat her to death.

The other soldier was acquitted; Boon and Smith, who blamed each other for the crime, were convicted and sentenced to death. Although Smith chose to appeal, Boon decided not to, but his execution was postponed until the result of Smith's appeal was heard. Following a dismissal of the appeal the two men were hanged in October, and, amid fears of disturbing scenes if the convicts met on the scaffold, Boon went to his death on the 25th, Smith the following morning. Tom Pierrepoint carried out both executions; Phillips assisted at the execution of Smith.

Phillips assisted at the double execution of IRA men Peter Barnes and James Richards for the Coventry bomb outrage mentioned earlier, before receiving the offer to carry out another execution at Wandsworth, again as chief executioner.

Ernest Edmund Hamerton was a 25-year-old kitchen porter sentenced to death at the Old Bailey for the murder of Elsie Ellington, the assistant manageress at Lyon's Café, Camberwell Green. Hamerton left his native Blackpool early in 1940, to be near Elsie, whom he hoped to marry, and who had been transferred by Lyon's to work in their London branch. She took lodgings at Walworth, south London, and, on arriving in the capital, Hamerton took a room in the same house. No sooner had he moved in than they began arguing. On the morning of 16 January, they had another massive quarrel at breakfast. Hamerton was enraged that Elsie didn't seem to appreciate that he had given up a good job at home to be near her and when she said their relationship was over he picked up a knife and stabbed her 24 times, leaving the blade stuck through her heart. He fled London by train but was arrested on arrival in Manchester.

At the prison, it was noted that Phillips smelled of drink and appeared flushed. Later that night, as he and assistant Alex Riley relaxed in their quarters, Phillips demanded more drink, and when he was refused he told the warders that they could put it down as an expense. At 9 a.m. on 27 March, Hamerton walked to the drop. Phillips was seen to be fumbling with the rope as he adjusted the knot and it was also reported that there was a distinct lack of precision in his movements. Later that day the governor contacted the Prison Commissioners and he was removed from the official list with immediate effect.

Later that year, at the height of the Blitz, he returned north, settling in Ellis's hometown of Rochdale and finding work as caretaker at the local police station offices. On 27 March 1941 he died of chronic kidney failure and heart disease at the age of 51, exactly one year to the day after his last execution.

Chapter 6:

The Roaring Thirties

The short official list of hangmen and assistants was increased from six to eight names just after World War One and that number remained constant with just the personnel changing every few years. As we have seen, in 1921 assistant Seth Mills of Hengoed, south Wales, joined the list, but after half a dozen engagements he disappeared.

Robert Wilson of Manchester carried out his first engagement in December 1921, and between then and January 1923 he assisted at just 2 executions before his career began to pick up, and by the mid-1920s he was frequently assisting all three main executioners, with his notable engagements including the hanging of the Charing Cross trunk murderer John Robinson and police killer Patrick Kennedy.

He often assisted both Willis and Tom Pierrepoint on trips to Northern Ireland, and was the assistant at Birmingham when Albert Pierrepoint was present as an observer at his first execution in England. Despite Pierrepoint's version of events, the official files show that it was Wilson who carried out the assistant's duties that morning in Birmingham and that the younger Pierrepoint played no part in proceedings other than as a witness.

Wilson assisted Tom Pierrepoint in the execution of Dr Buck Ruxton at Manchester in May 1936, but, as the war clouds loomed closer, dates in Wilson's diary became fewer and fewer. His last engagement was at Durham in February 1939, and when he failed to acknowledge a number of Home Office letters his name was struck off the list, although it is more than likely that he had died around this time.

Two other Lancashire assistants joined the list in the early 1920s. Henry Pollard lived in Blackburn and for a decade assisted at more than a score of executions. Pollard's diary lacked any executions of killers that had gripped the nation, and, apart from a hectic period in early 1928 when he assisted at three executions in four days, his was one of the less newsworthy careers as a hangman. It is believed that he died around 1938, shortly after tendering his resignation in April that year.

Lionel Mann of Rochdale was probably friends, or at least acquainted, with John Ellis, the famous executioner from his hometown, who was touring with his macabre sideshow on executions when Mann was accepted as an assistant hangman in 1925. He more than likely trained in the company of Pollard, since both were in action for the first time in the summer of 1925.

Twenty-three-year-old Wilfred Fowler and his elder brother, Lawrence, led a gang of Sheffield protection racketeers who spread terror among local shopkeepers and publicans, as they impersonated American gangsters. Their path to the gallows began in April 1925, when a disturbance took place in a city-centre public house. An associate of the Fowlers, who went under the name of 'Trimmer' Welsh and was the muscle behind the gang, caused a scene with a new barmaid and, when she made it clear his advances weren't wanted, he made to lash out at her.

He was prevented from doing so by former boxer William Plommer, who, although he knew of Welsh's reputation, was tough enough not to be scared. They squared up and in the ensuing fight Plommer gave Welsh a heavy beating. Out for revenge, Fowler and several of his gang cornered Plommer as he stood talking to another former boxer, Jack Clay, and that confrontation ended when Clay beat Wilf Fowler unconscious. Enraged, the gang went looking for Plommer and, finding him at home, called him out into the street. A fight broke out and ended only when Plommer slumped to the ground mortally wounded, having been attacked with knives, chains and clubs.

Following an initial reluctance by witnesses to testify against the Fowler gang, they received reassurances from the police that they would be safe from reprisals, and the police soon had enough evidence to arrest seven members of the gang on a murder charge.

On 3 September Wilfred Fowler shared the gallows at Leeds with Alfred Bostock, who had committed a murder in Rotherham in Yorkshire, while his brother Lawrence was hanged alone 24 hours later. Pollard assisted Pierrepoint at the double execution; Mann made his debut as an assistant the following morning. All three men went to their deaths without undue incident.

Mann was the assistant at the last execution at Maidstone, when Sydney Fox was dragged in terror to the gallows, and for the next six years frequently assisted both Tom Pierrepoint and Robert Baxter around the country.

RULES FOR ASSISTANT EXECUTIONERS

1. Every person acting as an assistant executioner is required to conform to any instructions he may receive from or on behalf of the High Sheriff as to the day and hour and route for going to and leaving the place of execution.

2. He is required to report himself at the prison at which an execution is to take place, and for which he has been engaged, not later than 4 o'clock on the afternoon preceding the day of execution.

3. He is required to remain in the prison from the time of his arrival until the completion of the execution, and until permission is given him to leave.

4. During the time he is in the prison he will be provided with lodging and board.

5. He should clearly understand that his conduct and general behaviour should be respectable, not only at the place and time of the execution, but before and subsequently, that he should avoid attracting public attention in going to or from the prison, and he is prohibited from giving to any person particulars on the subject of his duty for publication.

6. His remuneration as an Assistant Executioner will be £1.11.6d or the performance of the duty required of him, to which will be added £1.11.6d if his conduct and

behaviour are satisfactory, during and subsequent to the execution. These fees will not be payable until a fortnight after the execution has taken place.

7. Records will be kept of his conduct and efficiency on each occasion of his being employed, and this record will be at the disposal of any High Sheriff who may have to engage an executioner.

8. The name of any person who does not give satisfaction or whose conduct is in any way objectionable so as to cast discredit on himself, either in connection with the duties or otherwise, will be removed from the list.

9. It will be considered as objectionable conduct for any person to make an application to a sheriff or under-sheriff for employment in connection with an execution, and such conduct may involve removal of such person's name from the list.

10. The Assistant Executioner will give such information or make such record of the occurrences as the Governor of the prison may require.

By May 1928, the number of executioners had dropped and no replacements had been recruited. First, the dismissal of William Willis left a vacancy for an executioner, and the voluntary retirement of Edward Taylor meant that there was now also a vacancy for an assistant. To bring the quota of hangmen back up to the normal number, and recruit two new assistants, it was decided, on 7 May, to open the file of applicants received in the previous months and to see if any of them were suitable replacements.

Among them was Charles Edward Green, a forty-year-old former soldier from Braintree, Essex. In February 1928 Green had written directly to the Home Secretary William Joynson-Hicks offering his services 'as hangman or as his assistant'. In his letter Green wrote that he had served four years and 227 days in World War One, came from a military family and was a working man with a family.

He was invited for interview at Pentonville on Saturday, 23 June at 3 p.m. It wasn't a successful interview, as the governor's report later showed.

HM Pentonville
23 June 1928
Mr C. E. Green. Candidate for Applicant for
Assistant Executioner or Assistant
Most unsuitable, the only point in his favour is
I fear his total disregard for the sanctity of
human life.
Common, rough type, smelt of drink and probably
already boasted in Braintree about what he would
do if he became executioner.
Uneducated to the degree that he could not spell
'June', Irish' and 'driller' etc. without assistance.
His application is written in another person's hand.
No enquiry to the local police deemed necessary.
Maj. A. Benke
Governor

Another unsuccessful candidate was Alexander Taylor of Liverpool, who wrote stating that he was thirty years old, married with two children and had served in France between

Above left: William Willis, sacked in 1926 after officiating at 116 executions.

Above right: Jean Pierre Vaquier arriving at court following his arrest for murder.

Below left: 'Nurse' Dorothea Waddingham, hanged at Birmingham in 1936 by Tom Pierrepoint and his nephew Albert.

Below right: A typical letter sent to the Home Office applying for the post of executioner.

Above: Robert Orridge Baxter. His first execution as chief was that of Vaquier at Wandsworth in August 1924.

Above right: Frederick Field – hanged at Wandsworth in 1936. He was one of only three men hanged by Alfred Allen.

Below: Wealthy abolitionist Mrs Violet Van der Elst outside Wandsworth Gaol on the morning of the execution of Percy Anderson.

LIST OF CANDIDATES REPORTED TO BE COMPETENT FOR THE OFFICE OF EXECUTIONER, OR WHO HAVE ACTED AS ASSISTANTS AT EXECUTIONS.

October, 1938.

Name and Address.	Remarks.
Thomas W. Pierrepoint, 2, Turner Avenue, Lidget Green, Bradford, Yorkshire.	Has satisfactorily conducted executions, has assisted at executions, and has been practically trained at Pentonville Prison.
Robert Wilson, 325, North Road, Clayton, Manchester.	Has assisted at executions, and has been practically trained at Pentonville Prison.
Thomas M. Phillips, 38, Park Parade, Harlesden, London, N.W.10.	Has assisted at executions, and has been practically trained at Pentonville Prison.
Stanley William Cross, 11, Dancer Road, Fulham, London, S.W.6.	Has assisted at executions, and has been practically trained at Pentonville Prison.
Albert Pierrepoint, 2, East Street, Newton Heath, Manchester.	Has assisted at executions and has been practically trained at Pentonville Prison.
Herbert Morris, 42, Marton Drive, Blackpool, Lancashire.	Has worked at executions and Has been practically trained at Pentonville Prison.
Alexander Riley, 2, Bland Street, Moss Side, Manchester.	Has assisted at executions and has Has been practically trained at Pentonville Prison.

A list of qualified executioners in late 1938.

Above: Thomas Mather Phillips around the time of his application to be a hangman. After acting as an assistant for over 18 years he was finally promoted to a chief executioner in March 1939.

Above right: Stephen Wade – one of four assistant executioners added to the list in 1940 following the dismissal of Tom Phillips.

Below: Karel Richter *(in trilby hat)* at the spot where he parachuted into England. Richter's execution was described by Albert Pierrepoint as his toughest job on the scaffold.

1939 =				as used in all practice. 1904 - 1958					
118	8	6	138	7	3	167	6	0
119	8	5	140	7	2	169	6	1
120	8	4	141	7	1	171	5	9
121	8	3	143	7	0	174	5	8
122	8	2	145	6	11	176	5	7
124	8	1	146	6	10	179	5	7
125	8	0	148	6	9	182	5	6
126	7	11	150	6	8	186	5	5
128	7	10	152	6	7	188	5	4
129	7	9	154	6	6	190	5	3
130	7	8	156	6	5	194	5	2
132	7	7	158	6	4	197	5	1
133	7	6	160	6	3	200	5	0
135	7	5	162	6	2			
136	7	4	164	6	1			

9" Must be added to all weights

Top left: John Leatherberry – American soldier hanged by Tom Pierrepoint at Shepton Mallet.

Top right: Pierre Neukermans – hanged at Pentonville in June 1944. He was one of the last foreign spies to be hanged in England.

Above: Harry Allen's own table of drops. Like all modern executioners, Allen added extra inches to the Home Office recommendations.

Left: Hangman Albert Pierrepoint and assistant Syd Dernley in 1952.

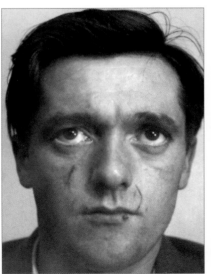 

Above: Alec Wilkinson with his wife and mother-in-law. In August 1955 he was hanged for the murder of the latter. It was the last execution in the pre-Homicide Act days.

Below left: John Willson Vickers – the first man to hang under the 1957 Homicide Act.

Below right: Assistant executioner Harry Smith and Harry Allen who carried out the first execution following the passing of the Homicide Act.

Robert Leslie 'Jock' Stewart – one of the last two hangmen of England.

44, Park Place,
Cardiff

26th March 1958

Dear Sir,

Vivian Frederick TEED

    I thank you for your letter of yesterday from which I see that you are available to officiate at the execution of the above named if his appeal is unsuccessful.

    I will write to you again as soon as I have further information.

    I also acknowledge the Memorandum of Conditions which you have duly signed. I have heard from the Governor of H.M. Prison, Swansea to the effect that he has engaged the services of Mr. H.F. Robinson as assistant executioner.

Yours faithfully,

Under Sheriff.

Mr.R.L. Stewart,
2, Birchenlea Street,
Chadderton,
Lancs.

Above: Typical letter requesting the services of an executioner.

Below: Allen and Evans – the last two to hang, sent to their deaths in August 1964.

1915 and 1918 His short letter of application ended by stating he had recently been pensioned out of Liverpool City Police Force, having lost a testicle when 'assaulted on duty by 3 persons who were afterwards sentenced for causing grievous bodily harm to me'.

Joseph Forrest wrote from Blackburn stating that '... this is my fourth application in the last three years'. Forrest claimed he was 'steady and sober' and that he had two certificates from the Royal Humane Society. On 18 June 1928 he was invited for interview at Strangeways Prison in nearby Manchester. Forrest made a favourable impression and the governor authorised a police report into his conduct before forwarding his details back to the Home Office.

Two days later the governor received back the police report, showing that Forrest was addicted to drink and associated with other women. The chief constable also noted in his report that Forrest had frequently boasted in licensed premises of becoming an executioner. The report concluded that in the opinion of the investigating officer, Detective Inspector Shimmin, Forrest was not a suitable person to be entrusted in the position for which he had applied.

Following interviews at various prisons around the country that summer, by Monday, 6 August, two applicants had been shortlisted to attend at Pentonville Gaol for an interview with the governor prior to training by Officer Townsend. The first to report was retired Metropolitan police officer Henry Durling of Fernham Common, Buckinghamshire. Stating that he still wished to be of service to the state, Durling failed at the first hurdle when he was reported to be grossly overweight with a pendulous abdomen and his vision to be poor, 'only partially corrected by a pair of badly fitting glasses that weren't his own'. The medical officer noted on his file that in his view Durling did not have the freedom of movement or manual dexterity needed to be an executioner.

Frank Rowe of Birmingham applied for the post in February 1928. At the time of application he was 45 years old and had served for 25 years in the Coldstream Guards. He had seen action both in South Africa and in World War One, during which time he had been a prisoner of war. In a long and distinguished military career he had been awarded numerous bravery and good-conduct medals, including the Military Medal. Although at his interview Rowe was noted as being sullen and not endowed with any fine feeling, he nevertheless successfully overcame the medical examination and, following a week of instruction, he passed the training course.

It was decided to wait until another suitable candidate could be found so that the two could be sent for training together, and a few days later the governor of Pentonville wrote that he had interviewed a potential candidate. Alfred Allen was a forty-year-old ex-sergeant in the 6th South Staffordshire Regiment who was employed as a wheeler at the Sunbeam motor factory in Birmingham. Allen returned to Pentonville in October for a period of instruction and on 11 November 1928 he and Rowe were notified that their names had now been added to the official list of executioners.

Rowe's name was to stay on that short list for just a matter of weeks. A few days before he had travelled to London to undertake training, at the village of Norton on the outskirts of Stockton in County Durham a gruesome killing took place that was to lead to a young man's conviction for the murder of his grandparents. Emily and Thomas Kirkby were battered to death and buried in a shallow grave after being lured out of their home by their grandson, Charles Conlin. A neighbour had seen Conlin walking from where the bodies had been found, carrying a shovel, shortly before they were discovered.

He was arrested a few days later, having recently purchased a motorbike for cash stolen from his grandparents. Conlin was convicted at Durham Assizes in November and sentenced to be hanged on 4 December 1928.

Letters were sent engaging Tom Pierrepoint as chief executioner with Rowe as his assistant. An appeal shifted the date of execution and on 3 January 1929 Rowe travelled up to Durham to prepare for the execution planned for the following morning. Quite what he had expected or had been told during his training isn't clear, but he was nevertheless shocked to learn that he was seemingly expected to find board and lodging on the night prior to the execution. He was also enraged to discover that he was expected to pay his own rail fare from Birmingham to Durham and two days before he set out he penned the governor a letter.

241 King Edwards Rd
Ladywood
B'ham

Sir

I am in receipt of your letter dated 1st inst and you are informed you have sent me no Railway Warrant which I fully expected, as I got one from the Governor of Pentonville Prison, London when I went there to be trained, and was found lodgings, and 7s 10d a day was paid to me while I was there. I do not know whose ridiculous idea it is that I am going to pay about £4.0.0 railway fare, out of my own pocket, and forfeit two days pay at work which is £1.6.0 total £5.6s and I receive £3.3.0 for my services I should be about £2.1 out of pocket, besides the expense of the journey, and there is

the trouble and expense I have been put to,
preparing for the journey, the whole business
looked ridiculous on the face of it. I never heard
of anyone being confronted with such a ridiculous
situation in my life. I think it is a case of the
'Charge of the Light Brigade', Someone has
blundered.

   I am yours, very disappointed
   F Rowe MM

The governor received the letter on the day prior to the execution and with little time to make alternate arrangements wired Rowe back with a short note: 'Travelling expenses will be refunded – are you coming?'

It seems apparent that Rowe decided to make the journey only once he had received the telegram, for it was reported that he didn't arrive at the prison until 8.28 in the evening. By the time he reached Durham, Pierrepoint had already rigged the drop and was waiting in his quarters.

Rowe was noted as being slow in his duties on the following morning but the execution was carried out satisfactorily, although the governor was told by the Prison Commissioners that it seemed Rowe had misunderstood the letter offering him the engagement, since there was no mention that he would receive board and lodgings in the prison and that the railway fare would be refunded on his arrival. He did note that Rowe had had ample time to make enquiries after receiving the engagement as to the arrangements relating to travel and accommodation. It was the last time Frank Rowe appeared at an execution, and it was noted that he tendered his resignation days after returning from Durham.

As we saw earlier, Alfred Allen's first experience at an execution nearly resulted in a serious accident, but following the inquiry at Pentonville early in 1929 no blame was attached and he was free to continue. There was a footnote on the file following the inquiry to the effect that the Prison Commissioners felt they were having no luck with their new assistants – one resigning almost immediately and the other 'almost hanging himself at his first execution!'

Allen may have felt something was amiss when he failed to receive any engagements in 1929, and, when he was next called into action, it was to hang a man who had been convicted of a brutal murder in Southampton during the previous year.

On 10 January 1929, 58-year-old Vivian Messiter was found dead in the locked garage he owned in Southampton. At first it appeared that he had been shot in the head. Pathologist Bernard Spilsbury was called in and confirmed that Messiter had been battered to death with the hammer, found beside the body. A search of his lodgings discovered a note bearing the name of W F Thomas, an agent who did business with Messiter, a man police suspected may be involved, and who had since disappeared. Thomas's hideout was traced and police found evidence that suggested his real name was William Henry Podmore, a motor mechanic and small-time criminal, wanted by the police in Manchester for fraud.

Messiter worked as an agent for an oil company and was killed after discovering that Podmore, whom he knew as Thomas, was defrauding the company. Podmore worked on commission and it was found he was making commission on fictitious sales and then tampering with the books to cover his tracks. Podmore was arrested and, though evidence linking him to the murder was not conclusive, he was strongly suspected. Detectives charged him with fraud and he was sentenced to six months in prison as officers built up a murder case against him.

Podmore was duly arrested on his release and later convicted before Lord Chief Justice Gordon Hewart in March. He was hanged at Winchester on 8 April 1930 by Tom Pierrepoint, assisted by Alfred Allen, protesting his innocence to the last.

Allen was present at three executions in 1931 at Birmingham, Manchester and Oxford, and the following year he assisted at Leeds and made a second trip to Manchester, where he assisted at the dispatch of the youngest man to be executed for over a decade.

Charles James Cowle was an eighteen-year-old unemployed labourer, of Darwen in Lancashire. Naomi Farnworth, the six-year-old daughter of his next-door neighbour, would often run errands for Cowle, and, when she failed to appear for afternoon school on 22 March 1932, enquiries led police to him. They called at his house after she had been missing for two days and Cowle immediately led the officer up to his bedroom, where the body of Naomi was hidden in a trunk. She had been raped and then strangled.

Cowle pleaded insanity at his Manchester Assizes trial, and it was revealed in court that he had been sent to borstal at the age of nine for the attempted murder of a two-year-old boy. There was no recommendation for mercy from the jury as they returned their guilty verdict and a medical examination found that Cowle was neither insane nor mentally defective. He was hanged in May, by Tom Pierrepoint, with Allen assisting at his seventh execution.

There was no further work that summer and, when Allen next received a letter requesting his services, he was probably shocked to find he was being engaged to carry out an execution as a principal, despite there being two recognised executioners and three assistant executioners holding seniority, in the case of Tom Phillips by over a decade. The execution that marked Allen's promotion took place at Oxford in November.

On 14 September, the body of Gwendoline Warren was found concealed under a bed at her home in Maidenhead, after a concerned neighbour forced entry into the house. She had wounds to her head but had died from suffocation. Death had taken place four days earlier and a nationwide search was launched for Ernest Hutchinson, with whom Mrs Warren shared a house and who had since disappeared.

Arrested in a boarding house at Southend the following day, Hutchinson said that, following quarrels over money, Gwendoline Warren had stormed out of the bedroom saying she would sleep on the sofa, and when he went downstairs the following morning he found her body. He had then panicked and concealed the body under the bed and fled, thinking he would be blamed for the murder. As sentence of death was passed upon him, Hutchinson, who had spent over twenty years in prison, burst out laughing in the dock.

Allen carried out the execution to everyone's satisfaction and even had the confidence to deviate from the official table of drops. Noting that Hutchinson had a 'bull' type of neck, he decided that a drop of 6 feet 6½ inches was sufficient. There seems no real reason why such an inexperienced assistant should be entrusted to carry out an execution as chief so early in his career. Although such an occurrence was commonplace at the turn of the century, it was almost unheard of in more modern times. As we have seen, during 1932 there were moves to get all persons on the official list to sign a confidentiality bond. When Tom Pierrepoint failed to return his signed bond a list was sent out with a line through his name and therefore another executioner was needed.

Executions were something of a rarity at Oxford and it could be that Allen had impressed the authorities when he assisted at the execution of Henry Seymour in 1931. His conduct was noted as being 'very satisfactory' on the official record of execution and so, when they were looking for a suitable man to carry out the execution, they chose him.

He reverted to assistant throughout the mid-1930s, and, following the execution of Harry Tuffney at Pentonville in 1934, his conduct was questioned when he was alleged to have turned up drunk. Allen received a temporary, unofficial suspension. The governor questioned chief hangman Baxter about his assistant, and, although Baxter mentioned that he found Allen an unpleasant person to share sleeping quarters with, he did not wish to go on record as having stated this. Baxter also said Allen seemed to neglect his assistant duties and was prepared to leave a lot of work to the chief.

Allen was allowed to continue as an assistant but his conduct was monitored and, on the two occasions when he officiated in 1935, the comments were favourable. Governor Harry Whyte at Leeds, where Allen assisted Tom Pierrepoint at the execution of David Blake on 7 February, confirmed that Allen was perfectly sober on arrival there, and Governor Clayton at Wandsworth reported that there was 'no fault to find' when he assisted at the execution of Percy Anderson in April.

Although a memo was now circulated that the monitoring of Alfred Allen had been lifted, it was to be over a year before he next officiated at an execution. When he was next engaged – at Wandsworth in June for the execution of Frederick Herbert Charles Field – it was as chief executioner, replacing the now retired Baxter.

In October 1931, workers renovating an empty building on Shaftesbury Avenue, London, discovered the body of Norah Upchurch. She had been strangled and Field became a suspect because he had once been a key holder for the building, although he claimed that he had since lost this key. Unable to prove a case, the coroner recorded an open verdict.

Two years later, while serving in the RAF, Field came to an arrangement with a newspaper that they would pay the costs of his defence if he confessed to the murder of Norah Upchurch. He retracted his confession but was unable to tell the police anything they did not already know about the case, and his trial at the Old Bailey ended with an acquittal.

In 1936, Field went AWOL from the air force and when he was picked up by the military police he immediately confessed to the murder of a woman, Beatrice Sutton, who had been discovered suffocated in a flat in Clapham in April. Tried again at the Old Bailey, Field, as before, retracted his confession, but this time he revealed information not released in the press – information that at that time could be known only to the killer. He was convicted at his second Old Bailey trial and detectives investigating the case wrote later that if Field had not made the second confession it was doubtful whether he would have been arrested.

Allen's skill as an executioner was brought into question following this execution and it became the subject of a medical debate over the placing of the noose.

HM Prison
Wandsworth
June 30th 1936

RE execution of 1054 Frederick Field
    The post-mortem on this man revealed that,
although there were fracture dislocations
between the first and second vertebrae and
between the second and third, yet the

displacement of the vertebrae was so small as to spare the spinal cord, which, to macrospection, remained uninjured. In actual fact there was no doubt at all about the efficiency of the hanging, but St sic Bernard Spilsbury, who performed the post-mortem, suggested that it would be well that instantaneous death would not depend solely on concussion as was here the case, and that a method which involved laceration of the cord, as was usually found, would be preferable. He considered that the essential difference between this case and former cases of judicial hanging which he had seen was that in former cases the knot had been taken well forward on the jaw, whilst in this case it lay below the ear. He suggested that the former method is preferable.

   Sgd. W F Roper

   Medical Officer

Allen was to officiate just twice more, in August 1937 at Pentonville. On 13 August he assisted Tom Pierrepoint and four days later he officiated as chief executioner of an Irish labourer who had strangled a prostitute. There is nothing to suggest he was dismissed following this execution, but, after his return to Wolverhampton that morning, he was never again called upon by the Prison Commissioners. He worked for a while as a caretaker at Wolverhampton labour exchange and it is believed he died sometime around 1938.

Chapter 7:

Wartime Executioners

Lionel S. Mann
170 Milnrow Road
ROCHDALE
Lancs
March 26.32

To:
His Majesties Commissioners of Prisons
Whitehall, London

Gentlemen,
   It is with much regret that I am compelled to
offer you my resignation as ASSISTANT
EXECUTIONER. It is not my wish to do so, but my
employer considers it detrimental to his business
interests, my holding such a post.
   Therefore I am faced with either resigning,
or standing a chance of being overstepped at

my regular employment. As I now hold the
position of Manager, I obviously do not want
to jeopardise that.

If however I at any time sever my connections
with my present employer, I will apply for reinstatement, trusting that then you will re-
instate me.

An acknowledgement of this resignation would
oblige. Hoping that my duties have at all times
been carried out satisfactorily.

I remain Gentlemen
Yours Faithfully
Lionel S Mann

The resignation of Lionel Mann, coming just a few years after Frank Rowe's short career had ended, left a vacancy for at least one assistant and on 14 April 1932 the commissioners opened the file of recent applicants and shortlisted six. Letters were sent to various local prisons and the prospective candidates were invited for interview. By the end of April the list had been whittled down to six suitable applicants. Those shortlisted and the result of the prison interview were reported back to the commissioners:

- Brixton – Fuller – no reply
- Manchester – Greenwood – suitable
- Manchester – Pierrepoint – suitable
- Manchester – Swindlehurst – adverse police report
- Pentonville – Jameson – declined
- Wormwood Scrubs – Cross – suitable

Swindlehurst was a former tram driver from Preston who had lost his job, and several previous situations, through his own misconduct. He was noted to have deserted his wife and for a time lived with another woman.

Jameson of Wembley wrote back to say that, since he had made his application, he had found a position that prevented him from having time off work. Fuller finally responded to the letter, having changed his address since applying, and was granted an interview at Brixton Prison. Although it was satisfactory and his details were passed to the Prison Commissioners, by now they had made a shortlist of three names and it was decided that two would be sent to Pentonville for training. A short note was made of each one on the file.

S. W. Cross age 38, single. Height 5ft 8ins. Is a member of the Metropolitan Special Constabulary Reserve. Ex-Serviceman. Presently un-employed.

W. J. Greenwood. Age 41. Married. Height 5ft 8ins. Is a postman (not about to give up this role) Ex-Serviceman (22½ years in RAMC).

A Pierrepoint. Age 27. Single. Height 5ft 6½ ins. Motor driver – No Army service – Is a nephew of the present Executioner.

A team of medical officers headed by Dr William Norwood East were furnished with all the papers relating to the interviews and police checks, and decided that Cross and Greenwood should be invited for training. Early in June, letters were sent out. East noted that he felt Pierrepoint was too young for the role. Cross wrote back at once to accept, but a week later Greenwood replied stating he would have to withdraw his application.

... under post-office regulations I am not allowed
to have any other employment under another
government department. I cannot afford to give up
my appointment as postman at present so I think I
will have to cancel my application for the office
of Executioner. The Postmaster at Rochdale will
not sanction me leave of absence ...

With one of their chosen candidates now out of the
running, the commissioners wrote again to East, saying there
was another clutch of applicants on file but '... one cannot
gather much from them, but I do not see any that promise
better than Pierrepoint. If however you still consider his age
a bar we will try a few others.'

On 28 June, East wrote back to say that in the
circumstances he thought that Pierrepoint should be given a
trial. Cross and Pierrepoint were invited for one week's
training at Pentonville Prison, starting on 25 July 1932. On 1
August, both were informed they had successfully passed the
course and their names would be placed on the list. Fuller
wrote to the commissioners on 6 August asking why he had
not heard back. Four days later he received word that the
Prison Commissioners regretted they were unable to select
him on this occasion but that his application would remain
noted for consideration in the event of a further vacancy.

Stanley William Cross was born in Fulham in September
1892. At his prison interview he stated that he was a former
soldier in the 3rd Battalion of the Dorset Regiment, serving
six years and 160 days. His first experience of an execution
was at Oxford in November 1932, when he witnessed new
executioner Alfred Allen carrying out his first senior
engagement. Coming through this observation with credit,
Cross received his first proper engagement in June 1933 when

he was invited to assist Baxter in the execution of boot repairer Jack Puttnam at Pentonville.

In December he assisted Tom Pierrepoint for the first time when he travelled to Manchester for the execution of William Burtoft. On 19 July, the body of Mrs Francis Levine, a wealthy Jewess, was found battered to death at her home in Cheetham Hill, Manchester. A week later, Burtoft, a one-eyed, meths-drinking vagrant, was arrested on a charge of being drunk and disorderly. Taken into custody at Hyde, Burtoft fitted the description of the man wanted for the murder. He was interrogated by detectives and confessed.

At his trial his counsel claimed that the evidence against him was very suspect. Although Burtoft had admitted being in the Cheetham Hill area at the time of the murder, there was little evidence, other than his 'confession', linking him to the crime. Also in his favour was a lack of bloodstains on his only set of clothes. Testimony came from investigating officers, who surmised that, from the state of the bloodstained house, the killer's clothes would show traces of blood. The prosecution's evidence was based on the confession and the fact that Burtoft had spent a little money after the murder, whereas before it he was short. Despite his counsel appealing to the jury for an acquittal, the jury seemingly believed the police version of events and returned a guilty verdict.

Cross worked with his fellow training partner Albert Pierrepoint at Wandsworth in May 1934 in a double execution that was witnessed by press representatives for the last time, and spent the last day of the year at Leeds Gaol in preparation for an execution to take place on New Year's Day 1935.

Frederick Rushworth was a 29-year-old farm labourer convicted along with Mrs Lydia Binks of the murder of their unnamed, one-month-old daughter. The couple were living together when in the summer of 1933 Binks fell pregnant. In

January 1934, she obtained employment at a holiday camp near Wensleydale, where on 1 March she gave birth to the child, but concealed it from the camp owner.

When the owner discovered the child, Binks told him she was looking after her for a friend who was in hospital. Told by the owner he didn't want a crying child disturbing holidaymakers, Binks said she would return her to the mother and a few days later she was seen with the child cycling away from the camp. She met with Rushworth, telling him she wanted the child to be looked after by a nurse. He told her they couldn't afford to do this and suggested they 'put it away quietly'.

Binks said she had refused and alleged that, as they walked through a field, he had snatched the child and buried her alive in a hole he had dug with a spade. Rushworth claimed he thought the child was dead when he buried her and that he had done it only to help Binks out. Both were sentenced to death in the November. Binks, described as simple and of below average intelligence, was reprieved on 28 December, leaving Rushworth to face the hangman alone.

Cross averaged just one or two engagements a year before he received promotion following the sacking of Tom Phillips. In July 1940 he hanged Udham Singh at Pentonville, assisted by Albert Pierrepoint. Readers of the autobiography Executioner: Pierrepoint (in which Cross is referred to as Stan Collins) will have read that the hangman apparently went to pieces during the execution and that afterwards he was never called back into service. Pierrepoint was not entirely accurate in his assessment of the situation. Cross did get muddled with his calculations and the governor noted this on the LPC4 sheet, but the execution was satisfactorily carried out and did not prevent Cross from receiving more work.

In December 1940, Cross carried out the first executions on enemy agents when three spies were hanged in a week at

Pentonville. On 10 December, with Albert Pierrepoint again among his assistants, Cross hanged Karl Heindrich Meier and Jose Waldberg, two of four enemy agents who on 2 September landed near Dungeness, Kent. Meier and Waldberg, both German-born, were arrested shortly after landing. Meier had called into a pub at Lydd, where, ignorant of the British licensing laws, he asked to buy a glass of cider. The suspicious licensee, warned to be on the lookout for spies, called the police and he was arrested later that afternoon.

Waldberg was arrested on the following day. He was stopped by a policeman and his suspicious reply in French led to his being detained. Like all subsequent spies caught during the war, they were tried under the 1940 Treason Act. The trials were held in camera so that the enemy would be unaware of their capture and bogus information could be sent back purporting to be from the agents. Evidence was heard in court that Waldberg had sent back radio messages prior to their arrest. Meier was later said to have tried to commit suicide before he was hanged and is probably the enemy agent a prison official later claimed had been hanged strapped to a wooden board.

Charles Van Der Keiboom was born in Japan to a Japanese mother and Dutch father. He and another spy, Dutchman Sjoerd Pons, had landed further up the coast at Dymchurch, Kent, from the first pair, and Van Der Keiboom immediately attracted attention by virtue of his marked Oriental features and because he was carrying a large suitcase. Pons saved his neck by immediately turning King's evidence and testifying against the others. Van Der Keiboom appealed against conviction, claiming that he had been blackmailed into spying by the Germans after threats were made against his family. The appeal court rejected this, stating that it was the most common defence to such a charge and there was nothing to substantiate it.

Again, it was noted that Cross did not seem to understand how to calculate drops correctly and he was never asked to carry out another execution. He did assist Tom Pierrepoint on occasions in 1941 but his name disappeared from the list later that year. Cross last appeared at an execution in September 1941 and his removal from the list opened the door for Albert Pierrepoint to rise up the rankings.

Albert Pierrepoint was born on 30 March 1905 at Clayton, Bradford, the middle child of former executioner Harry Pierrepoint and his wife Mary. Schooled in Huddersfield, where the family moved following the dismissal of his father from the official list, he was eleven years old when he set his ambition to paper. During a lesson the children were asked what they wanted to do on leaving school. Pierrepoint wrote that he would like to be the official executioner.

At the age of 12½ he went to work at a local cotton mill and, following the death of his father in 1922, Albert, as the eldest son, became the breadwinner, working in the mills until at the end of the 1920s, when he took a job as a delivery man with a wholesale grocer.

At the age of 27 Pierrepoint attended Strangeways Prison, Manchester, where the governor recommended that he was a suitable applicant to be sent for training. While Pierrepoint was undoubtedly the junior man in execution circles, both in terms of age and experience, he was fortunate that he was able to assist his uncle without going through the official circles, unlike his contemporaries. He received his first offers to witness an execution in December 1932 – but on each occasion the prisoner was reprieved. However, his first experience came when he was assistant to his uncle at Mountjoy, Dublin, a few days after Christmas 1932.

On returning home, he penned a letter to the Prison

Commissioners asking if he could now go to work as an active assistant rather than as a witness. In the letter he stated that he had just returned from Dublin, where he had acted as assistant, and that 'the Prison Officials and my uncle are well pleased with my services'.

By return he was notified that he would still need to be formally observed as a second assistant in England before he could be regarded as competent to officiate at an execution. When a proposed engagement at Pentonville ended in a reprieve, it was decided to allow Pierrepoint to be present at Birmingham on the understanding that he should play no part in the execution beyond that of an observer.

On the afternoon of Monday, 1 February 1933, in the company of his uncle, Pierrepoint travelled to Winson Green Prison, Birmingham, where they met up with assistant Robert Wilson. They were there to hang 49-year-old Jeremiah Hanbury, who had stabbed and battered to death his paramour after she rejected him

On the morning of his execution, Hanbury ate a large breakfast and sang loudly in the cell as the clock approached the fatal hour. On the stroke of eight the hangmen entered and, as Hanbury stood on the drop, he called out in a firm voice, 'Be good, everybody. Thank you for your trouble.' Wilson strapped the ankles and quickly stepped off the drop as Tom Pierrepoint pushed the lever. The younger Pierrepoint had satisfied the authorities that he was now suitable to act as a bona fide assistant.

Pierrepoint went on to assist his uncle three times that year and, like most assistants on the list, received his share of engagements, assisted at a number of executions and had his share of reprieves too. He assisted his uncle at the executions of female poisoners Ethel Major and Dorothea Waddingham, and also accompanied him to jobs carried out at places such as Exeter, Gloucester, Liverpool, Manchester, Dublin and Durham.

At Birmingham in 1940 the Pierrepoints, along with Cross and Phillips, carried out the executions of two Irishmen convicted of what became known as the 'Coventry Outrage'. Both died without giving any trouble and, as they relaxed in their quarters on the evening before the execution, Phillips was asked by Albert about the rumours of what he had heard relating to the execution of Mrs Thompson at Holloway back in 1923. Phillips said that none of the gruesome details reported in the press had taken place, but it had been very upsetting.

Antonio 'Babe' Mancini was the 39-year-old manager of the Palm Beach Bottle Party club in Soho. On 1 May he was involved in a fight at the club during which Harry Distleman received a fatal knife wound. He died in hospital after claiming Mancini had stabbed him. Mancini, an Italian-born gangster, was one of three men charged with the murder, but the only one convicted of murder and sentenced to death.

Pierrepoint claimed to have received a letter at the end of 1940 stating that the Home Office intended to appoint an assistant executioner to act in future as executioner, and asking if he wished to be considered. It seems unlikely, since, with Phillips having been sacked and Cross not deemed competent, Pierrepoint, by virtue of his length of service, was the only suitable person who could have been promoted in any case.

Mancini was hanged at Pentonville on 31 October 1941. He was standing facing the door, and, dressed in his smart suit, he smiled as Pierrepoint entered the cell and walked bravely to the drop. 'Cheerio,' the prisoner said, as the noose was placed around his neck. Pierrepoint saw that assistant Stephen Wade had completed his duties and then darted to his left, pulled the safety pin and pushed the lever. The trapdoors crashed opened and held firm in the rubber springs.

Pierrepoint carried out two executions at Wandsworth in December, the second of which was of a German spy, Karel Richter, who fought for his life in the last terrifying seconds when the hangmen entered the cell. Sudeten-born Richter had been dropped by parachute near London Colney in Hertfordshire. His mission was to bring in a replacement radio for one of the agents already on the mainland. He carried large sums of sterling and US dollars along with a map of East Anglia. On removing his flying suit he changed into civilian clothes and from that moment on he became a spy.

He laid low until the following evening, when he ventured out at 10.15, and had covered just a few hundred yards when he was stopped and asked directions by a lorry driver. He was unable to understand the question or make himself understood, and the driver drove off. When he spotted a policeman a little way up the road he reported the suspicious stranger. PC Alec Scott cycled after the man and, when asked for his papers, Richter produced an alien's visa with an address in London. A condition of carrying such a card meant that the holder had to be home by 11 p.m. Scott asked where he had come from and was told by the spy that he had walked from Dover and that it had taken him two hours, when the journey, by foot, would take approximately 24 hours! Suspecting he was an enemy agent, Scott took Richter into custody and he was subsequently tried at the Old Bailey and sentenced to death.

Pierrepoint later recorded that it was his toughest session on the scaffold. Richter's brute strength was enough to break the arm pinion straps and he fought in vain with the hangmen and warder as he was dragged to the scaffold. As Pierrepoint pushed the lever, Richter jumped forward and as the noose slipped it caught on his bridge of nose. It didn't prevent the execution being carried out successfully and cause of death was a broken neck as planned. Assistant executioner Wade noted in his diary that the struggle lasted seventeen minutes with Richter continually screaming, 'Help me!'

By the end of the war Pierrepoint had gradually overtaken his uncle at the top of the list and in December 1945 he hanged thirteen convicted German war criminals in one day at Hameln in Germany. They were the first of more than two hundred executions carried out by him in Germany over the next four years.

Most of the notorious killers of the twentieth century became names in Pierrepoint's diary, including Neville Heath, John Haigh, John Christie and Ruth Ellis. Pierrepoint carried out just two further executioners after Ruth Ellis's July 1955 hanging, and offered his resignation the following year. He blamed his resignation on the derisory sum he was offered as compensation for an execution he had been due to carry out at Manchester in January – one that had been called off at the eleventh hour – but it's more likely that he resigned in order to be free to write his memoirs for a Sunday newspaper. The series ran for just a handful of issues before it was pulled, following pressure on the newspaper owners by the British government.

Pierrepoint continued to run his public house at Much Hoole near Preston before retiring to Southport in Lancashire, where he died in a nursing home in July 1992, a few weeks after his diaries and papers were offered for auction.

With no new assistants engaged since Albert Pierrepoint and Stanley Cross in 1932, by the end of 1937 the list now showed a number of gaps. The retirement of Robert Baxter, and the disappearance of Alfred Allen and long-serving assistant Henry Pollard prompted the Prison Commissioners to again ask the Home Office if there were any suitable candidates on file to fill the vacancies. Within several days a shortlist had been drawn up of prospective hangmen.

One Portsmouth applicant, David Powell, began his letter with, 'Pardon my temerity, I wish to offer my services as the Hangman's assistant ...' Invited for interview at Portsmouth Prison, Powell failed to impress the governor, who, in writing to the commissioners, noted that 'he appeared rather nerve strained after ten years service in submarines ...' and 'was stupid to give up his father's army discharge papers as his own – he did not know his own exact age, and his reason for applying was because: "the job would interest me like!"'

Alexander Riley wrote from Bland Street, Moss Side, Manchester on 30 December 1937, hoping that it met with their approval to be put on the list of 'Public Hangsman'. Riley added that he had experience with ropes, having served in the Royal Navy. He was invited to attend Strangeways Prison, Manchester, on 23 June 1938 and said that he was thirty years old, married and employed as a scaffolder for Dickinson & Co. in Bolton. Riley had a successful interview and was invited for further training.

The motivation of some candidates was always questionable. Daniel Clifford of Fulham wrote in his letter of application, '... being a staunch supporter of justice and capital punishment', he wanted 'to uphold the prestige of our justice', and was shortlisted for training before making the golden mistake of failing to show the necessary discretion. Confident that he was now on the way to becoming a hangman, Clifford took the government letters out with him when he visited a local pub and bragged of what he would do to the condemned murderers if they came his way. Privy to these boasts was a serving assistant, and he took it upon himself to notify the commissioners.

I am writing to inform you that a man named
Clifford has received a letter 'to interview you for
the position of assistant executioner.

The letter has been shown to a number of people
in and around Fulham. He lets his tongue run
away from him when he is in drink ... I know he is
not to be trusted in exercising the duties ...

I am sir your obedient servant
Stanley Wm Cross
Asst. Executioner

That was enough for Clifford's name to be deleted. Another candidate, Arthur Gill, a butcher from Harrogate, was also rejected following an interview at Leeds Prison. His application was blocked when the local police chief warned that he 'is known to my officers as being a man of loose morals', and was suspected of being involved in a theft from his place of employment, although it was unproven.

Harry Kirk, a forty-year-old Grimsby-born police officer with the London Port Authority, was also blocked at this stage. Following his interview, the governor of Brixton Gaol formed the impression that Kirk 'had the nerve and temperament equal to the work he applies for but he appears to have a somewhat morbid interest in the work, aroused through having a friend who carried out many executions in Arabia'.

Nevertheless, it was a different matter that prevented Kirk fulfilling his ambition. He had served for 24 years as a police constable without attaining any promotion, and, when he discovered that the emoluments of the executioner were not what he had been led to believe, he opted not to take early retirement, but instead to see out the remainder of his service. His terms of employment at the Port Authority prevented him from taking the necessary time off work to undergo training, and Kirk was therefore advised to wait until he retired from the police and to reapply in eighteen months' time.

One man whose credentials seemed impeccable was 51-year-old Herbert Morris, who wrote from his home in Blackpool applying for the post.

42 Marton Drive
Blackpool
Lancashire

Dear Sir,

I most respectfully beg to offer my services to the Prison Commissioners, as Executioner of the Condemned.

I am a Colonial Pensioner from the Federated Malay States Prisons Department in which for 10 years of my service I acted in the capacity of Executioner.

I am thoroughly experienced and competent to carry out executions. Having executed a large number of condemned in the F.M.S.

I am quite conversant with Heights and Drops. I shall be glad to furnish any particulars that may be required.

Thanking you in anticipation
I remain your obedient servant
Sgd. Herbert Morris

On 11 August Morris attended Liverpool's Walton Gaol for a formal interview, which he sailed through, and when his police report came back with positive comments he was offered a place on the next training course at Pentonville, beginning on Monday, 26 September 1938.

Morris was seemingly disappointed at having to attend the course when he already considered himself well qualified. He replied by return,

> Your offer of training is accepted though I am perfectly conversant with the scale of drops, Heights, the system of measuring the rope ... having already executed many. However I will report to the Governor of Pentonville on Monday next ...

Simon Shute was a 35-year-old Cumbria-born nurse working at Ryhope Mental Hospital, Sunderland, when he applied in spring 1938. On 27 August he was interviewed by Governor Ben Grew at Durham, who noted that he had interviewed him at length and found him intelligent, alert and very respectable. The only negative comment Grew made was that Shute was in full-time permanent employment as a nurse, but added that Shute had told him he was prepared to use his days off for the purpose.

Despite the positive response, it seems, as with Kirk, the Prison Commissioners questioned his ability to be at their command when having full-time work commitments, and his application went no further. Shute wrote asking why he had heard nothing in November that year but it is unclear whether he received any further communications, and he was never to make it onto the list of assistants.

Riley and Morris successfully came through their training course and on 3 October were notified that their names had been placed on the list.

Morris was the first into action when he observed the execution of George Brain at Wandsworth. It was to be almost a year before he would be called to act as a paid assistant, when he returned to Wandsworth to assist at the execution of Len Hucker, who was hanged for the murder of sixty-year-old Mary Fullick, whom he had stabbed to death at Kilburn. Hucker, a thirty-year-old wood machinist, had gone to her house to try to reconcile his broken romance with Mrs Fullick's daughter Beatrice.

During a quarrel he had picked up a knife and stabbed her, leaving the knife buried in her stomach up to the hilt. He then walked to the local police station and gave himself up. The execution passed off without incident and Hucker, who had gained 7 pounds in the condemned cell, was given a drop of 8 feet.

Morris's next two engagements were also both in London, and it wasn't until April 1941 that a job came closer to home, when he travelled to Liverpool to assist in the execution of Samuel Morgan, a soldier who had brutally raped and murdered a young girl.

During the war he assisted both Tom and Albert Pierrepoint at around a score of executions, including those of several American soldiers hanged at Shepton Mallet. In July 1946 he assisted Albert Pierrepoint at the execution in Liverpool of Thomas Hendren, who had killed a prostitute in a beauty salon while it was being staked out by police following reports of immoral goings-on.

Morris, who had also worked as a taxi driver during the war, left the list around this time and it wasn't until four years later that he reapplied to join it. Now living in London, he asked for his job back and was offered the engagement to hang Frank Griffin, a Bolton-born steelworker convicted of the murder of Jane Edge, the landlady of a public house at Ketley, Shropshire.

Griffin was hanged at Shrewsbury on 4 January 1951, and Morris assisted Albert Pierrepoint. It was not to be a successful second spell on the list, as the governor reported later that day.

On the morning in question this man (Morris)
stood at the entrance to the execution shed as he
should do, but when the condemned man entered he
made no effort to fasten on the ankle straps. He
appeared to be trying to assist Pierrepoint with
the rope. The latter had no time to do anything
except motion to Morris to do his job. Morris did
not respond. Pierrepoint however did not allow
this incident to interfere with his own work and
the execution was carried out without loss of
time. It could however have caused a good deal of
trouble or distress.

I do not know Morris' previous history, but it
appears difficult for him to act in a subordinate
role. He has obviously - and being Morris he let it
be known - done work on a higher level. For this
reason alone I do not think he and Pierrepoint are
temperamentally suited to work together.

In my humble opinion Morris is not suitable, or I
at least, cannot have anymore confidence in him.

Pierrepoint was, of course, completely
unruffled by the incident and was his usual
efficient self.

J. S. Haywood
Governor

Two weeks later Morris was contacted at home.

14 February 1951
Sir,

I am desired by the Prison Commissioners to
inform you that they have under consideration a
report on the recent execution at Shrewsbury, and

have decided not to call upon your services in
the future.

I am, Sir,

Your obedient Servant

Sgd. W. M. Lee

for Establishment Officer

Mr H Morris

125 Stephendale Road

Fulham

London SW6

Alexander Riley had a relatively lean start to his career. His
first execution was at Durham in February 1939, where he
witnessed teenager John Daymond hanged by Tom Pierrepoint
and Robert Wilson. It was Wilson's last appearance at an
execution and it was to be over twelve months later before
Riley was called to act as a fully fledged assistant, when Ernest
Hammerton was hanged at Wandsworth by Tom Phillips.

Riley assisted in a double execution at Durham that
summer, but it was to be over a year before he was next
engaged, when he assisted at the last execution carried out at
Dorchester Prison.

During 1942 his name was deleted from the list at his own
request when he was engaged in war work, but Riley was
back on the list by September 1943 when he assisted at the
execution of Charles Gauthier at Wandsworth. The following
year he assisted at three executions of Americans at Shepton
Mallet, and also assisted at the execution of the last foreign
spy hanged at Pentonville in June 1944.

In November 1945, Riley assisted Albert Pierrepoint at the
double execution of two German prisoners of war who had
killed a fellow inmate at a camp in Sheffield. In early January

1946, Riley assisted at two executions in two days, the first being that of the notorious enemy sympathiser William Joyce, who had been convicted of treason for the radio broadcasts that earned him the moniker 'Lord Haw Haw'. Leaving Wandsworth on 3 January, Albert Pierrepoint and Riley travelled to north London, where Theodore Schurch was waiting in the condemned cell at Pentonville. Schurch had been convicted of treachery, having been found guilty of trying to persuade prisoners of war to side with the enemy during the war. It was the last execution for treachery.

Riley assisted again at Wandsworth in April 1946, and his final execution was at Strangeways, when Cheshire murderer Harold Berry was hanged for killing a Manchester moneylender. He was said to be a deeply religious man who would pray ardently before carrying out an execution. It is unknown why his short career ended as abruptly as it did. Perhaps the opportunities offered by the postwar economy made it impractical for him to continue.

Chapter 8:
Times of Change

When the Home Office decided upon action it moved quickly. Once word of Tom Phillips's indiscretions at Wandsworth had reached the ear of the Home Secretary, he issued a verbal order that the hangman should not be employed again. It would be several weeks following the incident before Phillips was informed officially that his career was over.

A letter to long-serving assistant Robert Wilson, who would have been the natural choice for promotion to succeed Phillips, wasn't answered. Wilson was questioned as to why he had failed to accept the last several engagements he had been invited to attend. When no reply was forthcoming, it was decided to delete his name from the list. It is believed that Wilson had died around this time.

On 22 April 1940 it was decided that there would be another recruitment drive. This time, possibly through a feeling of patriotic duty now that the war was on and there were spies to be hanged, the Prison Commissioners received an unprecedented volume of applications, with the number of applicants on file at the time numbering one hundred. They were filed as numbers 2282–2382, and the first review of the applicants whittled the numbers of those suitable for further investigation down to eight.

R E Humphries, an applicant from Stafford, was disqualified when his police report came back stating that he was only 'moderately sober', and another applicant who was interviewed by the governor of Lincoln Gaol turned down the offer of further training at Pentonville when he learned that the job was not a full-time salaried position.

By 4 June the commissioners ruefully noted on the file that only one applicant, number 2381, Stephen Wade of Doncaster, was suitable. Wade was 52 years old, according to his application form, on which he stated his date of birth as 14 December 1887. His true age posed a bit of a mystery: the Prison Commissioners listed on their file that he was 42 years old, and obituaries published after he died in 1956 give his age as both 62 and 67. On his application form he states that he has two children, a daughter aged 25 and a son two years younger. This does suggest that his age was 52 at application.

Wade was born in Droylsden, Manchester, and after attending St Patrick's school at Longsight, he became a clerk with a boot manufacturer. Immediately before the war he was running his own taxi business from an address in Harperhey, Manchester, a mile or so from where Albert Pierrepoint later ran a public house. He had first applied to be a hangman at the age of 21, around the time of Dr Crippen's execution.

WRITTEN EXAM PAPER

(as completed by Stephen Wade at Pentonville August 1940)

Q. What is the reason for leaving the sand bag suspended on the rope during night preceding the morning of the execution?

A. To stretch the rope to ensure that a perfect measure of the drop should be obtained.

Q. What measurement is allowed for a culprit's neck?

A. Thirteen inches

Q. Why is the copper wire used when 'setting' up the rope to the drop?

A. As a definite marking, which would not otherwise be obtained, when the sandbag is left from the trap, owing to the shrinkage of the rope ensuring the definite marking of the culprit's height.

Q. State details to be observed when placing the rope around the neck of the culprit.

A. That the cap is placed between the culprit's neck and the rope. Then the rope is tightened. The eyelet of the rope to be placed under the jaw with the eyelet or ring facing the hangsman.

Q. Give the length of drop you would state for a man of 158lbs

A. 6ft 3ins. The weight of the culprit is divided into 1,000. Weight of culprit 158lbs into 1,000 = 158/1,000 5ft 5 8/9 = 5ft 6ins + 9 ins as required by new 1913 regulations

'I hated murder,' he said in a newspaper interview in the mid-1950s. 'I felt so disturbed that I wrote to the Home Secretary and applied for the job of public executioner.' A few days later he received a replying stating he was too young. Unperturbed, he resolutely applied for the post every couple of years.

Wade was conscripted into the army in 1917, serving as a corporal in the RAMC until his discharge in May 1918. He returned to running a taxi service before owning his own haulage company with an address in St Peter's Square, Manchester. In 1935 he moved across the Pennines to Doncaster and had a partnership in a café on Station Road, when he applied to be a hangman.

With just one potential candidate for training, the original batch of applicants was reviewed again and this time a shortlist of nine was prepared. Again, just one was deemed fit for further training, this time 2369 Harry Bernard Allen, a 28-year-old lorry driver. Allen had presumably missed the first cut on account of his age. As seems clear from the case of Albert Pierrepoint a few years earlier, the commission preferred their assistants to be more mature in years.

Applicant 2383, H W Critchell of Enfield Highway, Middlesex, had applied at just the right moment. His letter was received on 12 July 1940 and in it he stated he was a British subject aged 39 with twelve years' military service 'man and boy' and currently employed as a mortuary keeper for Enfield Council. He clearly ticked all the right boxes as far as the commissioners were concerned. He was in the right age group and, as his letter showed, he had the required discretion and credentials. 'I would not hesitate to carry out the execution of any Male or Female sentenced to death by the laws of this country...' he wrote. 'I have been disciplined to obey orders at all times and treat the same confidentially.'

Critchell was contacted by return and invited for interview at Pentonville on 1 August. A police report compiled by Detective Inspector John Ball – later to have a glorious career with Scotland Yard's murder squad – found that there had been domestic trouble between Critchell and his wife, who was noted to be 'partial to drink and the company of other men'. On one occasion Critchell had inflicted rather heavy punishment with his fists on a male friend of his wife's to the extent that, concerned he had caused the man serious injury and that he might press charges, Critchell reported what he had done to the police. No complaint was made or further action taken. 'As far as can be ascertained Mrs Critchell is the cause of this trouble,' the report concluded.

On 2 August the commissioners contacted the governor of Brixton Prison and asked him to contact Harry Kirk, whose application in 1938 had been rejected due to his work commitments. He had been told to reapply in eighteen months: '... you should ascertain if his occupation will permit of his absenting himself for the purpose of assisting at executions.'

Two weeks later Kirk came through the interview and medical at Brixton, and on 15 August letters were sent out to the four men inviting them for training at Pentonville from 26–31 August. Although Kirk had been asked if absenting himself from work would cause him any problems, and had confirmed that it wouldn't, the amount of time needed to attend the training course did present difficulties. He replied, stating that, because he had used all his annual leave, he would esteem it a great favour if he could be allowed to attend all day on 26th, 28th and 31st but on the 27th, 29th and 30th he could attend only from 3 p.m., because he was on duty, but he was prepared to stay as long as needed. So keen was he to undertake this training that he offered to attend for six half-days the following week without pay if his first option was not acceptable. A note on the file shows that his request was acceptable.

The four applicants were offered a daily allowance of 10 shillings plus 10d. bonus for board and loss of time, and third-class railway fare from home to the prison.

The aspiring hangmen were trained by chief engineer Pugh and on 31 August medical officer James Murdoch at Pentonville contacted the Home Office to say that all four men had 'received a course of instruction in judicial execution, and they possess sufficient practical and theoretical knowledge to be fit to carry out this duty'.

TRAINING NOTES
(as dictated by Chief Officer Pugh and noted down by the trainees.)

To ascertain the drop 1913 scale.

With the modern scale of drops 9 inches is added. This is subject to departure from this table should the governor or medical officer advise though any special reason such as a diseased condition of the neck in any particular case. Also the culprit's age and physical conditions should be taken into consideration.

With the gallows rigged and adjusted the sandbag should be filled and attached to the rope and made ready for the Sheriff's test. On the arrival of the Sheriff, the Hangsman states his drop, to which the Sheriff should agree[;] also the MO who through some physical defect of the culprit may rule that an alteration may be made. Afterwards the bag is dropped, remaining suspended

---

until the following morning. The object being to give the rope its fullest stretch.

The morning of the execution the procedure is as follows. The assistant Hangsman goes below and holds the tape to the neck mark on the rope. The Hangsman marking off the length of drop on the rope with chalk. A piece of copper wire is then secured to the shackle[,] drawn straight down and cut off exactly to chalk mark on the rope. The bag is then raised[,] also the trap doors. The height of the culprit is then measured from the trap doors and the chain adjusted so that the end of the copper wire is exactly the height of the culprit. The slackness in the rope should be rolled up and fastened with twine. The noose set in position ready to place round culprit's neck.

At the appointed time the Hangsman will proceed to the condemned prisoner's cell (followed by the assistant) and adjust the straps to the prisoner's wrists, hands to the back. The culprit is then escorted to the scaffold and guided to position exactly central under the shackle. His feet to be in line with chalk mark on trap doors (this is to ensure that the culprit as far as possible drops plumb, and so has the full effect of the drop.

The Assistant Hangsman quickly adjusts the leg straps and steps back clear of trap doors. The Hangsman places white cap over the culprit's head then adjusts the rope tightly round the neck (with cap between rope and the neck)[,] the metal eye to be looking forward and placed in front of the angle of the lower jaw so that the constriction of the neck may come underneath the chin. The noose should be kept tight by means of a leather or

India rubber washer as a wedge. The Hangsman then goes quickly to the lever and lets down trap doors. The body is then to remain hanging for one hour.

Note: It is essential that the metal eye of the noose should be directed forwards. A failure to do this would cause the rope and metal eye to go to the back of the culprit's neck, which would prevent the full force of the drop.

All were notified that they had been added to the list of assistants and received a letter stating they would have to sign a bond for the sum of £50. The bond was in place to buy the assistants' silence and they would be liable to pay this fee should they be found guilty of breaching the Official Secrets Act. For one assistant this caused confusion. On 16 September Harry Allen wrote, '... does this mean I must provide £50 in cash? ... this is the first that has been mentioned of the financial side!'

It was decided to blood the new men as soon as possible and, on 31 October 1940, Critchell and Kirk were invited to observe the execution of Stanley Cole, who was hanged at Wandsworth for the murder of a soldier's wife found stabbed to death at Wimbledon. Wade and Allen witnessed their first job a month later at Bedford.

In December, Critchell and Kirk assisted Cross at the execution of the first spies hanged and each began to assist both Tom and Albert Pierrepoint throughout the war years. Critchell was present at Wandsworth in 1942, when Tom Pierrepoint was reported for his callous behaviour at the execution of Herbert Bounds.

One case that made headlines in both Great Britain and the

United States was the murder of a taxi driver in Middlesex. Twenty-three-year-old paratrooper Karl Gustav Hulten was on the run from his unit when he met Elizabeth Marina Jones in a London café in the autumn of 1944. Eighteen-year-old Jones left her native Wales to seek her fortune in the big city but had ended up working as a stripper under the alias of Georgina Grayson. They teamed up together and by night they cruised around in a stolen army truck attacking and robbing people in the blackout, living out a fantasy existence as a gangster and his moll.

On 7 October 1944 they hailed a taxi and, as they drove down a deserted lane, Hulten asked driver George Heath to pull over, then shot him dead while Jones rifled his pockets, stealing a small amount of money, a pen and a cigarette case. They then drove to Staines, hid the body in a ditch and sped off.

Hulten was arrested three days later still in possession of the stolen taxicab, and later that day Jones was also taken into custody. She claimed that Hulten had bullied her into helping him commit the murder, but, faced with this confession, Hulten passed on the blame, claiming Jones was the instigator, egging him on to do something 'exciting'.

Hulten was an American serviceman, but, unlike other Americans convicted of crimes in England, he wasn't court-martialled by the US government, and presumably, because it was a joint murder trial with a British citizen, Hulten was tried at the Old Bailey. Throughout the six-day trial Jones's defence maintained that it was Hulten alone who was guilty of murder, but the jury recorded a guilty verdict for both accused. Appeals to have the sentences reduced to manslaughter failed, although, much to the anger of Winston Churchill, Elizabeth Jones was reprieved two days before she was due to go to the gallows.

Critchell assisted Tom Pierrepoint on the aged hangman's

last visit to a London prison. Later that year he assisted Albert Pierrepoint at the execution of John Amery, convicted under the Treachery Act and hanged at Wandsworth.

In September 1946 Critchell was on duty at Wandsworth when it was decided that two men would be hanged an hour and a quarter apart. Sydney Smith was hanged at 9 a.m. for shooting dead a horse dealer near Hastings. There was no trouble at this execution, but, when David Mason, a 39-year-old Surrey engineer, was led to the gallows for the murder of his wife, a terrible scene broke out. Mason was unwilling to go without a fight and, as Critchell went to strap his arms, he spun round and punched the assistant in the face. He was quickly overpowered by the other assistant, Harry Allen, and the two prison officers and dragged struggling to the drop. Allen recorded in his diary later that the execution was very poor and they were very grateful for the work done by the 'screws'.

Critchell was the assistant when Walter Rowland was hanged at Manchester in February 1947 for a murder to which another man had confessed while Rowland waited in the condemned cell; and in the autumn of that year he assisted at a double at Pentonville.

Critchell's last execution was at Cardiff in December 1948, when he assisted Stephen Wade in the execution of Clifford Wills, who had murdered the woman he was having an affair with. There is nothing untoward noted at the execution but it seems that Critchell had now had enough. In January 1949 he turned down an engagement at Liverpool. He was contacted by the commissioners and asked why he had been unavailable for the execution and he replied that he was unable to assist at the present time. When asked when he would be available, Critchell ignored the letter and subsequent ones until in June of that year he received a letter saying that, if he did not reply to their last letter within fourteen days, they would be obliged to remove his name from the list. Critchell failed to reply.

In July 1955 he wrote to a Sunday newspaper following the execution of Ruth Ellis, the last woman to be hanged in the UK. Clearly now anti-hanging, Critchell put forward a very forthright opinion.

> I write this in good faith. I have entered that pit and shamed myself many times. I am thoroughly ashamed. The harm this job has done no doctor can remove. The memories and scenes of the Condemned Cell and the adjoining scaffold are forever embedded in my mind. No medicine can ever help me. I still suffer.

Harry Kirk's career lasted one year longer than that of his training partner. Having left the police he moved from London to Elton, near Peterborough, becoming the publican at the Black Horse. He assisted at the execution of several spies during the war and assisted Albert Pierrepoint when they were flown out to Gibraltar in January 1944 to hang two saboteurs at the Moorish Castle on the island.

Kirk also assisted at the high-profile executions of Neville Heath at Pentonville in October 1946, and three years later he helped hang John Haigh, the acid-bath murderer, at Wandsworth. 1949 was a busy year for Kirk. He was present at half of the executions carried out in England and Wales, starting in January, when he assisted at the execution of a woman for the only time when Margaret Allen was hanged at Manchester.

1950 started well for Kirk, with the execution of Daniel Raven at Pentonville. Raven had battered to death his wife's parents while she was in hospital following the birth of their first child. Kirk assisted in two executions in three days at

Durham in July, aiding Albert Pierrepoint on the 11th and, two days later, assisting Stephen Wade. They were the last occasions Kirk acted as an assistant.

On 23 November Kirk was entrusted with responsibilities to carry out an execution as number one. On 12 August, Emma Howe, a 66-year-old prostitute, had been found strangled in her home at Great Yarmouth. A neighbour identified Norman Goldthorpe leaving the house in the early hours and he was arrested the following afternoon. At his trial he claimed he had gone looking for a prostitute after being jilted by his girlfriend.

Assistant Syd Dernley told a story many years later that on the eve of the execution they had upset the condemned man by bursting into howls of laughter at a rude joke book the assistant had taken to the prison to relieve the atmosphere. They were unaware that their quarters were directly above the condemned cell and that their merriment could be heard by the prisoner. But it stopped abruptly when warders on death-watch duties knocked on the floor of their room.

The morning of the execution Kirk seemed unconcerned and wished the prisoner good morning as they entered the cell. On the drop Dernley noted that Kirk was slightly slower than Pierrepoint, but Goldthorpe soon plunged the 7 feet 8 inches to his death. Within seconds a snort came from under the hood of the prisoner followed by several loud moans. By the time they climbed down into the pit, the noises had stopped and the doctor confirmed the prisoner was dead, but when the assistant checked the noose he found that the cap had fouled into the noose and had not tightened correctly. Cause of death was due to dislocated vertebrae, as it should be, but in his haste to carry out the execution Kirk had failed to check that the hood was clear of the noose. It was a tiny error but enough to get his name struck off the list. Harry Kirk died from cancer in the mid-1960s.

Stephen Wade's first engagement was at Wandsworth. He was to hang George Armstrong, the first Britain to be hanged for treason during the war. 'I was never nervous,' said Wade later. 'It's a job which needs a special type of temperament. You're either fit to do it or you're not. And you soon find out!'

On 31 October he assisted Albert Pierrepoint for the first time on what was Pierrepoint's first job as senior executioner and he also assisted him again six weeks later, when they hanged spy Karel Richter, the man Pierrepoint later recalled had given him his most difficult experience on the scaffold. Wade recorded the execution in his diary.

Execution good in the circumstances. 8.58 a.m. On entering cell to take prisoner over and pinion him he made a bolt for the door. I warded him off and he then charged the wall at a terrific force with his head. This made him even more violent. We seized him and strapped his arms at rear. This new strap was faulty, not enough eyelet holes and he broke away from them. I shouted to Albert he is loose and he was held by warders until we made him secure. He could not take it and again charged for the wall screaming 'help me!'

Had to drag him to the scaffold and he then tried to get to the opposite wall over the trap with legs splayed. I drew them together and could see Albert going to the lever. I shouted 'wait - strap on legs and down he goes'. As the rope was fixed around his neck he shook his neck and the safety ring - too big - shifts. Noose slackens and in the drop the eyelet catches underneath his nose. Neck

```
broken immediately. 9-15 a.m. hanged. I said I
would not miss this execution for  £50 and well
worth it!
```

During the war Wade helped both Pierrepoints hang a
number of spies and murderers, and also helped Pierrepoint
hang five German prisoners of war at Pentonville in October
1945. He assisted Tom Pierrepoint at his last executions in the
summer of 1946, a few months after his appointment to chief.

In March 1946 Wade replaced Tom Pierrepoint as the
hangman for Durham prison and carried out almost every
execution at both Durham and Leeds until 1955. He was the
regular assistant to Albert Pierrepoint in Scotland, but once
he had gained promotion, Wade stopped receiving letters
asking him to assist at executions. During the early 1950s he
was called into action on only a handful of occasions.

Following Pierrepoint's resignation in February 1956, the
press was full of speculation that Wade would be promoted
to the country's chief executioner. However, moves behind the
scene had already led to the end of his career. A letter from
the commissioners in February 1956 stated that Wade's name
was removed from the list in October 1955 – before that of
Pierrepoint – due to minor fumblings on recent executions
and his failing eyesight. 'This action was a precaution against
what might happen rather than because of anything that had
happened,' it read.

On 25 February 1956 Wade wrote asking that the
commissioners reconsider their decision, but they had already
appointed a replacement and did not agree to his request. In
a newspaper article published before his death he told the
reporter that he believed that those condemned had received
a fair trial and been condemned by a learned judge. Asked
about the two local men he had hanged – men he knew well

– he said, 'What sympathies I had went to their victims, not to them.'

Asked why he chose a career as a hangman, he said that it was because he hated murder. 'That and nothing more,' he said, defending his decision, and adding, 'Don't think I do this for monetary reasons. In terms of money the reward is negligible. There are other things more important than money.'

Stephen Wade, known among his contemporaries and in the local press as 'the Quiet Man', died of stomach cancer in Doncaster in December 1956, a week after his 67th birthday.

Harry Bernard Allen was born to Scottish parents in Yorkshire on 5 November 1911. The family moved back to Scotland and lived for a time in Kirkcaldy, before returning south, settling in Ashton-under-Lyne, Manchester, when Allen was ten.

He learned to drive at eighteen and while living in Urmston, Manchester, he got a job as a van driver. Just before World War Two, while working as a lorry-driver, he applied for a job as a prison officer at Manchester's Strangeways Prison. Allen later wrote that, although he failed to become a prison officer, he was offered the chance to become an assistant hangman. This isn't strictly true: he also wrote applying to be an executioner at around the same time, and, when the Home Office decided to recruit a new batch of assistants, his was one of the names shortlisted.

He successfully passed the necessary interview at Strangeways Prison and was invited for training at Pentonville in the summer. He later said that his wife Marjorie was completely against it, but, 'I had no choice, I had to take it on,' he told her. It was later claimed that Allen's father, a staunch Roman Catholic, refused to speak to his son for five years when he learned of his appointment.

His first experience of an execution was at Bedford, where he witnessed the sentence carried out on William Cooper, who had battered to death a farmer at Ely. Cooper had been dismissed from the farm and was alleged to have hit the farmer several times about the head with a bottle in revenge. He claimed he had acted in self-defence.

Cooper had remained calm in the days leading up to his execution and on his final evening he played dominoes and chatted with the warders, seemingly unafraid of what awaited him the following morning. Allen spent his first pre-execution night in the company of Tom and Albert Pierrepoint, the appointed hangmen, and fellow trainee Stephen Wade. All that was expected of Allen was that he witness proceedings, stay on his feet and show the right nerve and temperament for the post for which he had been trained.

As it turned out, Cooper's execution was to be a good test of the type of character needed to be a hangman. The prisoner went to pieces as the fateful hour approached and, as Tom Pierrepoint and his nephew entered his cell, Cooper became overcome with terror and had to be dragged semiconscious to the scaffold. Bedford was one of the few prisons that still had execution sheds in the grounds, and this necessitated a long walk from the condemned cell to the execution chamber. Allen and Wade experienced first hand what all their training had failed to show them: while you could plan meticulously for the execution to go smoothly, you could never anticipate the behaviour of the condemned man or woman during those final moments with all hope lost and with death just a few footsteps away.

Asked later about his experiences, Allen said that he was very relieved it had passed off without serious incident, and that 'it wasn't half as gruesome as I expected.'

Now that he had overcome this test of nerve, Allen's first

official appointment as an assistant was at his local prison, where he was engaged to help Tom Pierrepoint hang Clifford Holmes at Strangeways in February 1941. Holmes was a serving soldier who had shot dead his wife while on leave. Allen also worked as assistant to Tom Pierrepoint on the next execution at Manchester, when John Smith, a soldier in the Home Guard, was hanged for the murder of his girlfriend, who had left him.

By strange coincidence, the next man Allen was engaged to execute was also called John Smith, but this John Smith was a Londoner who had stabbed his girlfriend in a crime of passion after her father had forbidden their courting. Smith was hanged at Wandsworth in December 1941 and it was the first time that Allen had worked as assistant to Albert Pierrepoint. It was in fact only the second senior execution the younger Pierrepoint had carried out.

What happened to Harry Allen between 1942 and 1945 is something of a mystery, and even his family have been unable to shed any light on the reason why he was forced to leave the list of executioners in 1942.

On 1 May 1943 he was issued with a permit to drive single- and double-decker buses under the Defence Regulations 1939, and for the remainder of the war he worked as a bus driver for the Manchester Corporation. But it seems unlikely that it was an occupation that would have prevented a man taking two days' leave three or four times a year. An official Home Office list of assistants clearly has a note against Allen's name stating he was not to be engaged due to wartime duties. Perhaps he was involved in some official wartime activities, but a search through armed-service records has so far drawn a blank.

His son mentioned a conversation between Pierrepoint and Harry Allen, when both were long retired, in which it seemed they had fallen out when Allen failed to lend Pierrepoint some money, saying he did not have the money to lend him. Pierrepoint was alleged to have replied, 'You made enough money during the war, and that should have been mine.' It's another mystery that may eventually be solved.

In 1945, with the war in Europe at an end, Allen wrote to the Prison Commissioners and asked for his name to be added back to the list of assistants. This was done and in October 1945 he assisted Albert Pierrepoint and Stephen Wade in the execution of five German prisoners of war who had been convicted of the murder of a fellow prisoner at Comrie POW camp in Scotland.

Allen assisted at two executions in the first part of 1946. In January he assisted Tom Pierrepoint for the last time when the aged hangman hanged William Batty at Leeds, and in March he assisted at Durham in what was Stephen Wade's debut as chief executioner. Allen assisted at two further executions in 1946 and began 1947 assisting Wade at Liverpool. It was to be a quiet year, with Allen employed on just two further occasions; but the first of these was one of the most notorious postwar executions, when two young thugs were hanged for what became known as the Antiques Murder.

Alec de Antiquis was a 31-year-old father of six shot dead as he attempted to stop the escape of a gang who had just robbed a West End jewellery shop. On 29 April 1947, three masked men raided the shop, striking the manager with a revolver, before running into the street and firing a warning shot as they made their escape.

Antiquis was riding his motorcycle along Charlotte Street when he saw the getaway car and bravely – or foolishly – chose to drive into the path of the fleeing gang. When he refused their shout to move he was shot once in the head and fell dying to the pavement as they made their escape.

A taxi driver told police he had seen a group of men running into a house off Tottenham Court Road, and when police searched the premises they found a raincoat and a scarf that had been knotted to form a mask. The coat was traced to twenty-three-year-old Charles Henry Jenkins, a criminal with a long record of robbery and violence, and this led them to pick up two other men, twenty-year-old Christopher James Geraghty and Terence Peter Rolt, aged seventeen. Geraghty blamed Rolt who in turn blamed Jenkins.

After a trial lasting a week, all three were found guilty. Rolt, because under eighteen at the time of the crime, was sentenced to be detained at His Majesty's Pleasure. Jenkins and Geraghty were both sentenced to death and hanged at Pentonville Prison on 19 September. It was the first double execution for several years, since, in more recent times when two men were to hang together, the executions had been carried out separately, usually an hour apart.

Rolt was released on licence in June 1956, while the double execution has often since been cited as a case in which the death penalty has perhaps acted as a deterrent to others who might be tempted to go down that murderous path. With Geraghty and Jenkins each in a felon's grave inside Pentonville, the gang they had led broke up and a large number of guns were abandoned or handed in during an unofficial gun amnesty.

By now Allen had taken over the running of the Rawson Arms public house in Farnworth, Bolton. Being a publican was a popular occupation among the hangmen. As we have seen, Billington was a publican at the turn of the century, and John Ellis had a spell running the Jolly Butcher in Rochdale. Besides Harry Allen, both Albert Pierrepoint and Harry Kirk were running hostelries while working as executioners.

When Allen officiated at the execution of Walter Cross at

Pentonville in February 1948, it seemed for a while that he had helped execute the last person to be hanged in Great Britain. For a period of over six months all death sentences were suspended while the Royal Commission debated the validity of the death penalty, and a number of brutal killers avoided the gallows, including Donald Thomas, who had shot dead PC Nathan Edgar after the officer apprehended him following a burglary in Enfield.

The death penalty was eventually restored in the autumn of 1948 and Allen was present at just two cases that year, including that of Peter Griffiths, who had carried out the horrific murder of a child at Blackburn's Queen's Park Hospital.

Allen had a good run in 1949, being present at almost a third of all hangings, the most notable being that of ex-soldier William Jones at Pentonville. Jones had been serving a six-year sentence at Dartmoor when in the summer of 1949 he asked to be transferred to a prison in the north of England so he could be near his family. When the request was refused, he asked a warder for a pencil and a piece of paper, and wrote out the confession to the murder of a woman that had taken place four years earlier while he was stationed in Germany.

By contrast, in the following year, Allen received just two engagements. The first of these was at Liverpool, where George Kelly was hanged for what was known as the Cameo Cinema murder. On 19 March 1949, Leonard Thomas and John Bernard Catterall, the manager and assistant manager of the Cameo Cinema at Wavertree, Liverpool, were shot dead during a bungled robbery. It was over six months later that a tip-off led police to two local small-time criminals, George Kelly and Charles Connolly. Kelly was alleged to be the killer, while Connolly supposedly kept lookout.

They were tried together at Liverpool Assizes and, when the jury failed to reach a verdict, a retrial was ordered. This time they were tried separately and, although Kelly maintained he did not know the co-accused, with Connolly persuaded to plead guilty to robbery, the fact that Kelly was deemed to be in league with him was enough to convince the jury of his guilt, and he was convicted. Kelly was hanged on Tuesday, 28 March 1950, at Liverpool, by Pierrepoint and Harry Allen.

The chief executioner travelled down to Birmingham for another execution the following morning and on arrival told his assistant that Kelly had been terrified when they went for him. On removing the body from the rope they found that 'the tough Liverpool gangster had shit himself!' Although it was thought that most of those condemned lost control of their bodily function when hanged, assistant Syd Dernley claimed it was untrue and that in his experience it had happened only once.

In June 2003, the Court of Criminal Appeal overturned the verdict, stating that George Kelly's conviction was unsafe. They found that evidence of a confession made to the police during the original investigation had been withheld at the original trial.

Over the next two years, Allen assisted both Pierrepoint and Wade at executions in all parts of the country, including the last one at Cardiff and one carried out at Durham on Christmas Eve 1952.

A fellow assistant commented that he couldn't believe the flamboyant bow ties that Harry Allen used to wear when he arrived at a prison, but Allen claimed he wore them to help him get inside a prison if demonstrations were taking place prior to the execution. He said that anyone questioning him outside a gaol on his way in to an execution would believe he was either a lawyer or a doctor.

He would have needed this disguise to get through the large

crowds that congregated on the afternoon before Derek Bentley was hanged at Wandsworth in January 1953. Bentley had been convicted of the murder of PC Sydney Miles, who had been shot dead during a robbery at a Croydon warehouse in November 1952. Police had thwarted Bentley and sixteen-year-old Christopher Craig after they had attempted to break into the warehouse. Bentley was taken into custody, and, while he was under arrest, Craig shot the officer and Bentley was alleged to have shouted, 'Let him have it!'

Allen contacted the Home Office after accepting the engagement, asking them to reconsider their decision, and later told friends, 'He's the only one I wish I had never hanged; it was wrong that he was executed for what his friend did.'

Allen carried out his first execution in Scotland when he travelled to Edinburgh to assist Pierrepoint. George Robertson was hanged for the murder of his wife and son.

At the end of the year he assisted for the only time at the execution of a woman. Fifty-three-year-old Mrs Styllou Christofi had been sentenced to death at the Old Bailey for the murder of her German-born daughter-in-law Hella Christofi, whom she had battered to death at her home in Hampstead. She had left Cyprus to move in with her son and daughter-in-law in the summer of 1953. The two women did not get along and, shortly after Hella had told her husband his mother must leave the house, she was found dead.

Police investigations found that Hella had been strangled, then battered about the head with a heavy ash plate, before paraffin was poured onto her stricken body. Mrs Christofi claimed it had been an accident, but at the trial it was shown that, almost thirty years earlier, she had stood trial for the murder of her own mother-in-law by ramming a burning wooden torch down her throat. On that occasion she had been found not guilty.

Allen carried out just three more executions as an assistant in 1955 before he received promotion on 25 October that year. No sooner had he received promotion than, in November 1955, an abolition Bill came before Parliament, and, although it was ultimately to be rejected by the House of Lords in July 1956, there were no further executions in Britain until July 1957, by which time the newly devised Homicide Act had restricted the scope of the death penalty by introducing some exceptions, such as provocation and diminished responsibility.

Throughout 1956 a number of executions took place in Cyprus during the troubles involving the EOKA terrorists. Many sources claim that Harry Allen carried out these executions but it does not appear to be the case. His diary and papers make no mention of any executions in 1956, but his passport did contain Cypriot stamps dated December 1958 and January 1959. On these occasions he did travel to Cyprus, accompanied on at least one occasion by assistant hangman Harry Smith. On 17 December 1958, they flew to Cyprus to hang two men but by the time they had landed a reprieve had been granted; and on the second occasion the prisoner was granted a last-minute reprieve.

After he had received almost forty requests to officiate, all of which were in due course cancelled as the condemned men were reprieved, Allen's first execution as number one was at Durham Prison on 23 July 1957, when Carlisle labourer John Vickers was hanged for beating to death a shopkeeper in the city during a robbery.

On Sunday 14 April, Vickers broke into a general store at Carlisle. The elderly proprietor, Jane Duckett, was partially deaf, and Vickers, knowing the money was kept in the cellar, assumed she would not hear him force entry. Failing to locate the money, Vickers emerged from the cellar only to find the old lady approaching. Aware that she recognised him, he struck her, and, as she fell down the stairs, he kicked her in the face several times as she lay dying. Vickers fled empty-handed, but, being well known to the local police, he was quickly arrested. He admitted the crime – and to striking her – but denied intending to kill.

At his trial at Cumberland Assizes, the evidence against Vickers was mainly his damning statement that he had gone to the shop to 'rob the woman after hours', that she rushed at him, and he struck her 'in a panic'. By admitting he had gone with the intention to steal he became liable to a verdict of capital murder – murder committed in the course or furtherance of theft – under the newly passed Homicide Act (1957).

Allen conducted this, his first hanging as chief executioner, assisted by Harry Smith. Under the Homicide Act, notice of execution was no longer to be placed on the prison gate and this was the first execution without such notices.

There was one further execution that year, at Birmingham, but the next time Allen was called to action was to officiate at Glasgow, where Peter Manuel was hanged for a series of murders that had caused terror in Scotland and the borders for several years. Born in New York of English parents, Manuel came to England in his youth and soon fell foul of the law. He spent time in borstal for theft and assault before being released in 1945, when he went to live with his family in Scotland. In March 1946, Manuel was sent to prison for eight years following conviction in fifteen cases of housebreaking and one of rape.

In January 1956, seventeen-year-old Anne Kneilands was found battered to death and sexually assaulted on a golf course in East Kilbride. Manuel was questioned but released, and, even though it seems that detectives believed him guilty, they lacked evidence to secure a conviction. Later that year, sisters Marion Watt and Margaret Brown, along with Watt's sixteen-year-old daughter Vivienne, were found shot dead in a house in Lanarkshire. Marion's husband, William Watt, who had been away on a fishing trip at the time of the murder, was questioned, as was Manuel, but it was Watt who was charged with the murder of his family and detained.

On 8 December, taxi driver Sidney Dunn was shot dead near Newcastle. Less than a month later seventeen-year-old Isabelle Cooke was reported missing after attending a dance in Lanarkshire, and on 1 January 1958, as detectives searched for her, reports came in that a family of three had been shot dead at nearby Uddington. Manuel was interviewed again on 18 January and this time he made a full confession to all the crimes.

Although Harry Smith assisted, in Scottish newspaper accounts of the execution, Harry's son, Brian Allen, is named as the assistant. It appears that, while Allen was on duty in Scotland, his wife Marjorie took the opportunity to leave her husband, and she fled their home at the Junction Hotel, Whitefield, which Allen had been managing for most of the decade. On Sunday night, 14 December 1958, a fight broke out outside a nightclub in Holloway, London. Twenty-three-year-old PC Ray Summers tried to break up the disturbance and was fatally stabbed in the back with a frogman's knife. Ronald Marwood, a scaffolder from Islington, had been out celebrating his first wedding anniversary and was very drunk, when he and his friends became involved in the fight. It was a large brawl involving more than twenty young men, many armed with knives, bottles and knuckledusters. Marwood later claimed he had heard the police telling the men to disperse, and had struck at PC Summers, intending to push him away. He said he did not have a knife in his hand.

Marwood was one of those initially questioned but, following a statement, he was released. In the following

January, as evidence mounted, police announced that they wished to reinterview Marwood, who was by now in hiding. On 27 January, he gave himself up, allegedly confessing, 'I did stab that copper that night …'

Tried at the Old Bailey in March, he denied making the confession, claiming that the police 'had put things down'. His defence counsel claimed that, apart from this damning statement, there was no other evidence to connect Marwood with the killing or even the fight, and certainly not the knife.

Harry Robinson assisted Allen for the first time and recorded later that, as the hangmen rested in their quarters after rigging the gallows, demonstrations from the prisoners echoed loudly throughout the prison. So deafening was the banging and shouting that Marwood eventually asked the guards if they would relay a message for them to stop so he could have a peaceful last night on earth.

On 9 October, Allen and assistant Royston Rickard made a rare trip to Jersey. Francis Huchett was a 32-year-old fitter convicted of the murder of John Perree, whose body had been discovered by children playing on the sand dunes adjacent to Jersey's airport at St Brelade. He had been shot in the head. It was alleged that Huchett had lured the man onto the dunes before shooting him dead, then stealing a large amount of cash he was known to be carrying. This was the first execution on the island since 1907 and the last to be carried out in the Channel Islands.

Allen celebrated his 48th birthday by carrying out the execution of Guenther Fritz Erwin Podola at Wandsworth. On 3 July, a flat belonging to an American model in Kensington, south London, was burgled, and a couple of days later she received a phone call from a man attempting to blackmail her. She contacted the police, the phone was tapped, and on 13 July, when he rang back, she kept him talking as the call was traced to a call box outside South Kensington tube station.

As German-born criminal Podola was arrested by DS Ray Purdy and a colleague, a scuffle broke out. Podola broke free and fled to a nearby block of flats, where he was rearrested. As he was led outside to the police car he drew a gun and shot Purdy through the heart. He was identified by fingerprints at the scene and on 16 July was arrested in a Kensington hotel, where he received a heavy blow to the head as detectives burst into the room.

At the Old Bailey in September, Podola's defence team pleaded that, since Podola was suffering from amnesia caused by the blow to the head, he could not be tried, as they had been unable to plan a defence. The prisoner was remanded in Brixton prison, as doctors argued whether or not he was faking his memory loss. At the end of the first pretrial hearing in English legal history, it was decided Podola was fit to stand trial, and, on 24 September, the murder trial began.

Podola simply stated at the outset, 'I cannot put forward a defence ... I cannot remember this crime.' Evidence of the crime and arrest were heard and on the following day the jury needed just half an hour to find Podola guilty. He was the last man hanged for the murder of a policeman.

A few days after Christmas 1959, Allen travelled to Bermuda for the execution of nineteen-year-old Wendell Lightbourne, who had battered an English secretary with a rock after she had chastised him on a beach for making a rude remark about her. The execution was due to take place on 30 December and Allen flew to Bermuda via the USA on 27 December. Lightbourne's execution was postponed 24 hours before he was to hang following numerous petitions, including several to the Queen, and a stay of execution. It was rescheduled for 20 January, but there is no proof that Allen flew back on what would have been another wasted journey, since again, with just hours to go, the execution was postponed before a reprieve was eventually granted.

In November 1960 Allen hanged eighteen-year-old Francis Forsyth for his part in the Hounslow Footpath Murder. Inmates at Wandsworth claimed they heard Forsyth crying on the eve of his execution that he didn't want to die.

The next date in Allen's diary was also to hang a teenager. Nineteen-year-old Anthony Miller had been convicted at Glasgow High Court of the capital murder of John Cremin, a Dundee shopkeeper who was in Glasgow for a football match. Cremin, a homosexual, had been robbed and beaten to death with a plank of wood by Miller and his seventeen-year-old accomplice. The younger of the two would lure homosexuals to a secluded area of the park, where Miller would carry out vicious muggings and assaults. It was the last execution at Glasgow's Barlinnie Prison and Allen was assisted by Jock Stewart. Miller seemed overawed by events and had tears in his eyes as he was led to the gallows. He looked meekly at Stewart and pleaded, 'Please, mister' as the cap was placed over his head and he fell into the pit.

Allen officiated at all nine executions carried out in 1961. In February he hanged George Riley at Shrewsbury, who many to this day believe was innocent. On 6 July he carried out the last execution at Pentonville, when Edwin Bush was hanged for the murder of a shopkeeper in London. Bush's execution was historic, because it was the first time the Identikit system of identification had been used in a murder case, and it led to Bush's immediate arrest when a likeness appeared in the evening paper the day after the murder.

Later that month Allen made the first of two trips to Belfast. On the first occasion he hanged Samuel McClaughlin, who had strangled his wife after she had taken out maintenance proceedings against him. His plea of insanity, due to the amount of drink he had consumed prior to the murder, was rejected and he was hanged by Allen and Royston Rickard. Unlike England, Scotland and Wales, Northern Ireland had not adopted the Homicide Act of 1957 – which allowed for some partial defences, as we have seen, such as provocation and diminished responsibility – so, although McClaughlin would have been convicted of non-capital murder on the mainland and received a life sentence, in Northern Ireland he received the mandatory death sentence for murder.

Between the two trips to Ireland Allen carried out the last execution at Wandsworth when Hendryk Neimasz was hanged for the murder by shooting of his mistress's husband, and also convicted of the non-capital murder of her.

On 20 December he hanged Robert McGladdery for the brutal sex murder of a young woman. Nineteen-year-old Pearl Gamble's naked, mutilated body was discovered in a desolate spot near Newry, County Armagh. She had been battered and stabbed, and evidence suggested she had been sexually assaulted. Cause of death was later found to be strangulation.

She had last been seen at a dance in Newry on the night before her murder and among those interviewed was McGladdery, an unemployed labourer from nearby Damolly, a distant cousin of Pearl's, who had been seen dancing with her. McGladdery lied about the clothes he had been wearing on the night before the murder and was sporting scratches on his face that he did not have the night before. His bloodstained clothing was later found hidden, and hairs matching those of Pearl Gamble were discovered clinging to the fibres.

McGladdery was found guilty of the murder and duly sentenced to death, but he maintained he was innocent of the crime with such conviction that strenuous efforts were made for a reprieve. On the eve of the execution with all hope gone he made a full and detailed confession.

On 4 April 1962, James Hanratty walked to the execution shed and paid the supreme penalty for the rape and murder of Valerie Storie and her lover Michael Gregsten. On the night of 22 August 1961, Gregsten and Storie were disturbed as they were courting in his car. At gunpoint Gregsten was made to drive for several hours before he was shot dead on the A6 at Deadman's Hill, near Ampthill, Bedfordshire. Storie was then raped before the killer fired several shots at her, leaving her paralysed for the rest of her life.

Petty thief Hanratty was arrested after his description matched that of the wanted man and he was picked out at an identity parade by Valerie Storie. He came over badly in court, changing his alibi halfway through proceedings, and was sentenced to death on 17 February after a nineteen-day trial, at the time the longest murder trial in English legal history.

Allen always maintained he was convinced of the killer's guilt and that he walked the last few paces to the gallows with a defiant stare in his eyes. Although campaigning went on for the next three decades, in 2001 DNA evidence seems to have finally proved that Hanratty was almost certainly the A6 killer.

In August 1963 Henry John Burnett became the last man to be hanged in Scotland, when he went to the gallows at Craiginches Prison, Aberdeen, for the shotgun murder of his girlfriend's husband.

Burnett had begun an affair with Margaret Guyan when they were both employed at an Aberdeen factory, and with her husband away at sea they moved in together. A short time later she wrote to her husband asking for a divorce, and on 31 May Thomas Guyan returned to shore and sought out

Margaret. She agreed to his plea for reconciliation and returned to the house she shared with Burnett to collect her two children and her belongings.

Burnett was enraged and began to fight with Margaret. She received minor stab wounds as she fought off his attempts to strangle her. Later that afternoon, Burnett called at Guyan's house and blasted his love rival in the face with a shotgun, killing him instantly. He then snatched Margaret and dragged her outside. Having hijacked a car from a petrol station, he drove away until they were spotted by a patrol car. Making Margaret promise to stand by him if he gave himself up, Burnett surrendered and was charged with wilful murder.

The previous hanging at Aberdeen had taken place 106 years earlier, but the gallows at the prison were the most modern in Great Britain, having been newly built and installed just twelve months earlier. A report of the execution later emerged, given to a Scottish newspaper by a witness.

The magistrates were led up to the first floor and stood on a landing opposite two doors.
Immediately, the one on the left opened and facing us were Allen, the prisoner, and Allen's assistant Plant. The prisoner was wearing a white loose open-necked shirt and blue trousers, his arms pinned to his sides by a leather strap. Another strap, loose, was wound around his thighs.
Without a word he walked forward. In fact he trotted into the execution room. As we followed through the door we saw two warders standing with their backs to us on either side of the trap. At the side, a minister and priest stood, both praying. The prison doctor was also in the room. Not a word was spoken. The assistant placed a

white cap over the prisoner's head as they walked
to the trap in the floor. As soon as the prisoner
reached the spot the assistant quickly tugged the
loose straps around the legs tight and stepped
away as Mr Allen was placing the noose around the
prisoner's neck. Mr Allen then stepped back and
as he did so he put his right hand out and pulled
a lever. It was soundless. The prisoner was dead
instantly. It had taken just nine seconds.

Burnett had been given a whisky the night before the
execution and had slept well. On the following morning as
the hour approached he was offered a last tot, but refused,
claiming the one he was given the previous night had been
drugged. He settled for a final cup of tea.

The body was left to hang for just a short time and within
the hour it had been carried out in a coffin for a short funeral
service and burial. As Burnett was lowered into the ground,
the principal warder and the two condemned-cell officers
who had guarded the prisoner up to his death were reported
to be crying like children.

Allen was to carry out just two further executions. At
Bristol in late December 1963 he hanged Russell Pascoe for
his part in the murder and robbery of a recluse, and in August
1964 he was on duty at Manchester when Gwynne Evans
made the 8 o'clock walk for his part in a murder at
Workington, more on which later. On both occasions he was
assisted by Roy Rickard.

Although capital punishment for murder was to all intents
abolished in England in November 1965, it remained on the
statute book in Northern Ireland, the Irish Republic, the West
Indies, the Channel Islands and on the Isle of Man. During
the next two decades a number of requests were made for

hangmen's services, including one from the Republic of Ireland in the mid-1970s, but it never usually got any further than a speculative letter.

Allen gave several newspaper and television interviews, in each saying that he believed capital punishment should be reinstated. 'It may be eighteen years since I last hanged a man,' he said, in 1983 during a debate on the reintroduction of the death penalty, 'but, even at seventy-one, I'm perfectly ready, willing and able to resume my duties.' He was also the last hangman to model for Madame Tussaud's. He did this in the mid-1960s, and for many years his wax figure stood in the Chamber of Horrors next to several of his customers, including the A6 murderer Hanratty.

In one of his later newspaper interviews Allen also commented on the state of law and order in the country: 'Since the rope was scrapped, discipline has gone right out of the window. It's the well meaning do-gooders that I blame for the mess society is in today.' He also claimed that he had never been bothered by dreams or nightmares and that, once he arrived home after an execution, he would have a bath and go to bed.

Following the end of capital punishment, Allen continued to run a number of public houses around Lancashire before working as a security guard at a Blackburn warehouse. With his second wife Doris he retired to Fleetwood, where he worked for a time as caretaker and security guard on the historic pier.

Harry Allen died on 14 August 1992, just a month after the last-ever death sentence was passed (though not carried out) in the British Isles – on the Isle of Man. He had suffered a stroke a few weeks earlier and, despite reports to the contrary, had been too ill to attend Pierrepoint's funeral, which had taken place a month earlier.

Allen maintained to the end that he never officially retired as a hangman following the abolition of the death penalty for murder, as it was still a punishment in English and Scottish law for high treason, piracy with violence and arson in the Royal Dockyards. The death sentence for the last offence was abolished in 1971.

Chapter 9:

The Homicide Act

O nce it had been decided that the death penalty was not to be abolished in 1948 and that executions were again to be sanctioned, it was decided to look to fill the vacancies created by the removal of Alexander Riley's and Herbert Morris's names from the list.

Syd Dernley, a 27-year-old Nottinghamshire pit welder, applied to be a hangman on 23 January 1947. Dernley had been interested in the subject for many years and, feeling that he was now of an age, had written to the News of the World letters page asking where to apply, and the paper duly printed his letter in the following week's paper. He penned his application and a week later received a preprinted letter from the Prison Commissioners.

Sir,

In reply to your letter of 23rd January I am
directed by the Prison Commissioners to inform
you that a note has been made of your application,
but that it is not proposed at present to add to the
list of persons already qualified to assist at
executions.

I am Sir,

Your obedient servant,

J Holt

Establishment Officer

Dernley was saddened to find that the standardised letter
had a space for the date to be added, which suggested there
were numerous applicants that necessitated such a letter. It
was to be almost a year before he was invited to attend an
interview at Lincoln Prison, when at the end of September
1948 he was 'requested to attend this prison at 10.30 a.m. on
Friday 8th October, in order that you may be medically
examined and interviewed with a view ascertaining your
fitness for the post of Assistant Executioner'.

Successfully coming through the interview, Dernley made a
startling revelation when he felt that it was going badly. When
asked if he enjoyed sport, he had replied no, but then admitted
he enjoyed shooting on the Duke of Portland's estate.

'You shoot with the Duke?' Governor Paton Walsh asked
the aspiring assistant.

'No, I shoot when the Duke's gone to bed,' Dernley replied.

Shouting for the medical officer to join him, the governor
roared with laughter. 'Come in here, Doc, we've got a
poacher who wants to be a hangman!'

Dernley was invited to attend Pentonville for a course
lasting one week, starting at 2 p.m. on 6 December 1948. He

was paid £5 per week of 42 hours with no further allowances paid, apart from third-class rail fare from home to the prison. 'It is understood that attendance at this course does not necessarily imply that the trainees have been accepted for appointment as Assistant Executioners,' the letter warned.

Also attending that course were three other men: Londoner William Pollard, who went on to fail the course; George Dickinson of Adlington, near Bolton; and Herbert Allen, a Wolverhampton ice-cream man. There is nothing on record to suggest that Allen was related to the other Wolverhampton hangman of the same name, Alfred Allen, who had been on the list over a decade before.

Dickinson had only the briefest stint as an assistant executioner. Dickinson would have been present as an observer, probably at Birmingham with his two training colleagues, but his first proper engagement was at Swansea, when he assisted at the double execution of two young miners who had both strangled their girlfriends in June of that year.

Rex Harvey Jones, a 21-year-old collier from the Rhondda Valley, had been convicted of the murder of Peggy Watts, whose body had been found on a mountainside near Port Talbot on 6 June. Hanged alongside him was Robert Mackintosh, also 21, who had strangled 16-year-old Beryl Beechey on Friday, 3 June, leaving her body on a railway embankment at Port Talbot. Pierrepoint later said that the execution had passed off without incident, but as he was giving Dickinson a lift back to Lancashire, the assistant had turned a deathly white colour.

'All of a sudden he groaned and the bastard was pissing himself,' Pierrepoint said. This happened on a further two occasions before they reached home, with Pierrepoint adamant that Dickinson would not work with him again. Dickinson turned down the offer of an engagement at Wandsworth a few days later, claiming he had now received his national service papers, and is said to have later emigrated to Canada.

Dernley and Herbert Allen were present as observers at Birmingham in March 1949 when they watched Pierrepoint and Kirk hang James Farrell, who had raped and strangled a fourteen-year-old girl at Sutton Coldfield. Both were invited to participate at their first executions in December 1949, when two men were hanged at Durham.

Benjamin Roberts had shot dead 21-year-old Lillian Vickers, the girlfriend of his childhood friend, when he realised she did not have the same feelings for him as he had for her. John Wilson was a collier who had strangled a seaman's wife. They had been out drinking and, as he walked her home, they began kissing and walked towards a hayfield. When Wilson suggested making love and she asked him for 10 shillings, in a rage he strangled her.

The double execution passed off without any undue incident, although Dernley recorded later that he had assisted hangman Stephen Wade in getting Wilson onto the drop, and, stepping back after strapping his ankles, he expected to see Kirk lead Roberts through onto the drop. With Wilson noosed and pinioned on the drop, the hangmen were horrified to find that Kirk was still in the condemned cell, as Roberts showed no inclination to get up from his chair until he had finished singing a hymn with the priest. Eventually, Kirk and assistant Herbert Allen had to lift him up forcibly, pinion his arms and escort him to the drop, arriving just as Wilson was about to collapse in a faint.

Allen was engaged at an execution at Norwich in March, assisting Pierrepoint for the first time, and Dernley carried out his first engagement with the noted number-one executioner the following day, when he assisted at the hanging of Timothy Evans.

The assistants worked together again at Winchester that year, when two bank robbers were hanged side by side for a murder in Bristol, and at a double execution at Wandsworth in April 1951, when two labourers were hanged for the murder of a shopkeeper in Chertsey. Assisting Pierrepoint, alongside the new assistants was Manchester hangman Harry Allen.

Herbert Allen officiated at the last two executions of 1951, the latter being that of Herbert Mills, who had strangled a woman in a wood near Nottingham before trying to sell the story of the discovery to a Sunday newspaper. Soon after this execution, Allen is supposed to have quit as an assistant after being told by his employers that ice cream and hangings don't mix. While going through some old papers relating to Pierrepoint there was discovered a note in his diary that suggests Allen was dismissed for stealing a jumper belonging to the man they had just executed – presumably Mills. Dernley records that Allen – who received no official notification – had approached Pierrepoint following an execution in Birmingham the following year, begging for his job back. 'He'll never do another,' Pierrepoint coldly told Dernley as they drove away from the prison.

Dernley's last execution was at Birmingham in December 1952, although he continued to receive engagements until spring 1954. In his memoirs, published in 1989, Dernley wrote that he believed his career as a hangman effectively ended when he made a tasteless remark after an execution at Wandsworth a week before he assisted at Birmingham. The truth is that his career ended when he became implicated in the trading of illegal books, and served a short prison sentence in April 1954. He was 33 years old and, after his release, he returned to the colliery, rising to become a foreman welder before changing career in the 1960s and becoming a postmaster in his hometown of Mansfield in Nottinghamshire. Following the publication of his book Dernley often appeared at lectures and on television. He died at his Mansfield bungalow on 1 November 1994.

Robert Leslie Stewart was born in Edinburgh in April 1918. The son of a sergeant major who had served in the Boer war, Les, as he preferred to be known, grew up within the shadows of the city's Saughton prison, and was ten years old when the idea of becoming a hangman first appealed to him. In the spring of 1928, Allen Wales, an unemployed labourer, murdered his wife at Leith and the subsequent trial and execution left a distinct impression on the young Stewart.

After working as a grocer's boy while at school, he became apprenticed to a firm of specialist architectural metalworkers before following in his father's footsteps in 1939, when he enlisted in the armed forces, becoming a technician in the RAF. War service took him to Blackpool, where he met his future wife, Marie, and after a brief wartime romance they married in 1940, settling after the war in his wife's hometown of Chadderton, near Oldham, Lancashire.

The couple had four daughters and, while Stewart found skilled work in his former trade, his wife got a job at a pub in nearby Hollinwood. The pub where Marie worked was called Help the Poor Struggler, the landlord being the country's chief hangman Albert Pierrepoint. Stewart had told his wife of his childhood ambition and Marie confided in Albert Pierrepoint. The Pierrepoints and the Stewarts had by this time become good friends and Pierrepoint told him to write directly to the Prison Commissioners in London.

At 2 p.m. on 3 August 1950 Stewart faced an interview with the governor of Strangeways Prison, Manchester, and in September 1950 was invited to attend a week's intensive training at London's Pentonville Prison. Also present at Pentonville was another aspiring hangman, Harry Smith of Doncaster.

Harry Smith lived for a time on the same Doncaster street as Stephen Wade and it is reasonable to assume that a friendship between the two may have been instrumental in Smith's applying to become an executioner. Smith carried out his first execution in the summer of 1951 and in the following year he was present at five, assisting both Pierrepoint and Wade, the most notable being the double execution of Alfred Burns and Edward Devlin at Liverpool (see below). The highlight in Smith's ten-year career took place in July of the following year, when he assisted Albert Pierrepoint in the execution of John Christie at Pentonville.

The majority of Smith's engagements came at Leeds Prison, where he acted as assistant to Stephen Wade. Smith assisted Harry Allen at his first execution in 1958 and travelled to Cyprus in that year, when their services were cancelled at the eleventh hour. He resigned in 1959, following the execution of Ernest Jones at Leeds.

In the autumn of 1950, both Smith and Stewart were informed they had passed the training and the next step would be to witness an execution as non-participating assistants, a role designed to test a man's nerve, and one that had been more than enough for a few would-be hangmen. Their first experience took place a week before Christmas 1950, when they watched Pierrepoint and his assistant Syd Dernley hang Nicholas Crosby at Manchester.

Crosby was a young gypsy convicted of the murder of Ruth Massey in Leeds. Ruth had been violently assaulted and her throat cut. Crosby, the last person to see her alive, gave varying accounts of what had happened that night but never admitted his guilt, although he based his defence on the fact that he was so drunk when he left the pub that he had no recollection of events from then on. He would normally have been hanged at Leeds, but, since the execution suite at Armley Gaol was being modernised, he was the first of three people convicted during this period to be sent over the Pennines for execution.

Stewart made the short journey to Manchester, but prison officials were so concerned about the behaviour of the condemned man that it was decided on the morning on the execution that both Stewart and Smith would stay on the landing and view proceedings through the doorway. This was preferable to having them present on the gallows, adding to the number of officials already present. This, it was felt, could cause overcrowding and possible trouble if there was an unpleasant scene on the gallows. As it turned out, Crosby did try to put up some resistance, glaring at his executioners and telling them he did not want his arms pinioned. Ignoring the pleas, Pierrepoint and Dernley secured his arms and led the terrified killer onto the drop.

It was to be seven months after witnessing this Manchester execution before Stewart finally got the opportunity to put his training into practice, when he received the offer of an engagement at Norwich.

On 4 February 1951, the body of Eileen Cullen was found at Norwich two weeks before she was due to marry. Her fiancé, Dennis Moore, led police to the body, telling them they had quarrelled after she refused to have sex with him until after the baby was born, and in a rage he strangled her. Moore was sentenced to death at Norfolk Assizes on 2 June, and two days later Alfred George Reynolds was convicted at the same court of the murder of his fiancée. Reynolds, a 24-year-old labourer from Dereham, had told the court his fiancée was pregnant and her father forbade marriage between them.

Reynolds said that, frustrated at being unable to wed, they

had made a suicide pact, but he had failed in his side of the agreement. He told police that she had begged him to help her commit suicide, and when he refused she had turned the gun on herself. His version of events was found to be untrue and at the trial evidence showed that, judging from the distance the gun was fired, there was no way Ellen could have shot herself. The two Norfolk men were hanged side by side at Norwich Prison by Albert Pierrepoint and three assistants, Dernley, Harry Allen and Stewart, who with his Scottish accent soon earned the nickname Jock.

After a quiet first year, 1952 was to find Jock Stewart being the busiest assistant, present at eight executions, all carried out by Albert Pierrepoint. The first call came in January, when he received a letter from the governor of Strangeways Prison, Manchester.

Alfred Bradley was a 24-year-old Macclesfield labourer convicted of the murder of George Camp, a night-watchman from Wythenshawe, Manchester, whom he had beaten to death with a plank after Camp threatened to tell Bradley's parents about their sexual relationship. Bradley confessed to the crime while on remand in Strangeways Gaol on a lesser charge, and at his first trial, in November 1951, he had hurled a bible at the judge while taking the oath. The trial was postponed to allow Bradley to be examined by doctors, and a week later, before a new judge, he was sentenced to death. Bradley was so calm on the morning of the execution that the prison governor recalled, 'Anyone would think he was going to the pictures instead of the scaffold.'

A month later Stewart was back at Strangeways to help hang Roy Herbert Harris, a silk worker from north Wales, convicted of the murder of his wife.

One of the most controversial executions that year took

place at Liverpool in April, when Alfred Burns and Edward Devlin were jointly convicted of the murder of Mrs Beatrice Rimmer in Wavertree, Liverpool. Mrs Rimmer had been a recluse for a number of years, and rumours that she had large amounts of money in the house had led to several break-ins. She was last seen alive on the night of Sunday, 19 August 1951, and on the following evening her son found her lying in a pool of blood on the hall floor. She had been attacked by two different weapons, suggesting two killers. Following the testimony of a soldier held on remand in Walton Prison, Burns and Devlin, both petty criminals, were arrested at their homes in Manchester.

At their ten-day trial, they offered a defence that they could not have been in Liverpool on the night of the murder because they were at the time carrying out a robbery in a factory in Manchester with a third man. This alibi was destroyed in court when the other man, who had already been arrested for this offence, admitted that the date of the Manchester robbery was 18 August, the night *before* the alleged murder.

Although there was widespread protest at the execution of two young men – Burns was 22, Devlin a year younger – it was later reported that both had confessed in the condemned cell before they were hanged by Pierrepoint, assisted by Dernley, Stewart and Smith.

In July Stewart assisted in the execution at Bristol of Thomas Eames, a Plymouth labourer who had murdered a woman – whom he had bigamously married – after she had left him. Eames did not go quietly to the gallows, having to be dragged fighting and kicking as he struggled all the way to the drop.

Maureen Cox had been engaged to film cameraman John Godar for almost a year before she discovered he had an ex-wife and a young child. She ended the relationship and began to date another man, and when on 6 June she told Godar she was meeting her new lover that night he stabbed her almost fifty times with a stiletto. Stewart assisted Pierrepoint in the Pentonville execution in September, Godar being the first of three men to die on the north London gallows that month.

In September Stewart assisted Pierrepoint in a double execution at Pentonville, and also at Lincoln in December, when Eric Northcliffe, an ex-RAF sergeant, was hanged for the murder of his wife.

After such a hectic year Stewart wasn't involved in any of the controversial executions that filled the papers in the early part of the following year, but his first engagement was to assist in an execution that was one of the most newsworthy, that of Louisa Merrifield.

In March 1953, Merrifield and her third husband Alfred became live-in housekeepers and companions to the twice-widowed Mrs Sarah Ann Ricketts in Blackpool, and within the month Mrs Ricketts had changed her will in favour of the Merrifields. By early April, Merrifield was telling friends she had been left a bungalow by the elderly widow, and, when Mrs Ricketts died on 14 April, one of the friends became suspicious and contacted the police. A postmortem found that Mrs Ricketts had died as a result of phosphorus poisoning and both Merrifield and her husband were charged with her murder.

Despite no trace of poison at the house and conflicting medical evidence suggesting that cause of death may have been liver failure, Louisa Merrifield was sentenced to death after an eleven-day trial. The jury failed to reach a verdict on Alfred Merrifield and he was released and later inherited a half-share in the bungalow. Louisa Merrifield walked bravely to the gallows at Strangeways, where she was given a drop of 6 feet 1 inch. It was Stewart's only execution of a woman.

In January 1954 Desmond Hooper was hanged at Shrewsbury protesting his innocence. Six months before, in July 1953, twelve-year-old Betty Smith had disappeared after a visit to the home of Keith Hooper, her seven-year-old friend and neighbour at Atcham, Shropshire. Betty's mother called at the Hoopers' house at midnight and was told that Betty had left to go home at 10.40 p.m. Keith's father had left the house a short time after Betty to see about some pigeons that had not returned to their coop at a nearby farm.

A search located the young girl's body less than two miles away, down a ventilation shaft at a disused part of the Shropshire Union Canal near Shrewsbury. She had been strangled with a tie and kicked repeatedly in the stomach before being thrown down the 40-foot shaft, where she had drowned in the shallow stagnant water. A jacket recovered from the mouth of the shaft was identified as belonging to Desmond Hooper.

Hooper was tried at Shrewsbury Assizes and the evidence against him was mainly circumstantial: primarily the jacket found at the scene of the crime and the fact that his claim to be tending to his pigeons at the time of the murder could not be corroborated.

In April 1954 Stewart assisted Pierrepoint on three executions in eight days, carrying out hangings in all parts of the UK and Ireland. On 20 April they were in Dublin for the execution of Michael Manning, a 25-year-old carter from Limerick, who had been convicted of the rape and murder of Catherine Cooper, a nursing sister at a Limerick hospital, in November 1953. Manning had dragged the 65-year-old nurse into a nearby field, where he raped and beat her, forcing grass into her mouth to stop her screaming. Death was due to suffocation caused by the grass. Manning had confessed at his trial and offered a defence of manslaughter on the grounds that he had been very drunk on the night of the attack. He was the last man hanged in the Irish Republic.

Three days later Stewart returned to his birthplace to carry out an execution for the first time when John Lynch was hanged at Saughton Prison for the murder of two young girls in an Edinburgh tenement block.

In the following week the executioners travelled down to Swansea for the execution of Thomas Ronald Lewis Harries.

Farmer John Harries and his wife Phoebe had last been seen alive after a visit to a harvest-festival service on 16 October 1953. Nephew 'Ronnie' Harries said he had driven them from their farm at St Clears in Carmarthenshire to a local railway station, where they had caught a train to London for a secret holiday. Suspecting foul play, Scotland Yard were called in, and investigations led police to the conclusion that Harries had killed his aunt and uncle after they refused to lend him money. A forged cheque was found made out to Ronnie Harries and friends of the missing couple told police they did not believe they would go away without informing them.

Detectives leading the hunt suspected that Harries had buried the bodies in kale fields close to his own farm at nearby Cadno. Thread was tied over entrances leading into the fields and a disturbance was made to make Harries think the fields had been searched. The following day he went to investigate and in doing so broke the thread and led police to a spot in the fields where they found the bodies buried in a shallow grave. They had been battered to death.

Harries was in sheer terror when the hangmen entered his cell and he collapsed in a heap as they reached the drop, having to be supported, unconscious, by Stewart as the noose was placed around his neck.

Jock Stewart was present at just two further executions

that year, both as assistant to Pierrepoint. At Liverpool in June he helped to hang Milton Taylor and in September he assisted at Wandsworth for the first time when he helped to hang Rupert Wells. Both men had strangled the women with whom they had been having relationships.

In 1955 Stewart assisted Pierrepoint at Wandsworth in April and that summer he twice assisted his friend at executions at Liverpool, the second of which was notable in that it was the last time Pierrepoint officiated at an execution.

When Stewart assisted at an execution at Birmingham on 9 August it was to help veteran Stephen Wade for the first time. Ten-year-old schoolgirl Evelyn Patricia Higgins had disappeared after visiting a Coventry hairdressing salon on the afternoon of 8 June. Two schoolgirls told police they had been approached by a man who had tried to lure them into the black car he was driving. Another witness gave a detailed description of the car, which led police to 42-year-old Ernest Harding, a bricklayer.

They found their suspect slumped in his car, a pipe attached to the exhaust pumping fumes to the inside. He was thwarted in his suicide bid and made a number of conflicting statements. First, he claimed to have no recollection of finding Evelyn inside the car; in another statement he said that when he realised she was dead he decided to bury her body. He led police to a shallow grave in a wood near Coventry. She had been raped and asphyxiated and then stabbed in the throat. Harding was the last man to be hanged for child murder.

Three days after the Birmingham execution, Stewart assisted Stephen Wade at the execution in Leeds of Alec Wilkinson, a Barnsley miner who had killed his mother-in-law. As he was led to the gallows Wilkinson joked, 'At least I know where I'm going, and can use a shovel.' This alluded to his occupation as a miner. It was the last execution carried out by Stephen Wade and the last execution to take place in Great Britain for almost two years.

Following government reforms that culminated in the passing of the Homicide Act, there were just two people executed in 1957, and Stewart had to wait until May 1958 before he was able to officiate at his first senior engagement.

Seventy-three-year-old William Williams had been a subpostmaster at Fforestfach, Glamorgan (it is now in the city and county of Swansea), for over forty years when, on Sunday, 17 November 1957, an intruder armed with a hammer entered the premises. Williams confronted the man and was struck 27 blows with the hammer. As he lay dead on the floor the assailant fled empty-handed.

Police interviewed a number of workmen who had been employed to renovate the post office a few months earlier and in due course spoke to 24-year-old Vivian Teed, who had a history of thefts and assault. A witness also told police that Teed had confided in him that he planned to rob the post office.

Teed appeared at Glamorgan Assizes in March charged with capital murder – i.e. murder in the furtherance of theft. After he had made a confession, his counsel pleaded manslaughter on the grounds of diminished responsibility.

Aided by new assistant Harry Robinson, Stewart carried out his senior duties for the first time to everyone's satisfaction. The chief executioner and the governor later noted that he had never seen an execution carried out more expeditiously.

THE HOMICIDE ACT

The biggest change in the execution procedure and protocol in the twentieth century took place with the passing of the Homicide Act 1957. Prior to this Act the mandatory sentence for murder was death by hanging. This was regardless of whether the murder was unpremeditated – such as the result of a drunken quarrel – or because of a coldly calculated plot.

The arbitrary way reprieves were handed down was questioned, as was the mounting number of controversial cases in the years after World War Two, in particular those of Timothy Evans, Derek Bentley and Ruth Ellis. The growing disquiet following Bentley's execution gained further momentum when John Christie was charged with multiple murder in the summer of 1953, three years after Timothy Evans had gone to the gallows largely on the testimony of Christie, whom he blamed for the murders he had been accused of.

The last straw seemed to be when Ruth Ellis went to the gallows in July 1955. Although she had admitted her guilt in shooting the lover who spurned her, her mental state following a recent miscarriage was not really taken into account.

In response to the numerous abolitionists' movements the Act was passed. It led to a revision of the whole structure of the legal system relating to capital punishment, restricting the death penalty in murder cases to five types of murder, now known as capital murder. From March 1957, the death penalty was restricted to those convicted of:

- any murder committed in the course or furtherance of theft;
- any murder committed by shooting or explosion;
- any murder committed in the course or for the purpose of resisting or avoiding or preventing a lawful arrest, or of effecting or assisting an escape or rescue from legal custody;
- any murder of a police officer acting in the execution of his/her duty or of a person assisting a police officer in so acting; and in the case of a person who was a prisoner at the time when he committed or was a party to a murder, any murder of a prison officer acting in the execution of his/her duty or of a prison officer so acting.

These new restrictions were an attempt to reserve the death penalty for those viewed as deserving the final and irreversible ultimate punishment. In providing for this, the Act also produced other issues: why could a strangler or poisoner not be eligible for hanging, while someone who used a gun could be so executed? Murder in the course of theft was punishable by death, while murder in the course of rape was not. And most controversially – certainly when viewed from today – child murder was now no longer punishable with the death penalty. These anomalies fuelled public disquiet against the death penalty, and gradually capital-murder convictions became less common.

The wording of the death sentence was also changed again. Instead of the lengthy wording based on that used from Victorian times, it now simply stated that the prisoner would 'suffer death in the manner authorised by law'. The posting of notices on the prison gates also ended, replaced with a short notification inserted in the *London Gazette* and national newspapers such as *The Times*.

Double executions, which had stopped three years earlier in 1954 as a recommendation of the Royal Commission report, were also officially outlawed, and, on the three occasions during the period of the Homicide Act that two killers were hanged for the same crime, their executions were carried out at different prisons at the same hour. This change also meant that no one executioner could state that he was the last hangman of Britain.

Brian Chandler, a twenty-year-old Middlesbrough-born private in the Royal Army Medical Corps, had gone absent without leave from his camp at Catterick, and had met up with two teenage girls who had run away from their homes, in Darlington, County Durham. They planned to head to London but, without any funds, they decided to find a house to rob. One of the girls suggested that the home of a widow, Mrs Martha Anne Dodd, a former employer, would make a suitable target. On 11 June 1958, Chandler called at the house asking for work. Invited inside, they entered the kitchen, where he struck her nineteen times with a hammer, stealing £4 from her handbag before fleeing.

Chandler was soon placed under arrest and claimed he had lost his temper after she had offered him gardening work for the paltry sum of 3 shillings an hour. Convicted of capital murder, he was executed on 17 December 1958. He was the last man to be hanged at Durham. Harry Allen was originally offered the engagement but had to turn it down because he was scheduled to be in Cyprus on government business.

Chandler was hanged by Stewart and assistant Thomas Cunliffe, Stewart noting in his diary that Chandler came onto the gallows with his eyes tightly closed and, despite what the authorities had feared, had not given them any trouble.

Stewart's third engagement as senior man was at Winchester for the execution of Michael Tatum in May 1959, and, although he continued to receive many offers of employment, there were now far more reprieves than executions and it was to be eighteen months before he next entered a prison to carry out an execution.

On 25 June 1960, after a heavy drinking session, four teddy boys decided to 'jump someone' as they waited on a secluded path at Hounslow. Alan Jee, a 23-year-old engineer, who had just bidden goodnight to his fiancée, approached and without warning was punched in the face by one of the men and knocked to the ground. The eldest of the gang, 23-year-old Norman Harris, rifled his pockets, trying to find his wallet, as the others held him down. Harris stopped when he saw blood on his hands and ran away, leaving the 10 shillings the victim was carrying still in his pocket. As Harris rummaged for the wallet eighteen-year-old Francis 'Flossie' Forsyth stood over the stricken man and repeatedly kicked him in the head with his pointed winkle-picker shoes, in order to 'keep him quiet'. Alan Jee died in hospital from his injuries two days later.

Forsyth bragged to a girlfriend that he had been in a fight and this soon led to his arrest. The others were quickly rounded up and taken to Hounslow police station. Questioned first, Harris denied any involvement in the assault but soon admitted he had held down the victim while Forsyth and one of the others attacked him.

Four men stood trial for murder, but evidence suggested one of the gang played only a minor role – he was standing away from the victim, acting as a lookout – and as a result he was convicted of non-capital murder and sentenced to life imprisonment. Another of the gang, being under eighteen, was detained at Her Majesty's Pleasure; the other two were sentenced to death. Forsyth, who had claimed at an earlier court appearance that they would get only 'about five years', was hanged at Wandsworth. Harris was hanged by Stewart at Pentonville. He tried to put his head through the noose as they walked onto the drop, but Stewart had to stop him, as the noose was facing the wrong way.

A month later Stewart assisted Harry Allen for the one and only time when both were engaged for an hanging in Glasgow. Nineteen-year-old Anthony Miller was hanged for the murder of a Dundee shopkeeper who was in Glasgow for a football match. The telegram requesting Stewart's services had arrived at the house on the morning of his daughter Thelma's wedding and was spotted at the last minute by his wife and removed from the collection of telegrams sending good wishes to the married couple.

Resigned to being the understudy to chief executioner Allen, Stewart found that work was sporadic, as the death penalty became less used. It was to be almost three years to the day before he was next called into action, although in early 1961 he was asked to officiate at the execution of Luigia Camilleri, who had been convicted of the murder of her young son in Malta. The engagement was cancelled when the Governor of Malta commuted the sentence to life imprisonment.

William Rowe had been a World War One deserter. Conscripted in 1917, he had fled from his unit one week later, and for 35 years had hidden on his parents' farm in the Cornish fishing village of Porthleven, then latterly at Nanjarrow Farm near the village of Constantine, seven miles from Falmouth. Friends and neighbours were told William had been killed in France.

Following her coronation in 1953, Queen Elizabeth II granted a pardon to all deserters, and although Rowe was now a free man he rarely left the farm, having become a reclusive hermit whose only pleasure was studying Esperanto. Locally it was rumoured he was a wealthy man and previously there had been a robbery at Nanjarrow in 1961.

On 15 August 1963, the body of William Rowe was discovered at the farm. He had massive head injuries; his throat was cut; he had five stab wounds in the chest, two in the neck and one across an ear. Police believed he had been killed the previous day and that robbery was the apparent motive, since the whole farmhouse had been turned over. Following initial investigations, police believed that more than £3,000 had been stolen.

The following day Russell Pascoe was stopped at a police roadblock. He gave his address as a caravan near Truro, which he shared with his teenage wife and young child, along with Dennis John Whitty and two teenage girls. Pascoe told police he was in Constantine to visit his parents and that he knew the deceased, having worked at the Nanjarrow farm three years earlier.

Believing that the killer was probably a local man who knew of the alleged wealth of the victim, police visited the caravan in Truro and interviewed Whitty and the three girls. They soon discovered that the two men had left Truro on Pascoe's motorcycle on the night of 14 August – the day of the murder – returning late in an excited and agitated state. Under questioning, Whitty eventually confessed that they had called at the house at 11 p.m., pretending to be helicopter pilots who had crashed nearby and wanted to use a phone. Pascoe had then hit Rowe with an iron bar. Their search failed to find any large sums of money and they had fled with a haul of just £4.

At their trial at Bodmin Assizes, it soon became clear Whitty was the leader who had planned the attack, caused the fatal wounds and threatened the others if they 'grassed'. Despite the fact that each counsel tried to blame the other's client, both men were deemed equally guilty and both were convicted of capital murder in the furtherance of theft.

Stewart hanged Whitty at Winchester a week before Christmas 1963, while Pascoe was hanged by Harry Allen at Bristol at the same moment. The £3,000 police originally believed stolen was discovered hidden in a safe in the cowshed, along with other large sums of money concealed around the farm in small amounts. The haul was discovered by following instructions left in a diary penned in Esperanto.

An offer of an engagement in Bermuda ended in a reprieve and Stewart was to be in action as a hangman just one more time – in the summer of 1964.

In the early hours of 7 April, John Alan West was found battered and stabbed to death at his home at Seaton, on the outskirts of Workington. A raincoat found at the house contained a medal inscribed 'G O Evans 1961' and a piece of paper with a Liverpool address. This soon led police to Preston dairy-workers Peter Allen and Gwynne Evans.

Placed under arrest, each blamed the other for the murder and, after police told Allen that his wife was having an affair with Evans, who had been living as a lodger at the house, the men had to be kept apart in the dock.

Stewart and his regular assistant Harry Robinson, who had worked with him on four of his six senior engagements, hanged Allen at Liverpool on 13 August 1964. Harry Allen hanged Evans at Manchester.

His wife and their two children visited Allen for the last

time on the day prior to the execution. The decision of the Home Secretary not to order a reprieve had been made known shortly before the visit and, as it came to an end, Allen went berserk, hurling himself at the bulletproof glass, breaking his wrist in the process. Stewart noted in his diary, 'He [Allen] smashed his head against a wall during his last visit and broke a finger. As I was strapping his wrist in the morning, he shouted, "Jesus". That was it. Not another word.'

Stewart emigrated to South Africa during the mid-1960s, working as an engineer for an airline company. He never discussed his career as a hangman in Britain and it remained a secret until long after his retirement in 1983. He died in April 1988, aged seventy, and a lone piper played 'Abide with Me' as he was laid to rest.

Chapter 10:

The Last Executioners

It seemed to be the usual way in modern times that new assistants were trained in pairs or occasionally three or four. In the spring of 1953 two new assistants were added to the list. Joseph Broadbent was from East Brierley, Bradford, and he graduated at the same time as Royston Laurence Rickard of Maidstone in Kent.

Broadbent was the first into action when he assisted Albert Pierrepoint at an execution in Liverpool. John Todd was hanged for the murder of an old man in what was known in the press as the 'Old Curiosity Shop Murder'. He assisted Pierrepoint again later that year at Wandsworth and did two further jobs in 1954: one at Manchester in January and another as one of three assistants at Pentonville in June of that year. Broadbent was offered the chance to assist at the execution of Alec Wilkinson in August 1955 but turned down the offer writing that he no longer wished to be considered for work as an assistant executioner and that he was sending his resignation to the prison commissioners. He passed into obscurity, although it was thought that he was still alive at the end of the last century.

Born in August 1919, Rickard performed his first job as an assistant to Albert Pierrepoint at Leeds in July 1953. In December of that year he assisted at two executions in two days, assisting Pierrepoint at Manchester before travelling down to Wandsworth to assist Stephen Wade. He assisted at the last double at Pentonville in June, and in August he was present at Wandsworth when 63-year-old Spanish-born artist William Sanchez De Pina Hepper was hanged for the brutal murder of a young girl.

Hepper lived in Chelsea, but kept a studio flat in Hove, Sussex, and when Margaret Spevick, the eleven-year-old schoolfriend of his youngest daughter, injured her arm in a fall, Hepper suggested to her mother that the young girl should accompany him for a short break to help her recovery. He said they had the services of a nurse at the sea-view flat, and he would also paint a picture of Margaret while she was there.

Mrs Spevick agreed, and on 3 February Hepper and the young girl caught a train to Sussex, it being agreed that he would meet Mrs Spevick at Brighton station on 7 February. She would then accompany her daughter back home. When no one met Mrs Spevick at the station she had to return to London to get the address, because, having trusted Hepper implicitly, she had not even bothered to ask the actual address of the studio. On returning to Hove, she got the caretaker to let her in and to her horror found Margaret's body on a bed beside a half-painted portrait. She was naked and had been raped and strangled.

The hunt for Hepper led detectives to Spain, where, shocked at the horrific nature of the crime, members of his family told police of his whereabouts. Hepper appealed, saying that, as a Spanish national, he should not be extradited, but there was little sympathy for him – on account of his crime and the fact that he had fought against the government in the Spanish Civil War.

Like many other executioners Rickard worked as a publican in Maidstone and, although he officiated at only one execution in 1955, it was at Holloway, where Ruth Ellis was hanged for the murder of her lover. Following the passing of the Homicide Act in 1957, Rickard was present at a number of high-profile executions, including those of Edwin Podola, Flossie Forsyth and James Hanratty. In 1964 he was on duty assisting Harry Allen at Manchester. He maintained a low profile and I am unaware of any press interviews or articles on his life or career. He died in the summer of 1999.

Only one new assistant was added before the temporary suspension of executions in 1955, when John Robert Barker of north London graduated from Pentonville in the summer of 1955. He was present as a trainee observer at Leeds when Alec Wilkinson was hanged in August, but the long period of inactivity caused him to rethink. When offered the role of assistant executioner in 1958, he wrote to the prison stating he had already tendered his resignation to the Home Office.

After the promotion of Allen and Stewart, a new batch of assistants was sought and on 4 June 1956, six would-be candidates arrived for training at Pentonville. They were to be the last batch of assistants trained at the north London gaol. By the end of the week two men had quit and two others failed the end of course test. The two who graduated were Tommy Cunliffe of Hindley, Wigan, in Lancashire, and Harry Robinson of Kingswinford, Staffordshire.

TYPICAL TRAINING SCHEDULE
(1950-1960s)

Day One
   Report to the establishment between 3 p.m. and 4 p.m. Seen by Chief Officer and then passed to Senior Foreman of Works, who will see that each applicant completes form E74 (official secrets).
   Applicants will then be taken to the Governor for an interview. Following this they will be allowed to leave the prison to arrange lodgings.

Day Two
Report 9 a.m.
Lecture on Prison procedure.
Memorandum of conditions to which Assistants will conform, explanation of form and what it implies.
Duties of Assistant Executioner and procedure.
The apparatus explained and how it is used.

Day Three
Lecture on table of drops and method of calculations.
Method of pinioning and practice.
Short visit to the chamber.

Day Four
Recapitalisation and practice pinioning
Demonstrations in the chamber.

> **Day Five**
> Morning. Written examination.
> Afternoon. Applicants to pass pinioning in the presence
> of the Governor and MO.
> Disperse.

Both received numerous requests to assist in 1956, but, with all jobs ending in reprieves while Parliament debated and planned the new Homicide Act, they didn't get the chance to visit a prison on official business until the winter of 1957, when at 9.30 a.m. both were present as observers when Dennis Howard was hanged at Birmingham. Robinson claimed that Harry Allen's son Brian also spent the night at the prison prior to the execution, but Allen's son always maintained he never officiated at an execution.

Cunliffe assisted at just four jobs before he was dismissed after he neglected to secure the leg strap on Bernard Walden at Leeds in August 1959. He died at the age of 68 in the 1980s.

Throughout the following years, Harry Robinson received many engagements, the majority of which were reprieved, being frequently paired with Jock Stewart. He assisted Stewart at the last execution in Wales, when Vivian Teed went to the gallows at Swansea in May 1958; and his first engagement assisting Harry Allen was at Pentonville, when Ronald Marwood was hanged – amid disturbances by fellow inmates – for the murder of a policeman. Years later Robinson said that the noise of the protestors outside was so loud that he was unable to sleep as he spent the night in his quarters.

Robinson assisted Jock Stewart at Pentonville in 1960 and assisted Allen twice in the following year, at Bedford and

Leeds, with his last engagements coming in 1963, when he assisted at Winchester, and eight months later at Manchester.

In the late 1990s, while living in retirement, with his past life on the scaffold a secret from even his immediate family, he gave several interviews, always incognito. He died in 2006.

After the Homicide Act, all would-be hangmen were trained at Wandsworth and the last two assistants to complete their training were both from the Berkshire area. The last training session for executioners took place on Monday, 25 April 1960. With the execution chamber adjacent to the condemned cell it was normal practice for the area to be clear of persons under sentence of death, but it seems that resident in one of the condemned cells at Wandsworth was James Smith, a 32-year-old gypsy, who had murdered a policeman who had tried to stop him as he drove a car containing stolen goods. Smith had failed to stop and the policeman was thrown into the road, where he was struck by another vehicle and died. Smith was on death row at Wandsworth pending his appeal. He later had his death sentence commuted.

The prison authorities must have felt the soundproofing in the gallows room to have been sufficient for the training to go ahead, because, under the guidance of Harry Rayfield, the senior foreman of works at the south London prison, the men did attend the five-day course – and both were successful.

John Edward Underhill was a Twickenham-born former public-school boy who had grown up in India, where his father was serving in the army. He trained as a Royal Marine Commando after the war and in 1947 joined the Reading Borough Police, serving two years before being seconded to the Federal States of Malay Police, where he commanded three companies of Malay Police antiterrorist units.

I have been told that he had experience of executions while stationed in Malaysia, assisting a man named Wood at seventeen executions, and carrying out nine himself as principal. Underhill returned to Reading in 1953 and was awarded the Queen's Police Medal. He later joined the SAS, rising to become a captain.

Opportunities were few once he had joined the Home Office list of assistants. He was present as an observer at Lincoln in 1960 and returned to the prison as assistant to Harry Allen in the last execution carried out there a year later. Underhill assisted at just two further executions: in June 1961 at Pentonville and in 1962 at Manchester.

With the death penalty in abeyance, he continued working with the SAS and during the Vietnam War operated with the Americans on special covert work. He retired to Singapore and may still be alive.

The other graduate was Newcastle-born Samuel Barrass Plant, who was living in Slough when he carried out just a handful of jobs in the latter days of capital punishment. He was present at the last executions in both Scotland and Northern Ireland, but wasn't called upon for the last executions in England in 1964. He died in 2002, aged 86. His notable victims were the bank robber Victor Terry, who believed he was the reincarnation of the American gangster Legs Diamond, and the shotgun killer Henry Burnett.

All hangmen and assistants on the last official government list remained on standby until capital punishment was finally abolished in November 1965. None were ever officially notified that their services would no longer be needed.

It is now over forty years since the gallows were last used in Great Britain, and all traces of them have been removed from the gaols that operated them. Those that survive are in museums or private collections. Of the men on the last list, one by one they died, with only Underhill possibly being still alive at the time of writing.

In 1983 a vote in Parliament went close enough for prison officials at Wakefield and Wandsworth to begin preparations in the event of restoration. But just a handful of votes prevented this, and the chance that a condemned criminal would again be hanged by the neck until dead passed for ever.

ABOLITION

A newly elected Labour government came to power in October 1964 with the promise to abolish the death penalty. Before the Murder (Abolition of the Death Penalty) Act 1965 received Royal Assent, the Home Office sanctioned the reburial of Timothy Evans, who was exhumed from his felon's grave inside Pentonville prison. In due course Evans was granted a posthumous free pardon in October 1966. He was the first of many who have since been granted posthumous pardons.

In July 1964, while the last two to hang were in the condemned cell awaiting their fate, Ronald Cooper committed murder during the course of theft in Barking. When Cooper was sentenced to death at the Old Bailey in December, he knew that he would not hang. The last death sentence passed in Great Britain was by Mr Justice Havers at Leeds Assizes on 1 November 1965, when David Stephen Chapman was convicted of capital murder at Scarborough.

A week later, on 8 November 1965, the Murder (Abolition of Death Penalty) Act was passed, which effectively abolished capital punishment but provided for another vote on it 'within five years'. High treason, piracy with violence and arson in the Royal Dockyards remained capital crimes.

A vote in the autumn of 1969 rubber-stamped the permanent abolition of the death penalty in Great Britain, and a similar vote in 1973 abolished it in Northern Ireland. There have been numerous attempts to restore the death penalty – usually after a controversial case has hit the headlines. The first major public clamouring for restoration came as early as 1966 when the Moors Murders and Shepherd's Bush police murders both hit the headlines. All failed, none going closer than in 1983, when a House of Commons vote narrowly went against reinstatement, despite early polls showing it would go in favour. In February 1994, a narrow majority of fewer than two hundred votes defeated a proposal to reintroduce the death penalty for the murder of a police officer on duty.

The last working gallows – kept oiled and ready at Wandsworth Gaol in south London – was dismantled in 1992, in the week that the last death sentence was pronounced in the Isle of Man. Despite reports to the contrary in the press, the Queen did not commute the sentence. The Manx Appeal Court ordered a retrial, carried out in 1994, and, by the time the jury came to the same conclusion as at the first trial, hanging had been removed from the Isle of Man Criminal Code. The new sentence was therefore life in prison.

In early 1998 the death penalty was abolished for crimes committed under military jurisdiction. On 20 May of that year, on a free vote during a debate on the

Human Rights Bill, MPs decided by a large majority (294 to 136) to adopt provisions of the European Convention on Human Rights outlawing capital punishment for murder except 'in times of war or imminent threat of war'. The Bill incorporates the European Convention on Human Rights into British law. On 31 July 1998, high treason and piracy with violence ceased to be capital crimes.

On 27 January 1999 Labour Home Secretary Jack Straw formally signed the 6th Protocol of the European Convention of Human Rights in Strasbourg, on behalf of the British government. This formally abolished the death penalty in the United Kingdom.

Appendix

Date of Execution	Name of Prisoner	Age at Execution	Prison	Hangman & Assistant(s)
1900				
January 9	Louisa MASSET	36	NEWGATE	JB/WWk
March 6	Ada Chard WILLIAMS	24	NEWGATE	JB/WB
April 10	Patrick DUNPHY	34	WATERFORD	TS
May 22	Henry GROVE	26	NEWGATE	JB
July 17	Alfred HIGHFIELD	21	NEWGATE	JB/WB
August 14	William IRWIN	59	NEWGATE	JB
August 16	Charles BACKHOUSE	23	LEEDS	JB/
August 16	Thomas MELLOR	29	LEEDS	/WB
August 21	William L'ACY	29	CARDIFF	JB
August 28	Charles BLEWITT	33	LEEDS	JB/WB
October 2	John PARR	19	NEWGATE	JB/WB
October 3	William BURRETT	35	CHELMSFORD	JB/WB
December 4	Joseph HOLDEN	57	MANCHESTER	JB/WB
December 12	John BOWES	50	DURHAM	JB/WB
December 27	James BERGIN	28	LIVERPOOL	JB/WB

Executioners	Assistants
James Billington	Thomas Billington
Thomas Scott	William Billington
	William Warbrick

The hangmen and assistants are listed in alphabetical order.

Date of Execution	Name of Prisoner	Age at Execution	Prison	Hangman & Assistant(s)
1901				
January 11	Thomas CADOGEN		CORK	JB/TB
January 11	William WOODS	58	BELFAST	TS/Sm
February 19	Sampson SALMON	29	NEWGATE	JB
March 7	John TOOLE	62	DUBLIN	TS/BB
March 19	George PARKER	23	WANDSWORTH	JB/WB
March 21	Herbert BENNETT	21	NORWICH	JB/TB

Date of Execution	Name of Prisoner	Age at Execution	Prison	Hangman & Assistant(s)
April 2	Joseph SHUFFLEBOTTOM	38	STAFFORD	JB/WB
July 9	Valeri GIOVANNI	31	BODMIN	JB/WB
July 30	Charles WATKINS	34	MAIDSTONE	JB/TB
August 13	Ernest WICKHAM	29	WANDSWORTH	JB/WB
August 20	John JOYCE	36	BIRMINGHAM	JB/WB
November 19	Marcel FAUGERON	23	NEWGATE	JB/HP
December 3	Patrick McKENNA	53	MANCHESTER	JB/HP
December 7	John MILLER	67	NEWCASTLE	WB/TB[1]
December 7	John R MILLER	37	NEWCASTLE	/JE
December 10	John THOMPSON	38	DURHAM	WB/TB
December 13	Alick CLAYDON	43	NORTHAMPTON	WB/TB
December 24	John HARRISON	31	LIVERPOOL	WB/TB

Executioners	Assistants
James Billington	Thomas Billington
William Billington	Bartholomew Binns
Thomas Scott	John Ellis
	Henry Pierrepoint
	Smyth

1902				
March 18	Harold APTED	20	MAIDSTONE	WB/JnB
March 18	Richard WIGLEY	25	SHREWSBURY	HP/JE
March 25	Arthur RICHARDSON	25	HULL	WB/JnB
April 23	Thomas KEELEY	35	GALWAY	WB/JnB
April 29	Charles EARL	56	WANDSWORTH	WB/HP
May 6	George WOOLFE	21	NEWGATE	WB/JE
May 20	Thomas MARSLAND	21	LIVERPOOL	WB/JnB
July 15	Samuel MIDDLETON	46	WORCESTER	WB/none
July 22	William CHURCHER	35	WINCHESTER	WB/none
July 30	John BEDFORD	41	DERBY	WB/HP
August 12	William LANE	47	STAFFORD	WB/JnB
August 13	George HIBBS	40	WANDSWORTH	WB/HP
September 30	John MacDONALD	23	PENTONVILLE	WB/HP
November 11	Henry WILLIAMS	32	PENTONVILLE	WB/HP
November 12	Patrick LEGGETT	30	GLASGOW	WB
December 2	Henry McWIGGINS	29	MANCHESTER	WB/HP
December 4	William CHAMBERS	47	BEDFORD	WB/JnB
December 9	Thomas F BARROW	49	PENTONVILLE	WB/JnB[2]
December 12	Jeremiah CALLAGHAN	42	USK	WB/JnB
December 16	William BROWN	42	WANDSWORTH	HP/JE
December 16	Thomas NICHOLSON	24	DURHAM	WB/
December 16	Samuel WALTON	31	DURHAM	/JnB
December 23	William BOLTON	44	HULL	WB/JnB
December 30	George PLACE	28	WARWICK	HP/JE
December 30	James DOCHERTY	65	SLIGO	WB/none

Executioners	Assistants
William Billington	John Billington
Henry Pierrepoint	John Ellis

---

1 Although the executions took place on the same day the men were hanged in two separate executions.

2 Henry Pierrepoint also claims to have assisted on this execution and notes drop details in his diary.

Appendix

Date of Execution	Name of Prisoner	Age at Execution	Prison	Hangman & Assistant(s)
1903				
January 7	Joseph TAYLOR	25	KILKENNY	WB/none
January 9	Mary DALY	40	TULLAMORE	WB/none
February 3	Amelia SACH	29	HOLLOWAY	WB/JnB
February 3	Annie WALTERS	54	HOLLOWAY	/HP
February 17	William HUGHES	42	RUTHIN	WB/JnB
March 3	Edgar EDWARDS	44	WANDSWORTH	WB/HP
March 10	Samuel SMITH	45	LINCOLN	WB/JnB
April 7	George CHAPMAN	37	WANDSWORTH	WB/JnB
May 12	William HUDSON	26	MANCHESTER	WB/HP
June 2	Gustav RAU	28	LIVERPOOL	WB/
June 2	Willem SCHMIDT	30	LIVERPOOL	/JnB
July 7	Charles HOWELL	30	CHELMSFORD	WB/JE
July 14	Samuel DOUGAL	57	CHELMSFORD	WB/JE
July 21	Thomas PORTER	29	LEICESTER	WB/
July 21	Thomas PRESTON	24	LEICESTER	/JnB
July 28	Leonard PATCHETT	26	LINCOLN	WB/JnB
August 11	William TUFFIN	23	WANDSWORTH	HP/JE
November 10	Charles SLOWE	29	PENTONVILLE	WB/JnB
November 17	Edward PALMER	24	DEVIZES	WB/HP
December 1	Bernard WHITE	21	CHELMSFORD	WB/JnB
December 2	Charles WHITTAKER	43	MANCHESTER	JnB/JE
December 8	James DUFFY	46	DURHAM	WB/JnB
December 15	William HAYWOOD	61	HEREFORD	HP/JE
December 16	William BROWN	27	WINCHESTER	WB/
December 16	Thomas COWDREY	36	WINCHESTER	/JnB
December 22	Charles ASHTON	19	HULL	WB/JnB
December 29	Henry STARR	31	LIVERPOOL	WB/HP
December 29	John GALLAGHER	30	LEEDS	JnB/
December 29	Emily SWANN	42	LEEDS	/JE

Executioners
John Billington
William Billington
Henry Pierrepoint

Assistants
John Ellis

Date of Execution	Name of Prisoner	Age at Execution	Prison	Hangman & Assistant(s)
1904				
January 5	Joseph MORAN	25	LONDONDERRY	WB/none
March 9	Sydney SMITH	23	GLOUCESTER	WB/JnB
March 29	James CLARKSON	19	LEEDS	WB/HP
March 29	Henry JONES	50	STAFFORD	JnB/JE
April 5	Charles DYER	27	BIRMINGHAM	WB/JnB
April 14	James CAMPION	37	KILKENNY	WB/none
April 15	John KELLY	43	KILKENNY	WB/none
May 31	William KIRWAN	39	LIVERPOOL	WB/
May 31	Pong LUN	43	LIVERPOOL	/HP
July 12	John SULLIVAN	40	PENTONVILLE	WB/JnB
July 13	Samuel ROWLEDGE	37	NORTHAMPTON	WB/HP
July 26	Thomas GUNNING	48	GLASGOW	WB/JnB
August 2	George BREEZE	21	DURHAM	WB/JE
August 16	Samuel HOLDEN	52	BIRMINGHAM	WB/JE
August 16	John KAY	52	LEEDS	JnB/HP

Date of Execution	Name of Prisoner	Age at Execution	Prison	Hangman & Assistant(s)
December 13	Conrad DONOVAN	34	PENTONVILLE	WB/
December 13	Charles WADE	22	PENTONVILLE	/HP
December 20	Edmund HALL	49	LEEDS	JnB/HP
December 21	Eric LANGE	30	CARDIFF	JnB/HP
December 22	Joseph FEE	23	ARMAGH	HP/none
December 28	Arthur JEFFRIES	44	LEEDS	JnB/HP

Executioners	Assistants
Henry Pierrepoint	John Ellis
John Billington	
William Billington	

1905

February 28	Edward HARRISON	62	WANDSWORTH	JnB/HP
March 29	John HUTCHINSON	29	NOTTINGHAM	JnB/JE
April 25	John FOSTER	50	CORK	WB/JE
April 26	Albert BRIDGEMAN	22	PENTONVILLE	JnB/HP
May 23	Albert STRATTON	20	WANDSWORTH	JnB/HP
May 23	Alfred STRATTON	23	WANDSWORTH	/JE
June 20	Alfred HEAL	29	WANDSWORTH	JnB/JE
August 1	Ferat BENALI	19	MAIDSTONE	HP/JE
August 9	William HANCOCKS	35	KNUTSFORD	JnB/HP
August 15	Thomas TATTERSALL	31	LEEDS	JnB/WWk[3]
August 15	Arthur DEVERAUX	45	PENTONVILLE	HP/JE
November 7	William BUTLER	50	PENTONVILLE	HP/JE
November 14	Pasha LIFFEY	20	GLASGOW	HP/none
December 5	William YARNOLD	50	WORCESTER	HP/JE
December 6	Henry PARKINS	40	NEWCASTLE	HP/JE
December 20	Samuel CURTIS	60	MAIDSTONE	HP/WF
December 27	Frederick EDGE	23	STAFFORD	HP/JE
December 28	George SMITH	50	LEEDS	HP/JE
December 29	John SILK	31	DERBY	HP/JE

Executioners	Assistants
Henry Pierrepoint	John Ellis
John Billington	William C. Fry
William Billington	William Warbrick

1906

February 27	John GRIFFITHS	19	MANCHESTER	HP/JE
April 10	Henry WALTERS	38	WAKEFIELD	HP/TWP
August 7	Edward GLYNN	26	NOTTINGHAM	HP/WW
August 9	Thomas MOUNCER	25	WAKEFIELD	HP/TWP
November 13	Frederick REYNOLDS	23	WANDSWORTH	HP/JE
November 27	Edward HARTIGAN	58	KNUTSFORD	HP/WW
December 4	Richard BUCKHAM	20	CHELMSFORD	HP/none
December 27	Walter MARSH	39	DERBY	HP/JE

Executioners	Assistants
Henry Pierrepoint	John Ellis
	Thomas W. Pierrepoint
	William Willis

---

3 John Billington fell through trap doors and received injuries which later led to his early death.

Date of Execution	Name of Prisoner	Age at Execution	Prison	Hangman & Assistant(s)
1907				
January 1	John DAVIES	53	WARWICK	JE/WW
February 19	Tomas CONNAN	29	ST HELIER	HP /none
March 26	Joseph JONES	60	STAFFORD	HP/WW
April 2	Edwin MOORE	33	WARWICK	JE/WW
July 16	William SLACK	47	DERBY	HP/JE
August 7	Charles PATTERSON	37	LIVERPOOL	HP/TWP
August 13	Richard BRINKLEY	53	WANDSWORTH	HP/JE
August 14	Rhoda WILLIS	37	CARDIFF	HP/TWP
November 5	William AUSTIN	31	READING	HP/TWP
November 20	William DUDDLES	47	LINCOLN	HP/TWP
December 13	George STILLS	30	CARDIFF	HP/TWP

Executioners	Assistants
Henry Pierrepoint	John Ellis
	William Willis

Date of Execution	Name of Prisoner	Age at Execution	Prison	Hangman & Assistant(s)
1908				
March 5	Joseph HUME	25	INVERNESS	HP/none
March 24	William LAWMAN	35	DURHAM	HP/
March 24	Joseph NOBLE	48	DURHAM	/TWP
May 12	John RAMSBOTTOM	24	MANCHESTER	HP/JE
July 28	Fred BALLINGTON	41	MANCHESTER	HP/WW
August 4	Thomas SIDDLE	29	HULL	HP/JE
August 5	Matthew DODDS	43	DURHAM	HP/TWP
August 19	Edward JOHNSTONE	32	PERTH	JE/WW
August 20	John BERRYMAN	55	LONDONDERRY	HP/TWP
November 12	James PHIPPS	21	KNUTSFORD	HP/TWP
December 2	James NICHOLLS	35	NORWICH	HP/TWP
December 3	John ELLWOOD	43	LEEDS	HP/TWP
December 8	William BOULDREY	41	MAIDSTONE	HP/WW
December 15	Henry PARKER	32	WARWICK	HP/JE
December 30	Noah COLLINS	24	CARDIFF	HP/JE

Executioners	Assistants
John Ellis	Thomas W. Pierrepoint
Henry Pierrepoint	William Willis

Date of Execution	Name of Prisoner	Age at Execution	Prison	Hangman & Assistant(s)
1909				
January 6	John MURPHY	21	PENTONVILLE	HP/WW
February 23	Jeremiah O'CONNOR	52	DURHAM	HP/WW
March 2	Ernest HUTCHINSON	24	WAKEFIELD	HP/TWP
March 12	Thomas MEADE	23	LEEDS	HP/JE
March 30	Edmund ELLIOTT	19	EXETER	JE/WW
March 30	See LEE	38	LIVERPOOL	HP/TWP
April 14	Joseph JONES	39	STAFFORD	HP/TWP
May 8	William FOY	25	SWANSEA	HP/JE
May 20	Marks REUBENS	22	PENTONVILLE	HP/
May 20	Morris REUBENS	23	PENTONVILLE	/TWP
July 3	John EDMUNDS	24	USK	HP/JE
July 6	Alexander EDMUNSTONE	23	PERTH	JE/WW[4]
July 9	Walter DAVIS	37	WAKEFIELD	HP/TWP

---

4 William Willis was present at the gaol but was taken ill in the evening prior to execution and was unable to officiate as assistant on the following morning.

Date of Execution	Name of Prisoner	Age at Execution	Prison	Hangman & Assistant(s)
July 20	William HAMPTON	23	BODMIN	HP/TWP
August 3	Mark SHAWCROSS	24	MANCHESTER	HP/TWP
August 10	Julius WAMMER	43	WANDSWORTH	HP/WW
August 17	Madar Dal DHINGRA	25	PENTONVILLE	HP/TWP
August 19	Richard JUSTIN	31	BELFAST	HP/JE
December 7	John FREEMAN	46	HULL	HP/JE
December 8	Abel ATHERTON	29	DURHAM	HP/WW
December 14	Samuel ATHERLEY	30	NOTTINGHAM	HP/TWP

Executioners	Assistants
John Ellis	Thomas W. Pierrepoint
Henry Pierrepoint	William Willis

1910

Date of Execution	Name of Prisoner	Age at Execution	Prison	Hangman & Assistant(s)
January 4	Joseph HEFFERMAN	27	DUBLIN	HP/TWP
February 15	William MURPHY	49	CAERNARVON	HP/WW
February 23	Joseph WREN	23	MANCHESTER	HP/JE
March 1	George PERRY	27	PENTONVILLE	HP/WW
March 24	William BUTLER	62	USK	HP/JE
May 25	Thomas JESSHOPE	32	WANDSWORTH	HP/WW
June 14	James HANCOCK	54	CAMBRIDGE	HP/TWP
July 12	Thomas CRAIG	26	DURHAM	HP/WW
July 14	Frederick FOREMAN	45	CHELMSFORD	HP/JE
August 9	John DICKMAN	45	NEWCASTLE	JE/WW
August 9	John COULSON	32	LEEDS	TWP/WWk
November 15	Thomas RAWCLIFFE	31	LANCASTER	JE/TWP
November 22	Henry THOMPSON	54	LIVERPOOL	JE/WW
November 23	Hawley CRIPPEN	48	PENTONVILLE	JE/WW
November 24	William BROOME	21	READING	JE/WW
December 21	Noah WOOLF	38	PENTONVILLE	JE/TWP
December 29	Henry ISON	45	LEEDS	TWP/WW

Executioners	Assistants
John Ellis	William Warbrick
Henry Pierrepoint	William Willis
Thomas W. Pierrepoint	

1911

Date of Execution	Name of Prisoner	Age at Execution	Prison	Hangman & Assistant(s)
January 4	William SCANLAN	43	CORK	JE/WW
January 31	George NEWTON	19	CHELMSFORD	JE/WC
May 9	Thomas SEYMOUR	64	LIVERPOOL	JE/TWP
May 24	Michael COLLINS	30	PENTONVILLE	JE/TWP
June 20	Arthur GARROD	49	IPSWICH	JE/WW
July 19	William PALMER	50	LEICESTER	JE/GB
October 17	Francisco GODHINO	40	PENTONVILLE	JE/AL
October 17	Edward HILL	41	PENTONVILLE	/WC
November 15	Frederick THOMAS	38	WANDSWORTH	JE/TWP
December 6	Michael FAGAN	27	LIVERPOOL	JE/WW
December 12	Walter MARTYN	23	MANCHESTER	JE/
December 12	John TARKENTER	41	MANCHESTER	/GB
December 14	Henry PHILLIPS	44	SWANSEA	JE/WW
December 15	Joseph FLETCHER	40	LIVERPOOL	JE/GB

Date of Execution	Name of Prisoner	Age at Execution	Prison	Hangman & Assistant(s)
December 19	George PARKER	26	MAIDSTONE	JE/AL[5]
December 21	Charles COLEMAN	31	ST ALBANS	JE/WW
December 28	George LOAKE	64	STAFFORD	TWP/WW

Executioners	Assistants
John Ellis	George Brown
Thomas W. Pierrepoint	William Conduit
	Albert Lumb
	William Willis

1912

Date of Execution	Name of Prisoner	Age at Execution	Prison	Hangman & Assistant(s)
March 6	Myer ABRAMOVICH	22	PENTONVILLE	JE/AL
March 19	John WILLIAMS	38	KNUTSFORD	JE/AL
April 18	Frederick SEDDON	40	PENTONVILLE	JE/TWP
July 23	Arthur BIRKETT	22	MANCHESTER	JE/AL
October 1	Sargent PHILP	33	WANDSWORTH	JE/TWP
November 5	Robert GALLOWAY	27	NORWICH	TWP/GB
November 26	Gilbert SMITH	35	GLOUCESTER	TWP/AL
December 10	William BEAL	20	CHELMSFORD	JE/WW
December 18	Alfred LAWRENCE	32	MAIDSTONE	JE/WW
December 20	William GALBRAITH	25	WAKEFIELD	TWP/WW

Executioners	Assistants
John Ellis	George Brown
Thomas W. Pierrepoint	Albert Lumb
	William Willis

1913

Date of Execution	Name of Prisoner	Age at Execution	Prison	Hangman & Assistant(s)
January 7	Albert RUMENS	44	LEWES	JE/WW
January 29	John WILLIAMS	29	LEWES	JE/WW
January 29	Edward HOPWOOD	45	PENTONVILLE	TWP/AL
February 4	Eric SEDGEWICK	27	READING	JE/GB
February 25	George CUNLIFFE	28	EXETER	JE/GB
March 19	Edward PALMER	22	BRISTOL	TWP/GB
April 23	Walter SYKES	24	WAKEFIELD	TWP/AL
June 24	William BURTON	29	DORCHESTER	TWP/GB
July 8	Henry LONGDEN	52	PENTONVILLE	JE/WW
July 9	Thomas FLETCHER	28	WORCESTER	JE/TWP
July 22	John AMOS	35	NEWCASTLE	TWP/WW
August 13	Frank GREENING	34	BIRMINGHAM	TWP/GB
August 13	James RYDER	47	MANCHESTER	JE/
August 14	Hugh McCLAREN	29	CARDIFF	JE/WW
October 2	Patrick HIGGINS	38	EDINBURGH	JE/WW
November 4	Frederick SEEKINGS	35	CAMBRIDGE	JE/TWP
November 26	Augustus PENNY	30	WINCHESTER	JE/AL
November 27	Frederick ROBERTSON	26	PENTONVILLE	JE/WW
December 17	Ernest KELLY	20	MANCHESTER	JE/GB
December 31	George LAW	34	WAKEFIELD	TWP/AL

---

5 Lumb's name is noted on the LPC4 sheet – but crossed out and no comments made as to his actual conduct. This would suggest he played no part in the actual execution.

Date of Execution	Name of Prisoner	Age at Execution	Prison	Hangman & Assistant(s)
Executioners		Assistants		
John Ellis		George Brown		
Thomas W. Pierrepoint		Albert Lumb		
		William Willis		
1914				
February 26	George BALL	22	LIVERPOOL	JE/WW
March 10	Josiah DAVIES	53	STAFFORD	JE/GB
March 12	James HONEYANDS	21	EXETER	JE/WW
March 24	Robert UPTON	50	DURHAM	JE/WW
March 25	Edgar BINDON	20	CARDIFF	JE/GB
May 14	JOSEPH SPOONER	42	LIVERPOOL	JE/WW
June 16	Walter WHITE	22	WINCHESTER	JE/TWP
July 28	Herbert BROOKER	32	LEWES	JE/TWP
August 11	Percy CLIFFORD	32	LEWES	JE/TWP
November 4	Charles FREMD	71	CHELMSFORD	JE/
November 10	John EAYRES	59	NORTHAMPTON	JE/WW
November 10	Henry QUARTLEY	55	SHEPTON MALLET	TWP/GB
November 12	Arnold WARREN	32	LEICESTER	JE/WW
December 23	George ANDERSON	59	ST ALBANS	JE/GB
Executioners		Assistants		
John Ellis		George Brown		
Thomas W. Pierrepoint		William Willis		
1915				
July 15	Robert ROSENTHAL	23	WANDSWORTH	TWP/RB
August 10	Walter MARRIOT	24	WAKEFIELD	TWP/WW
August 11	Frank STEELE	31	DURHAM	JE/RB
August 13	George SMITH	43	MAIDSTONE	JE/ET
August 17	George MARSHALL	43	WANDSWORTH	JE/GB
November 16	William REEVE	42	BEDFORD	JE/none[6]
December 1	Young HILL	28	LIVERPOOL	JE/
December 1	John THORNLEY	26	LIVERPOOL	/WW
December 22	Harry THOMPSON	55	WAKEFIELD	TWP/ET
December 29	John McCARTNEY	40	WAKEFIELD	TWP/RB
Executioners		Assistants		
John Ellis		Robert O. Baxter		
Thomas W. Pierrepoint		George Brown		
		Edward Taylor		
		William Willis		
1916				
January 1	Lee KUN	27	PENTONVILLE	JE/GB
March 8	Frederick HOLMES	44	MANCHESTER	JE/ET
March 29	Reginald HASLAM	25	MANCHESTER	JE/ET
August 3	Roger CASEMENT	51	PENTONVILLE	JE/RB
August 16	William BUTLER	39	BIRMINGHAM	JE/ET
September 6	Daniel SULLIVAN	36	SWANSEA	JE/GB
December 12	Fred BROOKS	28	EXETER	JE/WW

6 No assistant engaged due to new guidelines from prison commissioners. This new ruling was quickly revised and an assistant employed at subsequent executions.

Appendix

Date of Execution	Name of Prisoner	Age at Execution	Prison	Hangman & Assistant(s)
December 19	James HARGREAVES	54	MANCHESTER	JE/WW
December 20	Joseph DEANS	44	DURHAM	JE/GB

Executioners
John Ellis

Assistants
Robert O. Baxter
George Brown
Thomas W. Pierrepoint
Edwards Taylor
William Willis

1917

Date of Execution	Name of Prisoner	Age at Execution	Prison	Hangman & Assistant(s)
March 21	Thomas CLINTON	28	MANCHESTER	JE/
March 27	John THOMPSON	43	LEEDS	TWP/WW
March 29	Leo O'DONNELL	22	WINCHESTER	JE/RB
April 10	Alexanda BAKERLIS	43	CARDIFF	JE/ET
April 17	William ROBINSON	26	PENTONVILLE	JE/RB
April 18	Robert GADSBY	55	LEEDS	TWP/RB
May 16	Thomas McGUINESS	25	GLASGOW	JE/RB
August 16	William HODGSON	34	LIVERPOOL	JE/ET
December 18	William CAVANAGH	29	NEWCASTLE	TWP/RB
December 19	Thomas COX	59	SHREWSBURY	JE/WW

Executioners
John Ellis
Thomas W. Pierrepoint

Assistants
Robert O. Baxter
Edwards Taylor
William Willis

1918

Date of Execution	Name of Prisoner	Age at Execution	Prison	Hangman & Assistant(s)
February 12	Arthur DE STAMIR	25	WANDSWORTH	JE/GB
February 21	Joseph JONES	26	WANDSWORTH	JE/WW
March 2	Louis VOISON	42	PENTONVILLE	JE/ET
March 5	Verney ASSER	30	SHEPTON MALLET	JE/WW
April 9	Louis Van Der KERK-HOVE	32	BIRMINGHAM	JE/GB
December 17	William ROONEY	51	MANCHESTER	JE/
December 17	John WALSH	35	LEEDS	TWP/WW

Executioners
John Ellis
Thomas W. Pierrepoint

Assistants
Robert O. Baxter
George Brown
Edwards Taylor
William Willis

1919

Date of Execution	Name of Prisoner	Age at Execution	Prison	Hangman & Assistant(s)
January 7	Benjamin BENSON	41	LEEDS	TWP/RB
January 8	Percy BARRETT	19	LEEDS	TWP/
January 8	George CALDWELL	22	LEEDS	/RB
February 19	Joseph ROSE	25	OXFORD	JE/ET
July 10	Henry PERRY	37	PENTONVILLE	JE/WW
July 22	John CROSSLAND	33	LIVERPOOL	JE/RB
July 31	Thomas FOSTER	46	PENTONVILLE	JE/ET
August 8	Henry GASKIN	25	BIRMINGHAM	JE/WW
October 7	Frank WARREN	41	PENTONVILLE	JE/GB

Date of Execution	Name of Prisoner	Age at Execution	Prison	Hangman & Assistant(s)
November 11	James ADAMS	31	GLASGOW	JE/RB
November 26	Ernest SCOTT	28	NEWCASTLE	JE/RB[7]
November 26	Ambrose QUINN	28	NEWCASTLE	JE/RB
December 3	Djang Djang SUNG	23	WORCESTER	JE/RB

Executioners		Assistants	
John Ellis		Robert O. Baxter	
Thomas W. Pierrepoint		George Brown	
		Edwards Taylor	
		William Willis	

1920

Date of Execution	Name of Prisoner	Age at Execution	Prison	Hangman & Assistant(s)
January 6	David CAPLAN	42	MANCHESTER	JE/RB
January 6	Hyman PURDOVICH	39	MANCHESTER	/ET
January 6	Louis MASSEY	29	LEEDS	TWP/WW
March 10	William WRIGHT	39	LINCOLN	TWP/WW
March 23	William HALL	66	DURHAM	JE/RB
April 13	Frederick HOLT	31	MANCHESTER	JE/WW
April 14	Thomas CALER	23	CARDIFF	JE/WW
April 16	Miles McHUGH	32	LEEDS	TWP/ET
May 6	Thomas WILSON	45	LEEDS	TWP/RB
May 11	Herbert SALISBURY	35	LIVERPOOL	JE/ET
May 11	William WADDINGTON	34	LIVERPOOL	/RB
May 26	Albert FRASER	24	GLASGOW	JE/
May 26	James ROLLINS	23	GLASGOW	/WW
June 16	Frederick STOREY	42	IPSWICH	JE/RB
June 22	William ALDRED	54	MANCHESTER	JE/WW
July 27	Arthur GOSLETT	44	PENTONVILLE	JE/ET
August 11	James ELLOR	36	LIVERPOOL	JE/ET
November 1	Kevin BARRY	18	DUBLIN	JE/WW
November 30	James RILEY	51	DURHAM	TWP/ET
November 30	Cyril SAUNDERS	21	EXETER	JE/WW
December 30	Edwin SOWERBY	28	LEEDS	TWP/ET[8]
December 30	Marks GOODMARCHER	58	PENTONVILLE	WW/RB
December 30	Samuel WESTWOOD	26	BIRMINGHAM	JE/none[9]
December 31	Charles COLCLOUGH	45	MANCHESTER	JE/WW

Executioners		Assistants	
John Ellis		Robert O. Baxter	
Thomas W. Pierrepoint		Edward Taylor	
William Willis			

1921

Date of Execution	Name of Prisoner	Age at Execution	Prison	Hangman & Assistant(s)
January 7	George LEVER	51	MAIDSTONE	TWP/RB
February 4	Jack FIELD	19	WANDSWORTH	TP/RB
February 4	William GRAY	29	WANDSWORTH	/WW
March 2	George BAILEY	33	OXFORD	JE/RB
March 14	Thomas WHELAN	25	DUBLIN	JE/
March 14	Patrick MORAN	22	DUBLIN	/

---

7 As at the previous double execution at Newcastle the two men were hanged separately.

8 The only occasion in modern times when three executioners officiated at different prisons on the same day.

9 In an unusual set of circumstances, three executions were scheduled for the same day. With only five names remaining on the list, Ellis as the most experienced executioner was entrusted with carrying out the job with no assistant.

Appendix

Date of Execution	Name of Prisoner	Age at Execution	Prison	Hangman & Assistant(s)
March 14	Patrick DOYLE	25	DUBLIN	/
March 14	Bernard RYAN	28	DUBLIN	/
March 14	Thomas BRYAN	23	DUBLIN	/
March 14	Frank FLOOD	19	DUBLIN	/WW
April 5	Frederick QUARMBY	47	MANCHESTER	JE/WW
April 25	Thomas TRAYNOR	39	DUBLIN	JE/WW
May 24	Thomas WILSON	43	MANCHESTER	JE/ET
June 7	Patrick MAHER	32	DUBLIN	TWP/
June 7	Edmund FOLEY	23	DUBLIN	/
June 7	William MITCHELL		DUBLIN	/RB
August 16	Lester HAMILTON	25	CARDIFF	JE/SM[10]
December 22	Edward O'CONNOR	43	BIRMINGHAM	JE/RW

Executioners	Assistants
John Ellis	Robert O. Baxter
Thomas W. Pierrepoint	Seth Mills
William Willis	Edward Taylor
	Robert Wilson

1922

Date of Execution	Name of Prisoner	Age at Execution	Prison	Hangman & Assistant(s)
February 21	William HARKNESS	31	GLASGOW	JE/WW
March 21	James WILLIAMSON	37	DURHAM	TWP/WW
March 23	William SULLIVAN	41	USK	JE/TMP
March 24	Edward BLACK	36	EXETER	JE/SM
April 7	Percy ATKINS	29	NOTTINGHAM	JE/RB
April 11	Frederick KEELING	54	PENTONVILLE	JE/SM
April 18	Edmund TONBRIDGE	38	PENTONVILLE	JE/RB
May 30	Hyram THOMPSON	52	MANCHESTER	JE/WW
May 31	Herbert ARMSTRONG	53	GLOUCESTER	JE/ET
June 7	Henry JACOBY	18	PENTONVILLE	JE/TMP
August 10	Reginald DUNN	25	WANDSWORTH	JE/ET
August 10	Joseph O'SULLIVAN	24	WANDSWORTH	/SM
August 11	Elijah POUTNEY	48	BIRMINGHAM	JE/RB
August 17	Simon McGEOWN	30	BELFAST	JE/WW
August 19	Thomas ALLAWAY	36	WINCHESTER	JE/ET
September 5	William YELDHAM	23	PENTONVILLE	JE/WW
December 13	George ROBINSON	27	LINCOLN	TWP/
December 13	Frank FOWLER	35	LINCOLN	/RB
December 19	William RIDER	40	BIRMINGHAM	JE/WW

Executioners	Assistants
John Ellis	Robert O. Baxter
Thomas W. Pierrepoint	Seth Mills
William Willis	Thomas M. Phillips
	Edward Taylor
	Robert Wilson

1923

Date of Execution	Name of Prisoner	Age at Execution	Prison	Hangman & Assistant(s)
January 3	George EDISBURY	44	MANCHESTER	JE/RW
January 5	Lee DOON	27	LEEDS	TWP/TMP
January 9	Frederick BYWATERS	20	PENTONVILLE	WW/SM
January 9	Edith THOMPSON	28	HOLLOWAY	JE/TMP/RB

10 Phillips was originally offered the engagement.

Date of Execution	Name of Prisoner	Age at Execution	Prison	Hangman & Assistant(s)
February 8	William ROONEY	40	LONDONDERRY	WW/
March 28	George PERRY	50	MANCHESTER	JE/
April 3	Daniel CASSIDY	60	DURHAM	TWP/RW
April 5	Bernard POMROY	25	PENTONVILLE	JE/ET
April 10	Frederick WOOD	29	LIVERPOOL	JE/TMP
June 11	John SAVAGE	54	EDINBURGH	JE/WW
July 4	Rowland DUCK	25	PENTONVILLE	JE/RW
July 24	William GRIFFITHS	57	SHREWSBURY	JE/SM
August 8	Albert BURROWS	62	NOTTINGHAM	JE/WW
August 8	Hassan MUHAMED	33	DURHAM	TWP/RW
October 10	Susan NEWELL	30	GLASGOW	JE/WW
October 30	Phillip MURRAY	31	EDINBURGH	JE/WW
November 1	Frederick JESSE	26	WANDSWORTH	JE/RB
November 29	William DOWNES	25	DUBLIN	TWP/
December 12	Thomas DELANEY	38	DUBLIN	TWP/
December 12	Thomas McDONAGH	42	DUBLIN	/JR
December 15	Peter HYNES	40	DUBLIN	TWP/JR
December 28	John EASTWOOD	39	LEEDS	JE/SM

Executioners
John Ellis
Thomas W. Pierrepoint
William Willis

Assistants
Robert O. Baxter
Seth Mills
Thomas M. Phillips
'Joseph Robinson'
Edward Taylor
Robert Wilson

1924

January 2	Matthew NUNN	24	DURHAM	TWP/TMP
March 13	Jeremiah GAFFNEY	23	DUBLIN	TWP/JR
April 8	Francis BOOKER	28	MANCHESTER	WW/RB
May 8	Michael PRATLEY	30	BELFAST	WW/RW
June 18	William WARDELL	47	LEEDS	TWP/WW
July 30	Abraham GOLDENBERG	22	WINCHESTER	TWP/WW
August 1	Felix McMULLEN	26	DUBLIN	TWP/JR
August 12	Jean-Pierre VAQUIER	45	WANDSWORTH	RB/TMP/WW
August 13	John HORNER	23	MANCHESTER	WW/RW
September 3	Patrick MAHON	44	WANDSWORTH	TWP/TMP
November 27	Frederick SOUTHGATE	52	IPSWICH	RB/RW
December 9	William SMITH	26	HULL	TWP/RB
December 17	Arthur SIMS	25	NOTTINGHAM	TWP/RB

Executioners
Robert O. Baxter
Thomas W. Pierrepoint
William Willis

Assistants
Thomas M. Phillips
'Joseph Robinson'
Edward Taylor
Robert Wilson

1925

February 24	William BIGNALL	32	SHEPTON MALLET	TWP/RB
March 31	William BRESSINGTON	21	BRISTOL	TWP/TMP
April 2	George BARTON	59	PENTONVILLE	RB/RW
April 15	Henry GRAHAM	42	DURHAM	TWP/TMP
April 15	Thomas SHELTON	24	DURHAM	WW/RW

Appendix

Date of Execution	Name of Prisoner	Age at Execution	Prison	Hangman & Assistant(s)
April 22	John THORNE	22	WANDSWORTH	TWP/RW
May 26	Patrick POWER	41	MANCHESTER	WW/TMP
June 10	Hubert DALTON	39	HULL	TWP/RB
July 28	Cornelius O'LEARY	40	DUBLIN	TWP/JR
August 5	James WINSTANLEY	29	LIVERPOOL	WW/RW
August 5	Michael TALBOT	24	DUBLIN	TWP/
August 5	Annie WALSH	31	DUBLIN	/JR
August 11	James MAKIN	25	MANCHESTER	WW/RB
August 14	Arthur BISHOP	18	PENTONVILLE	RB/ET
August 14	William CRONIN	54	PENTONVILLE	RW/HP
September 3	Alfred BOSTOCK	25	LEEDS	TWP/RW
September 3	Wilfred FOWLER	23	LEEDS	/HP
September 4	Lawrence FOWLER	24	LEEDS	TWP/LM
September 24	John KEEN	22	GLASGOW	TWP/WW
November 12	Herbert BLOYE	27	NORWICH	RB/ET
December 15	Samuel JOHNSON	29	MANCHESTER	WW/TMP

Executioners
Robert O. Baxter
Thomas W. Pierrepoint
William Willis

Assistants
Lionel Mann
Thomas M. Phillips
Henry Pollard
'Joseph Robinson'
Edward Taylor
Robert Wilson

1926

Date of Execution	Name of Prisoner	Age at Execution	Prison	Hangman & Assistant(s)
January 5	John FISHER	58	BIRMINGHAM	WW/RW
January 7	Lorraine LAX	28	LEEDS	TWP/WW
February 17	Herbert BURROWS	22	GLOUCESTER	TWP/RB
March 2	John Ignatius LINCOLN	23	SHEPTON MALLET	TWP/LM
March 9	Henry THOMPSON	36	MAIDSTONE	TWP/WW
March 9	George THOMAS	26	CARDIFF	RB/TMP
March 16	William THORPE	45	MANCHESTER	WW/RW
March 23	Lock Ah TAM	54	LIVERPOOL	WW/HP
March 24	Eugene DEVERE	25	PENTONVILLE	RB/TMP
April 13	George SHARPES	20	BIRMINGHAM	WW/RB
June 24	Louie CALVERT	33	MANCHESTER	TWP/WW
July 27	Johannes MOMMERS	43	PENTONVILLE	RB/WW
July 15	James MYLES	22	DUBLIN	TWP/JR
August 10	James SMITH	23	DURHAM	TWP/TMP
August 12	Charles FINDEN	22	WINCHESTER	TWP/RB
November 2	Hassan SAMANDER	26	PENTONVILLE	RB/TMP
November 16	James LEAH	60	LIVERPOOL	TWP/LM
November 24	James McHUGH	31	DUBLIN	TWP/JR
December 3	Charles HOUGHTON	45	GLOUCESTER	TWP/RW
December 9	Henry McCABE	48	DUBLIN	TWP/JR

Executioners
Robert O. Baxter
Thomas W. Pierrepoint
William Willis

Assistants
Lionel Mann
Thomas M. Phillips
Henry Pollard
'Joseph Robinson'
Edward Taylor
Robert Wilson

Date of Execution	Name of Prisoner	Age at Execution	Prison	Hangman & Assistant(s)
1927				
January 5	William JONES	22	LEEDS	TWP/RB
March 29	James STRATTON	26	PENTONVILLE	RB/LM
April 27	William KNIGHTON	22	NOTTINGHAM	TWP/HP
August 3	Frederick FULLER	35	WANDSWORTH	RB/TMP
August 3	James MURPHY	29	WANDSWORTH	/LM/HP
August 12	John ROBINSON	36	PENTONVILLE	RB/RW
September 2	Arthur HARNETT	27	LEEDS	TWP/LM
December 6	William ROBERTSON	32	LIVERPOOL	TWP/TMP
December 29	William O'NEILL	19	DUBLIN	TWP/JR

Executioners	Assistants
Robert O. Baxter	Lionel Mann
Thomas W. Pierrepoint	Thomas M. Phillips
	Henry Pollard
	'Joseph Robinson'
	Robert Wilson

Date of Execution	Name of Prisoner	Age at Execution	Prison	Hangman & Assistant(s)
1928				
January 3	Frederick FIELDING	24	MANCHESTER	TWP/TMP
January 4	Bertram KIRBY	47	LINCOLN	TWP/HP
January 6	John DUNN	52	DURHAM	TWP/TMP
January 6	Sydney GOULTER	26	WANDSWORTH	RB/HP
January 7	Samuel CASE	27	LEEDS	TWP/HP
January 24	James McKAY	40	GLASGOW	RB/
January 27	Daniel DRISCOLL	34	CARDIFF	RB/TMP
January 27	Edward ROWLANDS	40	CARDIFF	RW/LM
January 31	James GILLON	30	WANDSWORTH	RB/TMP
January 31	James POWER	36	BIRMINGHAM	TWP/RW
April 10	George HAYWARD	32	NOTTINGHAM	TWP/HP
April 12	Frederick LOCK	39	WANDSWORTH	RB/LM
May 31	Frederick BROWNE	49	PENTONVILLE	RB/TMP
May 31	William KENNEDY	36	WANDSWORTH	TWP/RW
June 6	Frederick STEWART	28	PENTONVILLE	RB/HP
June 28	Walter BROOKS	48	MANCHESTER	TWP/LM
July 25	Albert ABSALOM	28	LIVERPOOL	TWP/HP
July 27	William MAYNARD	36	EXETER	TWP/TMP
August 3	George REYNOLDS	41	GLASGOW	RB/
August 8	William SMILEY	33	BELFAST	TWP/RB
August 10	Norman ELLIOTT	22	DURHAM	TWP/RW
August 13	Allen WALES	22	EDINBURGH	RB/HP
August 29	Gerard TOAL	18	DUBLIN	TWP/JR
November 20	William BENSON	25	WANDSWORTH	RB/LM
December 6	Chung Yi MIAO	28	MANCHESTER	TWP/HP
December 11	Trevor EDWARDS	20	SWANSEA	RB/AA

Executioners	Assistants
Robert O. Baxter	Alfred Allen
Thomas W. Pierrepoint	Lionel Mann
	Thomas M. Phillips
	Henry Pollard
	'Joseph Robinson'
	Frank Rowe
	Robert Wilson

Appendix

Date of Execution	Name of Prisoner	Age at Execution	Prison	Hangman & Assistant(s)
1929				
January 4	Charles CONLIN	22	DURHAM	TWP/FR
February 20	Frank HOLLINGTON	25	PENTONVILLE	RB/RW
February 27	William HOLMYARD	24	PENTONVILLE	RB/LM
March 12	Joseph CLARKE	21	LIVERPOOL	TWP/HP
April 4	George CARTLEDGE	31	MANCHESTER	TWP/RW
April 25	John COX	33	DUBLIN	TWP/JR
August 7	James JOHNSON	43	DURHAM	TWP/TMP
August 14	Arthur RAVENEY	24	LEEDS	TWP/RW
November 26	John MAGUIRE	43	LIVERPOOL	TWP/TMP

Executioners	Assistants
Robert O. Baxter	Alfred Allen
Thomas W. Pierrepoint	Lionel Mann
	Thomas M. Phillips
	Henry Pollard
	'Joseph Robinson'
	Frank Rowe
	Robert Wilson

Date of Execution	Name of Prisoner	Age at Execution	Prison	Hangman & Assistant(s)
1930				
April 8	Samuel CUSHNAN	26	BELFAST	TWP/RW
April 8	Sydney FOX	31	MAIDSTONE	RB/LM
April 22	William PODMORE	29	WINCHESTER	TWP/AA
June 11	Albert MARJERAM	23	WANDSWORTH	TWP/HP

Executioners	Assistants
Robert O. Baxter	Alfred Allen
Thomas W. Pierrepoint	Lionel Mann
	Thomas M. Phillips
	Henry Pollard
	Joseph Robinson
	Robert Wilson

Date of Execution	Name of Prisoner	Age at Execution	Prison	Hangman & Assistant(s)
1931				
January 3	Victor BETTS	21	BIRMINGHAM	TWP/AA
February 4	Frederick GILL	26	LEEDS	TWP/RW
March 10	Alfred ROUSE	36	BEDFORD	TWP/TMP
April 16	Francis LAND	41	MANCHESTER	TWP/AA
June 3	Alexander ANASTASSIOU	23	PENTONVILLE	RB/HP
July 31	Thomas DORNAN	46	BELFAST	TWP/RW
August 4	David O'SHEA	33	DUBLIN	TWP/JR
August 5	Oliver NEWMAN	61	PENTONVILLE	RB/LM
August 5	William SHELLEY	56	PENTONVILLE	RW/TMP
August 12	William CORBETT	32	CARDIFF	RB/HP
December 10	Henry SEYMOUR	52	OXFORD	TWP/AA
December 15	Solomon STEIN	21	MANCHESTER	TWP/TMP

Executioners	Assistants
Robert O. Baxter	Alfred Allen
Thomas W. Pierrepoint	Lionel Mann
	Thomas M. Phillips
	Henry Pollard
	'Joseph Robinson'
	Robert Wilson

Date of Execution	Name of Prisoner	Age at Execution	Prison	Hangman & Assistant(s)
1932				
January 13	Edward CULLENS	28	BELFAST	TWP/RW
February 3	George RICE	32	MANCHESTER	TWP/RW
February 23	William GODDARD	25	PENTONVILLE	RB/TMP
March 9	George POPLE	22	OXFORD	TWP/HP
April 27	George MICHAEL	49	HULL	TWP/HP[11]
April 28	Thomas RILEY	36	LEEDS	TWP/AA
April 28	John ROBERTS	27	LEEDS	RW/TMP
May 4	Maurice FREEDMAN	36	PENTONVILLE	RB/RW
May 18	Charles COWLE	18	MANCHESTER	TWP/AA
November 23	Ernest HUTCHINSON	42	OXFORD	AA/HP[12]
December 29	Patrick McDERMOTT	26	DUBLIN	TWP/AP

Executioners	Assistants
Alfred Allen	Stanley Cross
Robert O. Baxter	Thomas M. Phillips
Thomas W. Pierrepoint	Albert Pierrepoint
	Henry Pollard
	Robert Wilson

Date of Execution	Name of Prisoner	Age at Execution	Prison	Hangman & Assistant(s)
1933				
February 2	Jeremiah HANBURY	49	BIRMINGHAM	TWP/RW[13]
April 7	Harold COURTNEY	23	BELFAST	TWP/RW
June 8	Jack PUTTNAM	32	PENTONVILLE	RB/SC
June 20	Richard HETHERINGTON	36	LIVERPOOL	TWP/AP
July 25	Frederick MORSE	34	BRISTOL	TWP/TMP
August 10	Varnavas ANTORKA	31	PENTONVILLE	RB/HP
October 11	Robert KIRBY	26	PENTONVILLE	RB/RW
December 6	Ernest PARKER	25	DURHAM	TWP/AA
December 19	William BURTOFT	47	MANCHESTER	TWP/SC
December 28	Stanley HOBDAY	21	BIRMINGHAM	TWP/AA

Executioners	Assistants
Alfred Allen	Stanley Cross
Robert O. Baxter	Thomas M. Phillips
Thomas W. Pierrepoint	Albert Pierrepoint
	Henry Pollard
	Robert Wilson

Date of Execution	Name of Prisoner	Age at Execution	Prison	Hangman & Assistant(s)
1934				
January 3	Roy GREGORY	28	HULL	TWP/TMP
January 5	John FLEMING	32	DUBLIN	TWP/none
February 6	Ernest BROWN	35	LEEDS	TWP/RW
April 6	Lewis HAMILTON	25	LEEDS	TWP/AA
May 3	Reginald HINKS	32	BRISTOL	TWP/HP
May 4	Frederick PARKER	21	WANDSWORTH	TWP/TMP
May 4	Albert PROBERT	26	WANDSWORTH	/AP/SC[14]

---

11 Lionel Mann turned down the offer to officiate as assistant.
12 Stanley Cross present as trainee observer.
13 Albert Pierrepoint present as trainee observer.
14 Last execution witnessed by members of the press.

Date of Execution	Name of Prisoner	Age at Execution	Prison	Hangman & Assistant(s)
October 9	Harry TUFFNEY	36	PENTONVILLE	RB/AA
November 14	John STOCKWELL	19	PENTONVILLE	RB/RW
December 19	Ethel MAJOR	42	HULL	TWP/AP

Executioners	Assistants
Alfred Allen	Stanley Cross
Robert O. Baxter	Thomas M. Phillips
Thomas Pierrepoint	Henry Pollard
	Robert Wilson

1935

Date of Execution	Name of Prisoner	Age at Execution	Prison	Hangman & Assistant(s)
January 1	Frederick RUSHWORTH	29	LEEDS	TWP/SC
February 7	David BLAKE	24	LEEDS	TWP/AA
March 13	George HARVEY	37	PENTONVILLE	RB/HP
April 2	Leonard BRIGSTOCK	33	WANDSWORTH	RB/RW
April 16	Percy ANDERSON	21	WANDSWORTH	TWP/AA
May 9	John BAINBRIDGE	26	DURHAM	TWP/HP
May 30	John BRIDGE	25	MANCHESTER	TWP/TMP
June 25	Arthur FRANKLIN	44	GLOUCESTER	TWP/RW
July 16	George HAGUE	23	DURHAM	TWP/SC
July 10	Walter WORTHINGTON	56	BEDFORD	TWP/AP
October 29	Raymond BOUSQUET	30	WANDSWORTH	RB/TMP
October 30	Allan GRIERSON	27	PENTONVILLE	RB/HP

Executioners	Assistants
Alfred Allen	Stanley Cross
Robert O. Baxter	Thomas M. Phillips
Thomas W. Pierrepoint	Albert Pierrepoint
	Henry Pollard
	Robert Wilson

1936

Date of Execution	Name of Prisoner	Age at Execution	Prison	Hangman & Assistant(s)
April 16	Dorothea WADDINGHAM	36	BIRMINGHAM	TWP/AP
May 12	Buck RUXTON	37	MANCHESTER	TWP/RW
June 30	Frederick FIELD	32	WANDSWORTH	AA/SC
July 14	George BRYANT	38	WANDSWORTH	TWP/HP
July 15	Charlotte BRYANT	34	EXETER	TWP/TMP
August 5	Wallace JENDEN	58	WANDSWORTH	TWP/RW
December 16	Christopher JACKSON	24	DURHAM	TWP/AP

Executioners	Assistants
Alfred Allen	Stanley Cross
Thomas W. Pierrepoint	Thomas M. Phillips
	Albert Pierrepoint
	Henry Pollard
	Robert Wilson

1937

Date of Execution	Name of Prisoner	Age at Execution	Prison	Hangman & Assistant(s)
February 4	Max HASLAM	23	MANCHESTER	TWP/AP
February 10	Andrew BAGLEY	62	LEEDS	TWP/RW
June 17	John HORNICK	42	DUBLIN	TWP/AP
July 27	Philip DAVIS	30	EXETER	TWP/TMP

Date of Execution	Name of Prisoner	Age at Execution	Prison	Hangman & Assistant(s)
August 12	Horace BRUNT	32	MANCHESTER	TWP/SC
August 13	Leslie STONE	24	PENTONVILLE	TWP/AA
August 17	Frederick MURPHY	53	PENTONVILLE	AA/TMP
November 18	John ROGERS	22	PENTONVILLE	TWP/HP
December 7	Ernest MOSS	26	EXETER	TWP/AP
December 30	Frederick NODDER	43	LINCOLN	TWP/SC

Executioners	Assistants
Alfred Allen	Stanley Cross
Thomas W. Pierrepoint	Thomas M. Phillips
	Albert Pierrepoint
	Henry Pollard
	Robert Wilson

1938

March 8	Walter SMITH	34	NORWICH	TWP/TMP
April 20	Charles CALDWELL	49	MANCHESTER	TWP/AP
May 26	Robert HOOLHOUSE	21	DURHAM	TWP/
June 8	Jan MAHOMED	30	LIVERPOOL	TWP/AP[15]
July 12	Alfred RICHARDS	38	WANDSWORTH	TWP/AP
July 19	William GRAVES	38	WANDSWORTH	TWP/TMP
July 26	William PARKER	25	DURHAM	TWP/TMP
November 1	George BRAIN	27	WANDSWORTH	TWP/SC[16]

Executioners	Assistants
Thomas W. Pierrepoint	Stanley Cross
	Herbert Morris
	Thomas M. Phillips
	Albert Pierrepoint
	Alexander Riley
	Robert Wilson

1939

January 7	Dermot SMYTH	35	DUBLIN	TWP/AP
February 8	John DAYMOND	19	DURHAM	TWP/RW[17]
March 25	Harry ARMSTRONG	38	WANDSWORTH	TMP/AP
March 29	William BUTLER	29	WANDSWORTH	TWP/TMP
June 7	Ralph SMITH	41	GLOUCESTER	TWP/AP
October 10	Leonard HUCKER	30	WANDSWORTH	TWP/HM
October 25	Stanley BOON	28	WANDSWORTH	TWP/SC
October 26	Arthur SMITH	26	WANDSWORTH	TWP/TMP

Executioners	Assistants
Thomas M. Phillips	Stanley Cross
Thomas W. Pierrepoint	Herbert Morris
	Albert Pierrepoint
	Alexander Riley
	Robert Wilson

1940

February 7	Peter BARNES	32	BIRMINGHAM	TWP/TMP/
February 7	James RICHARDS	29	BIRMINGHAM	/AP/SC

15 Robert Wilson turned down the offer to assist as he was unable to get time off work.
16 Herbert Morris present as a trainee observer.
17 Alex Riley present as trainee observer.

Date of Execution	Name of Prisoner	Age at Execution	Prison	Hangman & Assistant(s)
March 27	Ernest HAMERTON	25	WANDSWORTH	TWP/AR
April 24	William COWELL	38	WANDSWORTH	TWP/SC
July 11	William APPLEBY	27	DURHAM	TWP/SC
July 11	Vincent OSTLER	24	DURHAM	AP/AR
July 31	Udham SINGH	37	PENTONVILLE	SC/AP
August 8	George ROBERTS	28	CARDIFF	TWP/SC
September 10	John WRIGHT	41	DURHAM	TWP/AP
October 31	Stanley COLE	23	WANDSWORTH	TWP/HM[18]
November 26	William COOPER	24	BEDFORD	TWP/AP[19]
December 10	Karl MEIER	24	PENTONVILLE	SC/AP
December 10	José WALDBERG	25	PENTONVILLE	HK/HC
December 17	Charles Van Der KEIBOOM	25	PENTONVILLE	SC/HM
December 24	Edward SCOLLEN	42	DURHAM	TWP/HC

Executioners
Stanley Cross
Thomas M. Phillips
Thomas W. Pierrepoint

Assistants
Harry B. Allen
Henry Critchell
Harry Kirk
Herbert Morris
Albert Pierrepoint
Alexander Riley
Stephen Wade

1941

Date of Execution	Name of Prisoner	Age at Execution	Prison	Hangman & Assistant(s)
January 7	David DOHERTY	29	DUBLIN	TWP/AP
February 11	Clifford HOLMES	24	MANCHESTER	TWP/HBA
March 6	Henry WHITE	39	DURHAM	TWP/HBA
April 9	Samuel MORGAN	28	LIVERPOOL	TWP/HM
April 23	Henry GLEESON	39	DUBLIN	TWP/AP
July 9	George ARMSTRONG	39	WANDSWORTH	TWP/SW
July 24	David JENNINGS	21	DORCHESTER	TWP/AR
July 31	Edward ANDERSON	19	DURHAM	TWP/HM
August 6	Karl DRUEKE	35	WANDSWORTH	TWP/AP
August 6	Werner WALTI	25	WANDSWORTH	/SC/HK
September 4	John SMITH	32	MANCHESTER	TWP/HBA
September 19	Eli RICHARDS	45	BIRMINGHAM	TWP/SC
October 31	Antonio MANCINI	39	PENTONVILLE	AP/SW
November 12	Lionel WATSON	30	PENTONVILLE	TWP/HC
December 3	John SMITH	21	WANDSWORTH	AP/HBA
December 10	Karel RICHTER	29	WANDSWORTH	AP/SW
December 18	Patrick KELLY	31	DUBLIN	TWP/AP
December 23	Thomas THORPE	61	LEICESTER	TWP/AP

Executioners
Stanley Cross
Thomas M. Phillips
Thomas W. Pierrepoint

Assistants
Harry B. Allen
Henry Critchell
Harry Kirk
Herbert Morris
Alexander Riley
Stephen Wade

---

18 Kirk and wade present as trainee observers.
19 Critchell and Allen present as trainee observers.

Date of Execution	Name of Prisoner	Age at Execution	Prison	Hangman & Assistant(s)
1942				
January 30	Arthur PEACH	23	BIRMINGHAM	TWP/HC
March 11	Harold TREVOR	62	WANDSWORTH	AP/HM
March 25	David WILLIAMS	33	LIVERPOOL	TWP/SW
April 15	Cyril JOHNSON	20	WANDSWORTH	TWP/HC
April 30	Frederick AUSTIN	28	BRISTOL	TWP/HK
May 1	Harold HILL	26	OXFORD	TWP/AP
June 24	Douglas EDMUNDSON	28	LIVERPOOL	TWP/HM
June 25	Gordon CUMMINS	28	WANDSWORTH	AP/HK
July 7	José KEY	34	WANDSWORTH	AP/HK
July 7	Alphonse TIMMERMAN	37	WANDSWORTH	/SW/HC
July 21	Arthur ANDERSON	52	WANDSWORTH	AP/HM
September 2	Thomas WILLIAMS	19	BELFAST	TWP/AP
September 10	Harold MERRY	40	BIRMINGHAM	TWP/HC
September 10	Samuel DASHWOOD	22	PENTONVILLE	AP/SW
September 10	George SILVEROSA	23	PENTONVILLE	/HM/HK
October 6	Patrick KINGSTON	38	WANDSWORTH	AP/HM
October 28	William COLLINS	21	DURHAM	TWP/AP
November 3	Duncan SCOTT-FORD	21	WANDSWORTH	AP/HK
November 6	Herbert BOUNDS	45	WANDSWORTH	TWP/HC
December 31	Johannes DRONKERS	46	WANDSWORTH	AP/SW

Executioners
Albert Pierrepoint
Thomas W. Pierrepoint

Assistants
Harry B. Allen*
Henry Critchell
Harry Kirk
Herbert Morris
Alexander Riley*
Stephen Wade

* Not employed due to war work.

Date of Execution	Name of Prisoner	Age at Execution	Prison	Hangman & Assistant(s)
1943				
January 26	Franciscus WINTER	40	WANDSWORTH	AP/HC
January 27	Harry DOBKIN	49	WANDSWORTH	AP/HM
February 10	Ronald ROBERTS	28	LIVERPOOL	TWP/HK
March 12	David COBB	21	SHEPTON MALLET	TWP/AP
March 24	William TURNER	19	PENTONVILLE	TWP/HC
March 31	Dudley RAYNOR	26	WANDSWORTH	AP/SW
April 6	Gordon TRENOWORTH	34	EXETER	TWP/HM
April 29	August SANGRET	30	WANDSWORTH	AP/HC
June 2	Bernard KIRWAN	25	DUBLIN	TWP/AP
June 25	Harold SMITH		SHEPTON MALLET	TWP/AP
July 10	Charles RAYMOND	23	WANDSWORTH	TWP/SW
August 3	Gerald ROE	41	PENTONVILLE	AP/SW
August 3	William QUAYLE	52	BIRMINGHAM	TWP/AR
August 12	William O'SHEA	24	DUBLIN	TWP/AP
September 10	Trevor ELVIN	21	LEEDS	TWP/HK
September 24	Charles GAUTHEIR	25	WANDSWORTH	AP/HK
November 19	Terence CASEY	22	WANDSWORTH	AP/HC
December 14	Lee DAVIS	18	SHEPTON MALLET	TWP/AR
December 15	Charles KOOPMAN	22	PENTONVILLE	TWP/SW

Date of Execution	Name of Prisoner	Age at Execution	Prison	Hangman & Assistant(s)
December 22	John DORGAN	46	WANDSWORTH	TWP/HC
December 29	Thomas JAMES	26	LIVERPOOL	TWP/HM

Executioners	Assistants
Albert Pierrepoint	Henry Critchell
Thomas W. Pierrepoint	Harry Kirk
	Herbert Morris
	Albert Pierrepoint
	Alexander Riley
	Stephen Wade

1944

Date of Execution	Name of Prisoner	Age at Execution	Prison	Hangman & Assistant(s)
February 2	Christos GEORGIOU	38	PENTONVILLE	AP/HM
February 3	Mervin McEWEN	35	LEEDS	TWP/SW
February 10	John WALTERS	38	SHEPTON MALLET	TWP/AR
March 16	Oswald JOB	58	PENTONVILLE	AP/HK
March 16	Ernest DIGBY	35	BRISTOL	TWP/SW
April 13	Sydney DELASALLE	39	DURHAM	TWP/HC
May 16	John LEATHERBERRY	21	SHEPTON MALLET	TWP/AP
May 26	Wiley HARRIS	26	SHEPTON MALLET	TWP/AR
June 6	Ernest KEMP	20	WANDSWORTH	AP/HM
June 23	Pierre NEUKERMANS	27	PENTONVILLE	AP/AR
July 12	John DAVIDSON	19	LIVERPOOL	TWP/AR
July 12	Joseph VANHOVE	27	PENTONVILLE	AP/SW
July 26	James GALBRAITH	26	MANCHESTER	TWP/HK
August 8	William COWLE	31	LEICESTER	TWP/ AR
August 8	William MEFFEN	52	LEICESTER	/AP/HK
August 11	Eliga BRINSON	25	SHEPTON MALLET	TWP/
August 11	Willie SMITH	21	SHEPTON MALLET	/AP
October 12	Madison THOMAS	23	SHEPTON MALLET	TWP/AP
December 1	Charles KERINS	26	DUBLIN	TWP/AP

Executioners	Assistants
Albert Pierrepoint	Harry B. Allen*
Thomas W. Pierrepoint	Henry Critchell
	Harry Kirk
	Herbert Morris
	Alexander Riley
	Stephen Wade

* Not employed due to war work.

1945

Date of Execution	Name of Prisoner	Age at Execution	Prison	Hangman & Assistant(s)
January 8	Ernest CLARK	23	SHEPTON MALLET	TWP/
January 8	Augustine GUERRA	20	SHEPTON MALLET	/AP
January 9	Horace GORDON	29	WANDSWORTH	AP/SW
January 30	Andrew BROWN	26	WANDSWORTH	AP/SW
January 31	Arthur THOMPSON	34	LEEDS	TWP/HM
March 8	Karl HULTEN	23	PENTONVILLE	TWP/HC
March 13	Arthur HEYS	37	NORWICH	TWP/SW
March 17	Robert PEARSON		SHEPTON MALLET	TWP
March 17	Cubia JONES		SHEPTON MALLET	/HM

Date of Execution	Name of Prisoner	Age at Execution	Prison	Hangman & Assistant(s)
March 19	James LEHMAN	45	DUBLIN	AP/TJ
April 7	William HARRISON		SHEPTON MALLET	TWP/HM
May 8	George SMITH	28	SHEPTON MALLET	TWP/HM
June 15	Aniceto MARTINEZ	24	SHEPTON MALLET	TWP/AP
September 5	Howard GROSSLEY	37	CARDIFF	TWP/SW
September 7	Thomas RICHARDSON	27	LEEDS	TWP/HM
October 6	Joachim GOLTZ	20	PENTONVILLE	AP/
October 6	Heinz BRUELING	21	PENTONVILLE	/
October 6	Josef MERTENS	21	PENTONVILLE	/
October 6	Kurt ZUEHLSDORFF	20	PENTONVILLE	/SW
October 6	Erich KOENIG	20	PENTONVILLE	/HBA
October 31	Ronald MAURI	32	WANDSWORTH	AP/HK
November 16	Arnim KUEHNE	21	PENTONVILLE	AP/
November 16	Emil SCHMITTENDORF	31	PENTONVILLE	/AR
December 19	John AMERY	33	WANDSWORTH	AP/HC
December 21	John YOUNG	40	PENTONVILLE	AP/HM
December 21	James McNICOL	27	PENTONVILLE	/SW
December 29	Robert BLAINE	24	WANDSWORTH	AP/HK

Executioners
Albert Pierrepoint
Thomas W. Pierrepoint

Assistants
Harry B. Allen
Henry Critchell
Harry Kirk
Thomas Johnstone
Herbert Morris
Alexander Riley
Stephen Wade

1946

Date of Execution	Name of Prisoner	Age at Execution	Prison	Hangman & Assistant(s)
January 3	William JOYCE	40	WANDSWORTH	AP/AR
January 4	Theodore SCHURCH	27	PENTONVILLE	AP/AR
January 8	William BATTY	27	LEEDS	TWP/HBA
January 31	Michael NIESCIOR	29	WANDSWORTH	AP/SW
February 8	John LYON	21	GLASGOW	TP/SW
March 5	Charles PRESCOTT	23	DURHAM	TP/HK
March 19	Arthur CLEGG	42	WANDSWORTH	AP/HM
March 26	Arthur CHARLES	34	DURHAM	SW/HBA
April 2	Marion GRONDKOWSKI	33	WANDSWORTH	AP/HK[20]
April 2	Henryk MALINAWOSKI	25	WANDSWORTH	AP/AR
April 6	Patrick CARRAHER	39	GLASGOW	TWP/SW
April 9	Harold BERRY	30	MANCHESTER	TWP/HC
April 24	Martin COFFEY	23	MANCHESTER	TWP/AR
May 28	Leonard HOLMES	32	LINCOLN	TWP/SW
July 17	Thomas HENDREN	31	LIVERPOOL	AP/HM
August 7	Walter CLAYTON	22	LIVERPOOL	AP/SW
August 10	John CALDWELL	20	GLASGOW	TWP/SW
September 6	Sydney SMITH	24	WANDSWORTH	AP/HBA
September 6	David MASON	39	WANDSWORTH	AP/HC
October 16	Neville HEATH	29	PENTONVILLE	AP/HK
November 1	Arthur BOYCE	45	PENTONVILLE	AP/HC

20 Single executions carried out 75 minutes apart (9 a.m. and 10.15 a.m.).

Date of Execution	Name of Prisoner	Age at Execution	Prison	Hangman & Assistant(s)
November 13	Frank FREIYER	26	WANDSWORTH	AP/HK
November 19	Arthur RUSHTON	31	LIVERPOOL	AP/HC
December 10	John MATHIESON	23	PENTONVILLE	AP/HBA

Executioners	Assistants
Albert Pierrepoint	Harry B. Allen
Thomas W. Pierrepoint	Henry Critchell
Stephen Wade	Harry Kirk
	Thomas Johnstone
	Herbert Morris
	Alexander Riley

1947

Date of Execution	Name of Prisoner	Age at Execution	Prison	Hangman & Assistant(s)
January 3	Stanley SHEMINANT	28	LIVERPOOL	SW/HBA
January 30	Albert SABIN	21	LEEDS	SW/HK
February 27	Walter ROWLAND	38	MANCHESTER	AP/HC
March 18	Harold HAGGER	45	WANDSWORTH	AP/HC
March 26	Frederick REYNOLDS	39	PENTONVILLE	AP/HK
March 31	Joseph McMANUS	41	DUBLIN	AP/TJ
April 15	David WILLIAMS	26	WANDSWORTH	AP/HK
June 20	Eric BRIGGS	40	LEEDS	SW/HK
August 14	William SMEDLEY	38	LEEDS	SW/HK
August 21	John GARTSIDE	24	LEEDS	SW/HC
September 19	Christopher GERAGHTY	20	PENTONVILLE	AP/HBA
September 19	Charles JENKINS	23	PENTONVILLE	/HC
December 30	Eugenius JURKIEWICZ	34	BRISTOL	AP/HBA

Executioners	Assistants
Albert Pierrepoint	Harry B. Allen
Stephen Wade	Henry Critchell
	Thomas Johnstone
	Harry Kirk

1948

Date of Execution	Name of Prisoner	Age at Execution	Prison	Hangman & Assistant(s)
January 7	George WHELPTON	31	LEEDS	SW/HK
February 3	Evan EVANS	22	CARDIFF	AP/HK
February 6	Stanislaw MYSZKA	23	PERTH	AP/SW
February 19	Walter CROSS	21	PENTONVILLE	AP/HBA
November 18	Stanley CLARKE	34	NORWICH	AP/HK
November 19	Peter GRIFFITHS	22	LIVERPOOL	AP/HBA
November 24	William GAMBON	28	DUBLIN	AP/none[21]
December 2	George RUSSELL	45	OXFORD	AP/SW
December 9	Clifford WILLS	31	CARDIFF	SW/HC
December 30	Arthur OSBORNE	28	LEEDS	SW/HBA

Executioners	Assistants
Albert Pierrepoint	Harry B. Allen
Stephen Wade	Henry Critchell
	Harry Kirk

20 The possible reason why no assistant executioner was present was due to the previous Irish assistant Johnstone failing to carry out his duties as a senior man and therefore attendance was not required.

Date of Execution	Name of Prisoner	Age at Execution	Prison	Hangman & Assistant(s)
1949				
January 12	Margaret ALLEN	43	MANCHESTER	AP/HK
January 27	George SEMINI	26	LIVERPOOL	AP/HBA
March 22	Kenneth STRICKSON	21	LINCOLN	AP/HK
March 29	James FARRELL	19	BIRMINGHAM	AP/HK[22]
April 21	Harry LEWIS	21	PENTONVILLE	AP/HBA
June 2	Dennis NEVILLE	22	LEEDS	SW/HBA
June 21	Bernard COOPER	49	PENTONVILLE	AP/HK[23]
July 28	Sydney CHAMBERLAIN	32	WINCHESTER	AP/HBA
August 4	Rex JONES	21	SWANSEA	AP/HK
August 4	Robert MACKINTOSH	21	SWANSEA	/GD
August 10	John HAIGH	39	WANDSWORTH	AP/HK
August 16	William DAVIES	30	WANDSWORTH	AP/HK
September 28	William JONES	31	PENTONVILLE	AP/HBA
December 13	Benjamin ROBERTS	23	DURHAM	SW/HK
December 13	John WILSON	26	DURHAM	/SD/HA
December 30	Ernest COUZINS	43	WANDSWORTH	AP/HBA

Executioners	Assistants
Albert Pierrepoint	Harry B. Allen
Stephen Wade	Herbert Allen
	Sydney Dernley
	George Dickinson
	Harry Kirk

Date of Execution	Name of Prisoner	Age at Execution	Prison	Hangman & Assistant(s)
1950				
January 6	Daniel RAVEN	23	PENTONVILLE	AP/HK
March 8	James RIVETT	21	NORWICH	AP/HA
March 9	Timothy EVANS	25	PENTONVILLE	AP/SD[24]
March 28	George KELLY	27	LIVERPOOL	AP/HBA[25]
March 29	Piotr MAKSIMOWSKI	33	BIRMINGHAM	AP/SD
March 30	Walter SHARPE	20	LEEDS	SW/HA
April 19	Albert JENKINS	37	SWANSEA	AP/HK
July 7	Zbigniew GOWER	23	WINCHESTER	AP/HK
July 7	Roman REDEL	23	WINCHESTER	/SD/HA
July 11	George BROWN	23	DURHAM	AP/HK
July 13	Ronald ATWELL	24	BRISTOL	AP/SD
July 13	John WALKER	48	DURHAM	SW/HK
August 16	Albert PRICE	32	WANDSWORTH	AP/HBA
October 30	Paul HARRIS	28	GLASGOW	AP/SW
November 14	Patrick TURNAGE	31	DURHAM	SW/SD
November 23	Norman GOLDTHORPE	40	NORWICH	HK/SD
November 28	James CORBITT	37	MANCHESTER	AP/HA
December 14	Edward WOODFIELD	49	BRISTOL	AP/HA
December 16	James ROBERTSON	33	GLASGOW	AP/SW
December 19	Nicholas CROSBY	22	MANCHESTER	AP/SD[26]

22 Dernley, Herbert Allen and probably George Dickinson present as observers.
23 On the evening prior to the execution, the rope snapped while Wade was making a test drop.
24 Conviction later overturned on appeal.
25 Conviction later overturned on appeal.
26 Stewart and Smith were present as trainee observers.

Appendix

Date of Execution	Name of Prisoner	Age at Execution	Prison	Hangman & Assistant(s)

Executioners		Assistants	
Harry Kirk		Harry B. Allen	
Albert Pierrepoint		Herbert Allen	
Stephen Wade		Sydney Dernley	
		Harry Smith	
		Robert L. Stewart	

1951

Date of Execution	Name of Prisoner	Age at Execution	Prison	Hangman & Assistant(s)
January 4	Frank GRIFFIN	40	SHREWSBURY	AP/HM
January 26	Nenad KOVASEVIC	29	MANCHESTER	AP/HA
April 3	William WATKINS	49	BIRMINGHAM	AP/HBA
April 25	Joseph BROWN	30	WANDSWORTH	AP/HBA/
April 25	Edward SMITH	30	WANDSWORTH	SD/HA
April 26	James VIRRELS	55	WANDSWORTH	AP/SD
May 8	James INGLIS	30	MANCHESTER	AP/SD
May 9	William SHAUGHNESSY	48	WINCHESTER	AP/HBA
June 12	John DAND	32	MANCHESTER	AP/HBA
July 3	Jack WRIGHT	30	MANCHESTER	AP/HS
July 19	Dennis MOORE	23	NORWICH	AP/HBA
July 19	Alfred REYNOLDS	24	NORWICH	SD/RLS
September 15	Robert SMITH	30	EDINBURGH	AP/SW
October 24	John O'CONNOR	29	PENTONVILLE	AP/HA
December 11	Herbert MILLS	19	LINCOLN	AP/HA

Executioners		Assistants	
Albert Pierrepoint		Harry B. Allen	
Stephen Wade		Herbert Allen	
		Sydney Dernley	
		Herbert Morris	
		Harry Smith	
		Robert L. Stewart	

1952

Date of Execution	Name of Prisoner	Age at Execution	Prison	Hangman & Assistant(s)
January 1	Horace CARTER	30	BIRMINGHAM	AP/SD
January 15	Alfred BRADLEY	24	MANCHESTER	AP/RLS
February 6	Alfred MOORE	36	LEEDS	SW/HBA
February 26	Herbert HARRIS	24	MANCHESTER	AP/RLS
March 21	Tahir ALI	39	DURHAM	SW/HA
April 12	James SMITH	21	GLASGOW	AP/SW
April 25	Alfred BURNS	21	LIVERPOOL	AP/SD/
April 25	Edward DEVLIN	22	LIVERPOOL	RLS/HS
May 7	Ajit SINGH	27	CARDIFF	AP/HBA[27]
May 27	Backary MAUNEH	25	PENTONVILLE	AP/HS
May 29	Peter DEVENEY	42	GLASGOW	AP/SW
July 8	Harry HUXLEY	42	SHREWSBURY	AP/HBA
July 15	Thomas EAMES	31	BRISTOL	AP/RLS
July 22	Frank BURGESS	21	WANDSWORTH	AP/SD
August 12	Oliver BUTLER	24	OXFORD	AP/HS
September 3	Mahmood MATTAN	29	CARDIFF	AP/RLS[28]

27 Following execution Singh was cremated as his religion dictated, before his ashes were returned to the gaol and buried in unconsecrated ground.

Date of Execution	Name of Prisoner	Age at Execution	Prison	Hangman & Assistant(s)
September 5	John GODAR	31	PENTONVILLE	APRLS
September 30	Raymond CULL	25	PENTONVILLE	AP/RLS
September 30	Dennis MULDOWNEY	41	PENTONVILLE	/HS
October 9	Peter JOHNSON	24	PENTONVILLE	AP/HBA
October 23	Donald SIMON	32	SHREWSBURY	AP/SD
December 12	Eric NORTHCLIFFE	30	LINCOLN	APRLS
December 17	John LIVESEY	23	WANDSWORTH	AP/SD
December 23	Leslie GREEN	29	BIRMINGHAM	AP/SD
December 24	Herbert APPLEBY	20	DURHAM	SW/HBA

Executioners
Albert Pierrepoint
Stephen Wade

Assistants
Harry B. Allen
Sydney Dernley
Harry Smith
Robert L. Stewart

1953				
January 2	James ALCOTT	29	WANDSWORTH	AP/HS
January 26	George SHAW	25	GLASGOW	AP/SW
January 28	Derek BENTLEY	19	WANDSWORTH	AP/HBA[29]
February 24	Miles GIFFARD	26	BRISTOL	AP/HS
May 19	John TODD	20	LIVERPOOL	AP/JB
July 15	John CHRISTIE	55	PENTONVILLE	AP/HS
July 30	Philip HENRY	25	LEEDS	AP/RR
September 18	Louisa MERRIFIELD	46	MANCHESTER	AP/RLS
October 20	John GREENWAY	27	BRISTOL	AP/HBA
November 17	Joseph REYNOLDS	31	LEICESTER	AP/RLS
December 17	Stanislaw JURAS	43	MANCHESTER	AP/RR
December 18	John WILKINSON	24	WANDSWORTH	SW/RR
December 22	Alfred WHITEWAY	22	WANDSWORTH	AP/JB
December 23	George NEWLAND	21	PENTONVILLE	AP/HBA

Executioners
Albert Pierrepoint
Stephen Wade

Assistants
Harry B. Allen
Joseph Broadbent
Royston L. Rickard
Harry Smith
Robert L. Stewart

1954				
January 5	Robert MOORE	27	LEEDS	SW/HS
January 8	Czeslaw KOWALSKI	32	MANCHESTER	AP/JB
January 26	Desmond HOOPER	27	SHREWSBURY	AP/RLS
January 27	William LUBINA	42	LEEDS	SW/HBA
April 14	James DOOHAN	24	WANDSWORTH	AP/HBA
April 20	Michael MANNING	25	DUBLIN	AP/RLS
April 22	Albert HALL	48	LEEDS	SW/HS
April 23	John LYNCH	43	EDINBURGH	AP/RLS
April 28	Thomas HARRIES	24	SWANSEA	AP/RLS
June 17	Kenneth GILBERT	21	PENTONVILLE	AP/RR

28 Conviction later overturned on appeal.
29 Conviction later overturned on appeal.

Date of Execution	Name of Prisoner	Age at Execution	Prison	Hangman & Assistant(s)
June 17	Ian GRANT	24	PENTONVILLE	HS/JB
June 22	Milton TAYLOR	23	LIVERPOOL	AP/RLS
June 23	George ROBERTSON	40	EDINBURGH	AP/HBA
August 11	William HEPPER	62	WANDSWORTH	AP/RR
August 12	Harold FOWLER	21	LINCOLN	AP/HBA
September 1	Edward REID	24	LEEDS	SW/HS
September 1	Rupert WELLS	53	WANDSWORTH	AP/RLS
December 15	Styllou CHRISTOFI	53	HOLLOWAY	AP/HBA

Executioners
Albert Pierrepoint
Stephen Wade

Assistants
Harry B. Allen
Joseph Broadbent
Royston L. Rickard
Harry Smith
Robert L. Stewart

1955

March 29	William SALT	45	LIVERPOOL	SW/HS
April 14	Sydney CLARKE	32	WANDSWORTH	AP/RLS
May 22	James ROBINSON	27	LINCOLN	AP/HBA
May 24	Winston SHAW	39	LEEDS	SW/HS
June 21	Richard GOWLER	43	LIVERPOOL	AP/RLS
July 12	Kenneth ROBERTS	24	LINCOLN	SW/HS
July 13	Ruth ELLIS	28	HOLLOWAY	AP/RR
July 26	Frederick CROSS	33	BIRMINGHAM	AP/HBA
July 27	Norman GREEN	25	LIVERPOOL	AP/RLS
August 2	Corbett ROBERTS	46	BIRMINGHAM	SW/HBA
August 9	Ernest HARDING	42	BIRMINGHAM	SW/RLS
August 12	Alec WILKINSON	21	LEEDS	SW/RLS[30]

Executioners
Albert Pierrepoint
Stephen Wade

Assistants
Harry B. Allen
John R. Barker
Royston L. Rickard
Harry Smith
Robert L. Stewart

1956
No executions.

1957

July 23	John VICKERS	22	DURHAM	HBA/HS
December 4	Dennis HOWARD	24	BIRMINGHAM	HBA/RR[31]

Executioners
Harry B. Allen
Robert L. Stewart

Assistants
Thomas Cunliffe
Royston L. Rickard
Harry F. Robinson
Harry Smith

---

30 Barker present as trainee observer.
31 Robinson and Cunliffe present as trainee observers.

Date of Execution	Name of Prisoner	Age at Execution	Prison	Hangman & Assistant(s)
1958				
May 6	Vivian TEED	24	SWANSEA	RLS/HR
July 11	Peter MANUEL	31	GLASGOW	HBA[32]
August 12	Matthew KAVANAGH	32	BIRMINGHAM	HBA/TC
September 3	Frank STOKES	44	DURHAM	HBA/HS
December 17	Brian CHANDLER	20	DURHAM	RLS/TC

Executioners	Assistants
Harry B. Allen	Thomas Cunliffe
Robert L. Stewart	Royston L. Rickard
	Harry F. Robinson
	Harry Smith

Date of Execution	Name of Prisoner	Age at Execution	Prison	Hangman & Assistant(s)
1959				
February 10	Ernest JONES	38	LEEDS	HBA/HS
April 28	Joseph CHRIMES	30	PENTONVILLE	HBA/RR[33]
May 8	Ronald MARWOOD	25	PENTONVILLE	HBA/HR
May 14	Michael TATUM	24	WINCHESTER	RLS/TC
August 14	Bernard WALDEN	33	LEEDS	HBA/TC
October 9	Francis HUCHET	33	JERSEY	HBA/RR
November 5	Guenther PODOLA	30	WANDSWORTH	HBA/RR

Executioners	Assistants
Harry B. Allen	Thomas Cunliffe
Robert L. Stewart	Samuel B. Plant
	Royston L. Rickard
	Harry F. Robinson
	Harry Smith
	John E. Underhill

Date of Execution	Name of Prisoner	Age at Execution	Prison	Hangman & Assistant(s)
1960				
September 1	John CONSTANTINE	22	LINCOLN	HBA/RR[34]
November 10	Francis FORSYTH	18	WANDSWORTH	HBA/RR
November 10	Norman HARRIS	23	PENTONVILLE	RLS/HR
December 22	Anthony MILLER	19	GLASGOW	HBA/RLS

Executioners	Assistants
Harry B. Allen	Harry F. Robinson
Robert L.Stewart	John E. Underhill
	Royston L. Rickard
	Samuel B. Plant

Date of Execution	Name of Prisoner	Age at Execution	Prison	Hangman & Assistant(s)
1961				
January 27	Wasyl GNYPIUK	34	LINCOLN	HBA/JU
February 9	George RILEY	21	SHREWSBURY	HBA/SP
March 29	Jack DAY	30	BEDFORD	HBA/HR
May 25	Victor TERRY	20	WANDSWORTH	HBA/SP

32 Scottish newspapers state the assistant as being Harry Allen's son Brian Allen.

33 Following an un-named execution in London early that year the body was removed from the noose shortly after the execution had been carried out and when examined by a doctor was found to be showing signs of life. It was re-suspended until life was seen to be extinct and henceforth all bodies were left to hang for 45 minutes.

34 Plant and Underhill were present as trainee observers.